A MILLEN

BALLINGARRY, GRANAGH AND CLOUNCAGH, COUNTY LIMERICK

Archival Records 1800 - 1900

COMPILED BY
Christopher Kerins

All rights reserved.
No part of this publication may be reproduced, stored in a retrieval system or transmitted in any form or by any means, electronic, mechanical, photocopying, recording or otherwise, without the prior, written permission of the publisher.

This book is sold subject to the condition that it shall not, by way of trade or otherwise, be lent, resold, hired out, or otherwise circulated without the publisher's prior consent in any form of binding or cover other than that in which it is published and without a similar condition including this condition being imposed on the subsequent purchaser.

Typeset by Artwerk, Dublin

Printed in Ireland, 2000
by ColourBooks Limited

Published by:
Christy Kerins

ISBN: 0-9538402-0-4

DEDICATION

My late father, Michael Kerins (1893-1973) had a life long interest in local history. He would have been most interested in a project like this. This book is dedicated to his memory.

Christy Kerins. Dublin, April, 2000.

AUTHOR PROFILE

Christy Kerins was born in Ballingarry in 1946. He was educated in the local National School and local Secondary School. He can trace his family back to the early 1800's in Ballingarry on his Mother's side. He is an Executive Officer in the Civil Service. He is married and has four children. He lives in Artane, Dublin.

CONTENTS

Foreword

I.	Topography. A Description of Ireland, Munster and Limerick taken from Pigot's Directory, 1826. Lewis Topographical Directory, 1837 and the Ordnance Survey, 1840 for Ballingarry, Granagh and Clouncagh.	5
II.	Early 19th Century Records. Vestry Book Records 1792-1870, Local Historical Incidents 1811- 1830, Local Genealogical Records 1806-1845, Grand Jury Records 1807-1846, the Survey of the Roads, 1814 and some miscellaneous records 1802-1850.	25
III.	The Tithes Records for Ballingarry and Granagh, 1826 and Clouncagh, 1833.	51
IV.	The People and the Land. Extracts from Government Investigations into land use in the early 1800's including extracts from the Devon Commission, 1844.	69
V.	Griffith's Valuation, Ballingarry, Granagh and Clouncagh, 1852.	79
VI.	Statistical Records From The Censii throughout the 1800's.	95
VII.	The Workhouses of Ballingarry, 1848 and 1850. Researched by Sr. Delia Curtin.	111
VIII.	The Encumbered Estates, 1850 - 1865.	122
IX.	History of the National Schools in Ballingarry and Granagh, 1841-1900, including the setting up of the Convent National School researched by Sr. Delia Curtin.	144
X.	Late 19th Century Records. Miscellaneous records of the late 1800's including Grand Jury records and extracts from Guy's and Slater's Directories.	155
XI.	Church of Ireland Records of Births, Deaths and Marriages.	161

CHRONOLOGY OF EVENTS 1800-1900

1801	The Act Of Union
1805	Thomas Lloyd bought Beechmount.
1812	New Church (C of I) built.
1814	Roads Surveyed in the barony of Connelloe Upper.
	Ballingarry designated a Post town.
1821	Census Of Ireland.
1822	Glebe House built.
1826	Ballingarry applotted for Tithes.
1829	William Lloyd dies in duel with Thomas Ocell.
1830	Glenbrook House built by Miles Jackson Mason.
1831	National Education Board established. National Schools set up.
	Census.
1833	Clouncagh applotted for Tithes
1836	Ballinamona House built.
1837	Lewis's Topographical Dictionary of Ballingarry and Clouncagh.
1838	The Tithe Act ends the tithe war.
	Workhouses Established by Law.
1840	Ordnance Survey
1841	National School in Ballingarry established.
	Census.
1843	Clontarf Monster Rally in Support of Catholic Emanciaption.
1844	The Devon Commission.
1845	The First year of the Famine.
	Civil Registration Introduced, but not for Catholics.
1847	Death of Daniel O'Connell.
1848	Workhouse in Ballingarry established.
1849	Archdeacon Fitzgerald transfers to Rathkeale.
1850	Sales of Encumbered Estates commence in Ballingarry.
	The Grove workhouse established.
1851	Census.
1852	Griffith's Valuation.
	Church in Knockfierna / Shanavoha built.
1854	St. Oswald's House built. Replaces Odell Ville Cottage.
1856	Granagh National School opened.
1858	Ballyneale House built.

1861	Census
1862	Protestant Church at Kilfinny built.
1864	Civil Registration introduced for everyone.
1866	Fair Field used for the last time.
1867	Fenian Uprising.
1871	Census.
1872	Foundation stone laid for new Roman Catholic church.
1881	Gladstone's Land Act.
	Census.
1884	G.A.A. established.
1885	Asbourne Land Act enables tenants buy their holdings.
1887	Charles Townley dies in the Turrett.
1888	Ballingarry Convent School established.
1891	Census.
1894	Irish Agricultural Organization Society (The Co-op. Movement) established.
1898	Grand Jury System abolished. Replaced by County Councils.
1900	St. Oswald's purchased by Wilfrid Francis Clenell Wilkinson.

INTRODUCTION

While researching my family tree I had occasion to visit the various archives in Dublin. I was under the impression that there was little or no records of ordinary people in the archives with the exception of the 1901 and 1911 censii. When I heard the people of Ballingarry, where I was born and raised, discuss local history I often wondered where they got their information from and whether it was true. So I was delighted to find that there was a treasure trove of archival material pertaining to the area of Ballingarry, Granagh and Clouncagh. I started to assemble this material and this is the result. This book is primarily a genealogical resource. Under the guise of the various records, they name people, in their place and in their time. Some of the records if on their own would not be of great interest. However, I have included all I could collect in the hope that someone somewhere may make use of them particularly the pre 1860 period. I have copied the various spellings of townland and people as I found them. These often varied in the same text. I have made no effort to interpret these records. The only editing I did was to decide how much of the records it was worth copying for this book. It is unfortunate that the Roman Catholic Church authorities refused me permission to copy the early 19th century Church records. This is the only major genealogical source not represented in these records. I was very conscious of the fact that the **Rev. G. F. Hamilton** had forged the way with his 'Records of Ballingarry' published in 1928. This book does not duplicate anything he did except in a few minor details. I see this book as an addition to the Rev. Hamilton's book. Like Rev. Hamilton, I hope these records will interest, not only the residents of Ballingarry, Granagh and Clouncagh, but also many in the county of Limerick and elsewhere for whom these parishes have tender associations. Every effort has been made to be as accurate as possible but in any case of doubt the original material should be researched.

ACKNOWLEDGEMENTS

My sincere thanks to

My wife, Mary, and family Rosaleen, Julie, Sara and James for their help.

The Representative Church Body for permission to quote from the Vestry Book. The entire Births, Deaths and Marriages section is taken from their Church records.

The Ordnance Survey, Ireland for permission to use extracts from the Ordnance Survey, 1840.

Sr. Delia Curtin, for permission to re-produce her two articles on the Workhouses in Ballingarry and for her valuable contribution to the National schools records. Also the Knockfierna Heritage and Folk Group in whose publication - Knockfierna Remembers, Vol 7, 1997 - the two workhouse articles were first published.

The Trustees of the National Library for permission to re-produce records under their control and the staff for their unfailing courtesy.

The Director of the National Archives for permission to re-produce records under their control and the staff for their unfailing courtesy.

The Gilbert Library, where I accessed most of this material, and the staff for their unfailing courtesy.

Irish Roots Magazine in whose various editions I got inspiration to attempt this work and in whose various issues I got many useful snippets of background information for use in this book. Thanks to the Editor Mr. Tony McCarthy.

Limerick County Council for permission to access the early Grand Jury

Books and Tony Storan for drawing my attention to the Donovan Name Books.

Brian Donnelly, Archivist, National Archives - for permission to extract from his work on Local Government.

My friends in the Raheny Heritage Society for their encouragement and advice when needed.

My brother-in-law, Thomas Houston, Ballybofey and Northampton, England and my niece Deborah Noonan, Fanningstown, Croom whose encouragement and financial assistance helped to get this book published.

The Ballingarry Community Council for their support of this project.

And finally, to our predecessors who saw fit to make these records and the archives who preserved them through the years for our use and the use of future generations.

PART I

Topography

Ireland, Munster, Limerick, Ballingarry, Granagh, And Clouncagh.

Ireland: This fertile and beautiful island appears to have been known to the Greeks some centuries before the Christian era and is described by them under the name of Juverna; but who were it's first inhabitants cannot be ascertained. Some historians venture to suppose they came from Persia, or Iraen; hence the vernacular term of Erin is thought to have been adopted.

In the Saxon Chronicle, the Irish are stated to be a colony from Armenia; but the presumption of this nation's being of Eastern origin is certainly corroborated by monuments which have been frequently discovered in the bogs, and which resemble the ancient buildings of Persia and India, by the numerous Persian and Indian words which occur in the language, and by the general strong resemblance in phraeseology between the Irish and the Zend and Pehlevi.

Ireland is situated West of England, from which it is separated by the Irish Sea, or St. George's Channel. The general figure of the island resembles a parallelogram. It's greatest length is about 300 English miles, it's breadth is very irregular, and varies from about 80 to 182 English miles. It is divided into four great provinces, viz. Leinster, Connaught, Munster and Ulster, which are again divided into thirty two counties, containing 3,436 parishes.

The soil varies from the stiffest clay to the lightest sand; of the latter not much is to be met with, neither is chalk to be found in any part of the island. The soil by nature is remarkably fertile, and the pasturage is generally very luxuriant; but whether it be owing to the soil or climate no serpents, toads or any venomous creature is ever seen in the country; nor is that delightful bird, the nightingale ever heard or seen there.

A great part of Ireland lies upon a stratum of rock at various depths; a great deal of it being limestone, greatly contributes to enrich and improve the land. Marble of great beauty is found in several of the counties; and mines of gypsum, coal, iron, lead and copper are not unfrequent, but none have been worked to any great advantage to the country. The bogs are numerous and supply most of the inland parts with fuel; their surfaces produce heath, rushes, and coarse grass, and these, in some situations by being drained, become excellent meadow land. The mountains of Ireland are few, but sufficient in number to give a pleasing variety to it's appearance: they generally form detached groups which are so dispersed through the country that there is scarcely any part in which the prospect is not terminated by this species of majestic scenery. The number of lakes, or loughs, is very great, and some of them are not only large, but extremely beautiful: the lake of Killarney is the most celebrated for magnificence. Among the principal rivers are the Shannon, Foyle, Bann, Liffey, Boyne, Slaney, Suir, Barrow, Erne and Moy; many of which are considerable in point of size, and navigable for large boats for many miles above their fall into the sea. The noble river Shannon may fairly rank among the most eminent rivers of Europe.

Ireland possesses many natural curiosities, some of which, if equalled, are not exceeded by any other country; and it's antiquities have engaged the attention of many authors of profound erudition. The climate owing to it's western position and it's exposure to the clouds driven from the Atlantic, is far more humid than in England; the dews are heavy, and the atmosphere always replete with moisture, yet the climate is healthful and the summers are not so hot, nor the winters so cold, as the sister kingdom.

The situation of this island is peculiarly favourable for receiving and bestowing the reciprocal benefits of external commerce: it's communication is open and direct with England, France, Spain, Portugal, the coast of Africa; the East Indies, South America, Newfoundland, Hudson's Bay,

Greenland &c. It possesses the privilege of trading with all the different colonies of the empire equally with England and Scotland, and it's position for navigation generally is more advantageous than either. The population of Ireland in the year 1821 was estimated at 6,846,949.

Historical Description of the Province of Munster.

This province, the largest of the four, occupies the south-western portion of the kingdom. It has Connaught on the north; the boundary marked by an irregular line from Galway Bay through the Slieve Baughta to the Shannon; on the north-east Leinster, from which it is parted by another imaginary and uneven line; commencing at the Shannon five miles south-west of Banagher and stretching south-south-east to Carrick on Suir, whence the river Suir distinguishes it's limits to the sea; on every other part it is bounded by the Atlantic Ocean. It is about 135 miles in length and 120 in breadth. There are 62 baronies; 686 parishes, and 3,377,149 acres. The number of houses together with the population of this province, according to the census of 1821 is as follows, viz.

County	Houses	Inhabitants
Clare	36, 312	209, 595
Cork	103, 622	802, 535
Kerry	34, 612	205, 037
Limerick	44, 357	280, 328
Tipperary	60, 200	353, 402
Waterford	25, 545	154, 466
Total	**304, 648**	**2,005, 363**

County Limerick.

The County of Limerick is bounded on the north, by the river Shannon, which separates it from the county of Clare; on the east by Tipperary, on the south by Cork and by Kerry on the west. Its extent from east to west is about 40 Irish miles; and from north to south about 25. Its surface comprehends 386,750 acres, Irish plantation measure; including bogs, mountains and waste. It is divided into nine baronies: Owneybog; Clanwilliam; Coonag; Small County; Coshlea; Coshma; Publeobrien; Kenry and Connillo, which last barony exceeds the other eight in magnitude. Limerick city, with its liberties, constitutes a distinct county. This county contains 126 parishes and is thickly inhabited.

It can boast of a large portion of some of the richest land in Ireland. The soil is a rich, mellow crumbling, sandy loam, and is fit for every kind of culture. Its most considerable collection of fresh water is Lough Gur, and Knock-patrick is the most elevated mountain. This county is watered by the following rivers:-the Maig, which receive a number of rivulets in its course to the Shannon, falls from the Galtic mountains south of Kilfannan, and from the high lands which mark the boundaries of Limerick and Cork, the two branches uniting five miles north-west of Kilmallock, join the Shannon at Carigagunell; the Deel, which from two sources in the same highlands, west of the preceding, falls into the Shannon at Askeyton. There is a coal mine at the western extremity of the county, but turf is the general fuel of the inhabitants. Lead occurs in the lime stone mountains above the Deel near Askeyton, and fine slate near Abbeyfeale on the borders of the county.

The above script has been taken entirely from Pigot's Directory, 1824, Nat. Library.

A Topographical Dictionary of Ireland by Samuel Lewis 1837.

Ballingarry, a market and a post-town, and a parish in the barony of Upper Connello, County of Limerick and a province of Munster, 16 miles SW x S from Limerick and 111 miles SW x W from Dublin; containing 8,651 inhabitants of which number 1,685 are in the town. Several religious houses appear to have been founded here at a very early period, and have been greatly confounded with each other by various writers. The earliest of which any account is preserved is one founded by **Donough Cairbre O'Brien**, for Conventual Franciscans, a little eastward of the town, but generally attributed to Fitzgerald, Lord of Clenlis; the walls which are tolerably perfect, and a beautiful square tower, are still remaining. A preceptory of Knights Templars was founded in 1172, which, after the suppression of that order in 1304, was granted to the Knights Hospitallers and in the immediate vicinity was a Cistercian Abbey, founded by the **Fitzgeralds,** in 1198, and dedicated to the Blessed Virgin, which afterwards became a cell to the Abbey of Corcomroe; it was also called Kilson, and from the similiarity of the name has often been mistaken for the Abbey of Kilshane. There was also a convent for Sisters of the Order of St. Augustine, of which no vestiges can be traced.

The town is situated on the road from Rathkeale to Charleville, and in a pleasing and sheltered valley which opens towards the West; it consists of one long irregular street and several smaller, and contains 276 houses, of which the greater number are small but tolerably well built. A building called the Turrett was erected by a branch of the **de Lacy** family, and repaired by Col. **O'Dell** in 1683. as appears by a stone in the chimney; it was lately the residence of Major O'Dell. Near the town are the Fort-William flour mills, the property of **Mrs. Graves,** and three miles to the east are the Kilmore flour-mills; the property of John Tuthill, Esq, of Kilmore House, adjacent to which is a good bridge, built by his grandfather. The markets are on a Tuesday and Friday, chiefly for the sale of vegetables; there is no market house and the public scales are in the open street. Fairs are held on Easter Monday; Whit Monday; July 4th and Dec.5th , chiefly for the sale of horses, horned cattle and pigs. Here is a station of the Constabulary Police, and petty sessions are held every Saturday.

The parish comprises 16,219 statute acres, as applotted under the tithe act, and valued at £16,013 per annum. About one hundred acres are common lands, and of the remainder, a large proportion is good arable land under an improved state of agriculture but the greater portion is pasture; there is scarcely any bog or waste land. The soil is very variable, in some parts remarkably fertile, and in others rocky, sterile and cold; it is for the greater part based on a substrata of silicious grit rising from the limestone vales into hills of considerable elevation in three different parts of the parish. To the south-west of the town rises the hill of Kilnamona, on which is a lake, supposed to have been formed by the excavation of a coal mine, and called Lough-na-Gual, or 'the lake of coal.' Directly opposite is Knockfiernha, which commands a most extensive prospect.

The principle seats are:

Ballyno Cox, handsome residence	of	W.	**Cox**, Esq.,
Glenwilliam Castle	of	W. H.	**Massey**, Esq.,
Ballino Kane	of	W.	**Scanlan,** Esq.,
The Grove	of	Major	**O'Dell**,
Odell Ville	of	T. A.	**O'Dell,** Esq.,
Rossmore	of	Capt. J.W.	**Shelton**,
Mount Brown	of	J. S.	**Brown**, Esq.,
Heathfield	of	E.	**LLoyd**, Esq.,
Fort-William	of	T.	**O'Dell,** Esq.,
Liskennet	of	R. K.	**Sheehy**, Esq.,
Woodstock	of	Richard D.	**Graves,** Esq.,
Ash Grove	of	D. D.	**Power**, Esq.,
Frankfort	of	R.	**Standish,** Esq.,
The Glebe	of	Rev. T.	**Gibbings**,
Ballynail	of	J.	**Cox**, Esq.,
Kilbeg	of	H.	**Scanlan,** Esq., and
Springmount	of	E.	**Fitzgerald**, Esq.

There are also many neat villas in the parish. The living is a rectory and a vicarage, in the diocese of Limerick, and in the patronage of the Earl of Cork; the tithes amount to £900. The church, a small but very neat edifice in the early English style, with a lofty square tower, was built in 1820. The glebe house was built by the aid of a loan of £500 from the late Board of First Fruits, in 1822. The R.C. parish is co-extensive with that of the Established Church; there are three chapels, one in the town, one near Knockfiernha and one near the south eastern extremity of the parish. The parochial school for male and female children is aided by the rector, who provides the school house rent-free; and there are eight pay schools, in which are about 420 children. A dispensary is supported by subscriptions. Adjoining the town are the remains of a very beautiful castle, of which the original name and the history are unknown; it is now called Parson's which perhaps might have been originally a window; it is seven feet high by about four feet (7'X 4'). The walls are about seventeen feet high (17') and two feet nine inches (2' 9") in thickness. The tower, which is square, springs from two large pointed arches about fifteen feet (15') high; seven and a half feet (7' 6") in width and three feet two inches (3' 2") in thickness; these arches are four and a half feet ($4^{1}/_{2}$') from each other.

On this tower there are several windows of the annexed form. There is also a small square narrow opening on the tower between the trace of the upper part of the roof of the nave and the top of the arch. A similar opening appears to have been on the opposite or east side of the tower, but it is now much shattered. The west gable of the nave is totally destroyed, but the bare traces of it's foundations which are observable, enable us to determine the length of this part of the Abbey, viz thirty nine feet (39'); it's breadth is nineteen feet eleven inches (19'11"). Of the south wall of the nave about eleven feet (11') in length near the west, retaining the original height and a portion about four and a half feet (4 6") high adjoining the former, remain. Only a small portion of the north wall retaining the original height and adjoining the tower, remains. Most of the breaches and features of (on?) this Abbey are filled up to the height of four or five feet with loose stones. The stones of this building are of a regular size and cemented with lime and sand mortar. There is at present no burial at this place. According to **Fitzgerald** *(History of Limerick, Vol 1, page 574)* the Abbey near Ballingarry belonged to the order of St. Francis.

Ballingarry Castle, the walls of which are in a state of perfect preservation, is situated in the townland of Knight Street immediatly adjoining the village of Ballingarry. It measures thirty eight feet by twenty six and a half feet (38' X 26' 6") on the outside. On the south east side there is a window, the frame of which is shaped thus.* Some of the glass still remains in it. Towards the east corner of the same side, there is a square port hole, and over it a small narrow glazed window. On the south west side there is a double pointed window, the framework of which is of wood; it has a very modern appearance. Above this on each side there are two windows of this form having still some glass in them.* On the north west side near the ground there is a window formed somewhat thus.* and near the top of this side there is a window having ornamental moulding of cut stone. On the north corner there is a square tower, the north west side of which is a continuation of the wall of the castle; this tower is about one hundred feet (100') in height, and contains several narrow square windows. The entrance is at the north east. On this side there is a window of ornamental cut-stone and two plain square windows having the glass still remaining in them. The walls of this castle are about sixty five feet (65') high, three feet nine inches (3'9") in thickness and built of regular sized stones cemented with lime and sand mortar. The tower contains the stairs leading to the top of the building. The castle consists of three stories, the ceiling over the second floor being arched and plastered. On the third floor there is fixed a large old chimney piece brought from Kilmallock by Mr. Gibbons, who at one period fitted up this castle as a dwelling place. On the centre of the upper part of this chimney piece there is a slab having the following letters and figures raised on it: 16 IHS 38. Towards the edges of the chimney piece on each side of this slab are the letters S.H. on the left, and E.H. on the right. Ballingarry castle is said traditionally to have been an erection of the Knights Templars, from whom the name of the townland in which it is situated, and a street in the village, is called Knight Street.

The inhabitants say that there was formerly a Castle called **Castle Rag,** the site of which is now occupied by a modern house in the village of Ballingarry, immediately adjoining the Protestant Church. In the townland of Rylaans, at a spot the ancient name of which is Ard Eaglais, now under cultivation and near the dwelling house of Major Odell, is pointed out by the people the site of a religious edifice called the '**Priory**' by some, by others the '**Friary.**' The foundation stones have been met with from time to time, in tilling the ground. The field on which it stood is to this day called 'the Friary (Priory) Garden.' This establishment is said to have belonged to the Knight's Bannerets. The local tradition says that in the time of Cromwell's Wars, (1649-1650), the Odell's retreated and took shelter here and that the valuable possessions of the Knights and of the Odell family are (have been) deposited at the Friary.

Near the east boundary of the same Townland of Rylaans there is a well, reputed holy and called **John's Well.** In the same townland and near the above, there remains a bastion or turret of an old Castle said to have belonged to the **Lacy** family. It is popularly called '**the Turrett.**' In the east of the townland of Grenagh are the ruins of an old church called **Shannaboha** (Seana Bhoithe) situated in a large grave yard still in use. This church is now all destroyed except a small fragment of the east gable and a smaller one of the north side wall, both of which are featureless.

In the townland of Lissamota on level ground about one mile and a half north of the village of Ballingarry there is an old Castle called by the name of the townland. The walls are still perfect and are about sixty feet (60') high and five and a half feet (5'6") in thickness. It measures fourteen and a half feet by eleven feet, ten inches (14'6" X 11'10") on the inside. There are two stone arches still remaining over the first and second floors; it originally contained three other floors, i.e. in all five floors. This is a very strong castle; it was surrounded by a lios or earthen rampart, whence the name **Lios A Mhota**. Of this lios not a vestige now remains, it having been entirely carried away for manure. Lisamota Castle belonged to the Desmond family.

Woodstock (Bun a Stoigh) Castle is situated in the townland of the same name on level ground in a valley less than half a mile north of Ballingarry. It measures twenty one feet, ten inches by fifteen feet, nine inches (21' 10"X 15' 9"), the walls being about thirty five feet high (35') at present and five feet, ten inches (5'10") in thickness. The first stone arch remains. This building looks very old and is all covered with ivy. There is no tradition concerning it's ancient possessors.

Of the old **Church of Kilmacow,** situated in the townland of the same name two and three quarter miles to the east of Ballingarry, the west gable is destroyed, but the east gable and the greater part of the side walls are standing. It is fifty eight feet long and eighteen feet, three inches in breadth (58' X 18'3"), the walls being two feet, ten inches (2'10") in thickness. The east window is about six inches wide outside, but towards it's top it is so covered with ivy that it's height inside could not be learned. On the outside it is four feet, ten inches high (4'10") and five feet (5') from the ground. It widens to four feet (4') on the inside. At the distance of three feet, ten inches (3'10") from the east gable, the south side wall has a small window which is reduced to a shapeless breach on the outside, where it was narrow. On the inside it widens to four feet, two inches (4'2"), but it's top is destroyed. Directly opposite this on the north wall, there is a small window, evidently old, in tolerable preservation, measuring on the inside four feet, three inches (4'3") in width and five and one third feet (5'4") in height and on the outside four feet, three inches (4'3") in height and six inches (6") in width, being six feet, two inches (6'2") from the ground. It is round headed both inside and outside. There is a breach on the south wall, evidently where the doorway was placed. There is a Castle-like house in ruins in this townland (i.e.Kilmacow). In this parish (Ballingarry) is situated the lofty hill of **Cnoc-Fir-Inne,** which is believed to be inhabited by the great fairy chief Donn-Firinne, who is often seen marshalling his warlike troops on the side of the hill. Nothing has yet turned up to shew whether this Donn was Dessa or Donn, the son of Milesius.

(Footnote: The antiquities of this parish were, with the exception of a few places in the more distant part of it, examined and described by Mr.O'Keeffe.) J. O'Donovan.
Note also re the stars *. In the text are hand drawn maps of windows. I did not reproduce them here.

Clooncagh. The O'Donovan Letters.

Situation. This Parish is in the Barony of Upper Connello and is bounded on the north by the Parish of Rathkeale; on the east by the Parish of Ballingarry; on the south by Kilmeedy, and on the west by Mahoonagh and Cloonelty. Name. This is supposed by Archdal and his followers to be the Cluain Claidheach - Maodhog of the ancient Irish authorities as quoted by Colgan, and I can very easily believe that it is, as the natives assert that St. Maidoc is still remembered in the Parish. The name however, is now pronounced by the natives as if written Cluain Cath, which if correct would signify Battle - Field. The old **Church of Clooncah** is in a great state of dilapidation but from what remains it appears to be a ruin of great antiquity. Its choir is entirely destroyed, as is also the south wall of the nave, except a very small fragment near the south west corner from which it appears that the wall was two feet eleven inches (2'11") thick. The choir arch is much injured in its sides, but its semicircular head remains which is eleven feet (11') from the present level of the ground. The north wall is in good preservation; it is nine feet seven inches (9' 7") in height and built of large stones cemented with very good mortar. The west gable is up, but its little belfry is nearly destroyed as well as its semi - Cyclopean doorway, which is now reduced to a formless breach. The nave is thirty seven feet

(37') in length and sixteen feet (16') in breadth, but the dimensions of the choir cannot be determined.

The following inscription is on a lime stone flag inserted in the north wall on the outside within about twelve feet of the north west corner :-
'Here lyeth the bodies of Daniel **Sulivan** who died Anno Domini 1682, Margaret his wife who died Anno Domini 1690, Derby his son who died on the 22nd day of July 1708, and Joane his wife who died the 28th of March 1693. Mathew Sullivan who died the 7th April 1716.'

I here insert what the Irish writers have collected of the history of Cluain Claidheach, which is very little. This Parish was examined by me. J. O'Donovan, July 25th, 1840. Ballingarry.

Cluainclaidheach. *(AA. SS. Page 212. C. 38. Vit. S. Maidoci. XXXI Janurii.)*

At another time, Saint Moedoc (he, S. Maidoc restored the dead daughter of the Chief to life) hearing that some of his own family were captives among the Momonians, namely in that territory which is called Hy Conaill Gabhra, proceeded to liberate them from their captivity. And when the Man of God had arrived there, the Chief of that Territory (illius terrae) was unwilling to give him audience, nor did he leave him to remain in his fort (in suo castello). Before the entrance of that fort the Man of God fasted three days. The fast being ended, the daughter of the Chief whom he loved very much died suddenly. The wife of the Chief, knowing that this fact was the cause of a miracle, brought the lifeless body to S. Moedoc. And the servant of God being requested by her mother and by her (own) attendants, resuscitated her from death. But the hard (hearted) Chief still (or as yet) resisted S. Moedoc with harsh words. And when Saint Moedoc began to curse the Chief, a certain boy who stood hard by said: Holy Senior (&) Sire, may your malediction be on this rock; and when he had said upon this rock be the curse, instantly was that rock divided into parts (by his curse, he (St. Moedoc) split the rock and thus converted the tyrant to penance). That Chief, seeing this now, did penance and left (or let) his relatives liberated (or free) to St. Moedoc, and offered him the place which is called Cluainchladh - bhaith (Cluain - claidblaim) (37) and the Holy Man erected a Monastery there, and blessing the place itself and the Chief who gave it, retired from thence. (There is more data of a technical nature as to what various historians like Archdall, Gough, Lanigan wrote but nothing of significance and some is a repeat of above.)

Ballingarry and Granagh. The Name Books.

Area is in acres, roods and perches

Ballangarry. Baile An Garraidh. Town of the Garden. Situated in the west part of Cloontemple townland with Knight Street and Rylanes.

Ballyeelan. Baile Ui Fhaolain. O'Phelan's Town. Property of Mr. **Pigott**, Limerick, 532-02-17. In the south west of this townland is St. Patrick's Holy Well. This well is resorted to from all parts by individuals affected with sore eyes.

Ballygreenan. Baile Ui Ghroidhnain. O'Grynan's Town. Property of John **Pigot**, Esq., Limerick, 950 acres. In the south is a Children's Burial Ground. Here also is a trigl. Station called Cill a Liatain.

BallyguilaTaggul. Baile Ghoill a' t-Seagail. Ballyguile of the Rye. Property of Wm. H. **Massy**, Esq., Clanwilliam, 483-01-13. In the north-east of the townland is Ballyguile Cottage. Here also is Graigue.

Ballyguilebeg. Baile Goill. Town of the Englishman. Property of John **Dwyer**, Esq., England, 95 acres..

Ballykeavin East. Baile Ui Caemhain. O'Kevan's Town. Property of **Lord Clare**, Mount Shannon, 147-02-34.

Ballykeavin West. See Supra. Property of **Trinity College Dublin,** 194-03-37. In the west of the townland is Fair Field Lodge, also known as Ballykevan Lodge, the residence of Crone **Odel**.

Ballyknockaun. Baile an Chnocain. Town of the Hillock. Property of Willian **Scanlan**, Esq., Ballynockaun, 145 acres of Demesne. In the south part is Ballyknockaun House, the residence of Counsellor **Scanlan.**

Ballynaha. Baile na h-Athach. (h-Aithe). Town of the Kiln. Property of John **Pigot** Esq., Cappard, 464-03-30. In the west-central part is Ballynahaha House, the residence of Counsellor Matthew **Scanlan,** Esq. In the west part is O'Brien's Fort and in the southern part are Keary's two forts.

Ballynaroogabeg East. Baile na Ruaige Beag. Town of the Rout. (Little). Property of Thomas Alexander **Odle,** Esq., Victoria Terrace, Limerick, 131 acres. About the centre of this townland is Ashburrow House, a seat of Mr. **Power** of Glenwilliam.

Ballynaroogabeg West. Vide Supra. Property of Thomas Alexander **Odle**, Esq., containing 209-02-11 of a demesne. In the south of this townland is an ancient fort in which is a Trigl. Station called Frankfort. In the east part of this townland is Odelville House, a seat of John **Odle,** Esq.

Ballynashig. Baile an Easaig. Town of the Waterfall. Property of John **Pigot**, Esq., 149 acres. This name (Ballynashig) is not known to the people.

Ballyneal. Baile Ui Neill. Town of O'Neill. Property of the Hon. John **Massy**, Limerick, 656-03-30. In the west of the townland is Ballinamona House, the residence of John **Cox,** Esq. Baile na Mona - Town of the Bog.

Ballyno. Baile No. Newtown. Property of William **Cox,** Esq., Vallynoe, 661-01-22. In the north-west part is Ballynoe House, the residence of Wm. **Cox,** Esq.

Ballyroe East. Baile Reo. Town of the Frost. Baile Ruadh would mean 'Redtown.' Property of Edmund **Nash,** Esq., Fort Edmund, 169 acres. About the centre of the townland are two ancient forts, Lissmote and Lissnakillode. Elsewhere this is given as Lissnakillove - Lios na Cille - Fort of the Burial Place.

Ballyroe West. See Above. Property of John **Odel,** Esq., Lissduane, 99-03-23.

Ballyvellogue. Baile Bholog. Town of the Bullocks. Property of Genrl. **Dixon**, England, 282 acres.

Caherhennesy. Cathair Aenghusa. The Stone Fort of Angus. (now Aeneas). Property of John **Odel,** Esq., Lisduane, 235-01-03. In the west part of the townland is Caherhenesy Lodge.

Cloonregan. Cluain Reagain. Reagan's Clon, lawn or bog island. Property of Major **Odel,** Odel Grove, 119-03-30.

Cloontemple. Cluain Teampuill. Clon, lawn or bog island of the Church. Property of Major **Odel,** Odel Grove, 78 acres, of which 48 acres is Demesne and the remainder arable land. In the south-west is by far the greater portion of the Village of Ballingarry. In the north is the Paddock Fort trigl. station. In the north-west of the townland is a Holy Well. This is also known as Tobhar Ri an Domhnaigh, Well of the King of Sunday. It is also known as Tubberindony or Sunday Well. It is noted for the curing of many diseases and it is frequented on Saturdays and Sundays.

Common. In the centre of the parish. Bounded on the north by Ballynahaha and Ballyroe East., on the west by Ballyroe W., Caherhenesy, Gorteen and Kilmihil: on the south by Ballyelan and Ballygrennan and on the east by Kilmacow, Killoughty and Ballyvologe. Contains 652-03-17, about half of which is arable, the remainder rough ground.

Coolrus. Cul Ros. Back of the Woods or Shrubberies. The people call this 'Coolrusk' but perhaps incorrectly. Property of Richard **Hart**, Esq., Coolrus, 1,030 acres. In the east boundary is a well called Patrick's Well. In the south part is Coolrus House, the residence of Richard **Harte,** Esq., and a single-arch Coolrus bridge.

Dollas Upper. Dola. Supposed to be a corruption of Tolaigh, a hill. Dullas in the barony map. Property of Lord **Langford,** $466^{1}/_{2}$ acres of which 90 acres are marshy bog.

Dollas Lower. See Dollas Upper above. Recte Dolla or Dola, the S being added to form the English plural. The property of Mrs. **Pigott,** $244^{1}/_{2}$ acres.

Downslara. Dun. This is the Irish name meaning an earthen Fort. Property of Alfred **Furlong**, Esq., Newcastle, 174-01-13.

Durlus. Durlas. A Strong Fort. Property of Richard **Hart**, Esq., Coolrus, 172-01-07.

Durraclogh. Durmhagh-Chloch. Stoney, Oak-Wood Plain. Property of William **Cox**, Esq., Ballynoe, 443-03-34.

Frankfort. Baile na Fraoingce. A fancy name. Phonetically - Town of the French. Property of Richard **Standish,** Esq., Frankfort, 518-02-09. In the south-east of the townland is Frankfort House the residence of Richard **Standish,** Esq.. In the south-west is Cloonready Cottage, the residence of Mr. **Browne**. Cluan Riada - Ready's clon, lawn or meadow.

Glanwilliam. Gleann na Reatha. Glen of the Running. Glenaraha is the old name. Property of William H. **Massy**, Esq., Glenwilliam, 552 acres. In the west boundary of this townland is Massy Tower, the residence of Mr. **Power.**

Glebe Of Knight Street. Called from the Knight's Templars. Property of the **Earl of Cork**, England, 07-00-14. Later shown as the property of the Revd. Mr. **Stuart,** Glebe House. In this townland is Glebe House, the residence of the Revd. Mr. **Steward**.

Graigbeg. Graig Bheag. The Little Village. Property of John **Dwyer**, Esq., England, 219 acres.

Graigacurragh. Graig a' Churraigh. Village of the moor or morass. Property of Genl. **Dixon,** England, 608-03-38.

Greenagh. Greanach. Gravelly. Property of Richard **Peppard,** Esq., Cappagh, 366-03-15. In the east of this townland is Shannonaboha Church (in ruins) and burying ground. Shaunaboha - Seana-Boithe - Old booths or tents. Near the north boundary is a R.C. Chapel.

Gurteen. Guirtin. The Little Garden, or cultivated field. Property of Major **Odel,** Odel Grove, 82 acres arable land. *(In my youth, I heard this townland referred to as Gorteen-na-mBo - the Little Garden of the Cows. C.K.)*

Kilbeg East. Cill Beag. Little Church. Property of Richard **Peppard**, Esq., Cappagh, 41-02-33.

Kilbeg West. See Above. Property of William **Scanlan**, Esq., Ballyknockaun, 164-02-26. In the south of the townland is Kilbeg Lodge, the seat of John **Scanlan.**

Killoughta. Cill Lachtin. St. Lachtin's Church. Pronounced by the people Killaughteen. Property of General **Dixon,** England, 202-02-14.

Kilmackanerla North. Cill Mhic an Iarla. The Church of the Earl's Son. Property of William H. **Franks,** Esq., Mallow, 460-03-09. About the central part is Kilmacanearla Abbey (in ruins.)

Kilmackanerla South. As above. Property of William H. **Franks**, Esq., Mallow, 116-03-14.

Kilmacow. Cill MoChuach. St. McDhuach's Church. Property of John **Pigot,** Esq., Cappard, 1,070-03-23. There is a castle here. In the north east of the townland are Kilmacow House, Kilmacow Church (in ruins) and Burial Ground. In this townland is Cnoc Firinne - Knockfeerina - the Hill of Truth. This is the barometer of the district.

Kilmeehill. Cill Mhichil. St. Michael's Church. Property of Major **Odel,** Odel Grove, 436-03-12. In the north central part is Kilmihil Burial Ground.

Kilmore. Cill Mor. The Great Church. Property of John **Tuthill,** Esq., Nenagh, 965-02-01. In this townland is Ballanleeny village. Baile an Line - The Town of the Line. Contains about eighteen or twenty scattered houses.

Kilmore Demesne. See above. Property of John **Tuthill,** Esq., 112-01-15. About the central part is Kilmore House.

Kilshaan. Cill Seain. John's Church. Property of John **Pigot,** Esq., Limerick, 28-02-25. Near the north-west boundary is Ballangarry Abbey, (in ruins), having a steeple to it of 60 ft. high. There were persons buried in this Abbey formerly.

Kingsland. Kingsland. Property of Charles **Tuthill,** Esq., Dublin, 216 acres.

Knight Street. Property of Mrs. C. E. **Greaves,** Woodstock, 97-00-26. In the north part of this townland is a Trigl. Station called Dunburns. In the north is Echo Lodge, the seat of Revd. Mr. **Fitzgerald,** R.C. Archdeacon. There is a beautiful echo here. In the east is a part of the Village of

Ballingarry. Here also is Old Castle, called Ballingarry Castle. It is in a good state of preservation.

Lissamota. Lios a' Mhota. Fort of the Moat. Property of **Lord Middleton,** England, 609-02-01. Near the north-east is a Children's Burial Ground. Near the west boundary is Lissamota Castle, (in ruins). This castle is supposed to have been built by the Fitzgerald family.

Lissavarra. Lios a' Bharraigh. Barry's Fort. Property of the **Earl of Dunraven**, Adare, 153-00-21. In the north-east boundary is Cohy's or Lissavarra Fort. Coohy's - or Cowhy (O Cobhthaigh) - is a family name.

Lissduff. Lios Dubh. Black Fort. Property of John **Pigot,** Esq., Limerick, 106-00-07.

Lissdooaun. Lios Dubhain. Duan's Fort. Property of **General Dixon,** England, 677-02-26. Near the east boundary is Jackson's Turret. There is a notable old chimney (in ruins) of about 50ft. high in this turret. In the east is Lisduane House, the seat of Walter **Mason.** Here also is Lissdooaun bridge. This bridge has three arches. In the south-west is Fort Edward (Edmond) House, the residence of Captain **Nash** and named from a small fort at the rere of the said house.

Lisskennet East. Lios Coinead. Lios is a Fort and Coinead seems a man's name. Property of C. **Heffernane,** Monasteranenagh, 235-01-20. In the east is Liskennett House, the residence of Roger **Sheehy**, Esq.

Lisskennett West. See above. Property of C. **Heffernane**, Monasteranenagh, 301-01-32.

Mournaan. Moirnean. Meaning uncertain. Property of Lord George **Quin,** England, 859-03-18. In the south part is Morenane Old Church, (in ruins). Here also is Crock Phadian Burial Ground. Cnoc Phaidin - Paddy's Hill. Knockphaudeen It appears there was here a church built by St. Patrick or dedicated to him..

Rylaans. Roidhlean - meaning uncertain. Property of Thomas **Odel**, Esq., Odel Grove, 88-03-22. About the west central part of the townland is an R.C. Chapel. At the south boundary is a part of the Village of Ballingarry. John's Well is near the east boundary. It is said to be holy, and has a large ash tree growing over it. Here is an Old Castle, in ruins, and Ballangarry Old Mill, also in ruins in the east boundary. *(This is the mill referred to in the sale of the Encumbered Estates records. C.K.)* The Friary Gardens - Ardeanglan ? - are situated in the centre of this townland about 200 links south of the R.C.Chapel of Ballangarry. This is a small garden enclosed by a stone wall in the centre of which was formerly a religious edifice called the Friary. It is now under cultivation and not even a vestige of the foundation can now be found. Situated in the centre of the townland and within sixty links of the Friary garden, on the south side, is the Turrett. This Turrett, (or House) was built by the Knight's Templars in 1575, and inhabited by the Odel family in 1783 as appears by an inscription on the wall of the house. Here is the Grove House, residence of Major **Odel.**

Woodstock. Bun a' Stoig. No meaning given. Property of John **Odel**, Esq., Lisduane. Area 27-01-15. In the west boundary is Woodstock Castle (in ruins.)

Clouncagh. The Name Books.

Clouncagh Parish. Cluain Cath. Plain or Meadow of the Battle. Area 4,542-01-02. There are only two principal roads extending through this parish.

Ballybeggaan. The property of Wm. **Smith O'Brien,** Esq., Near the centre of this townland, on the brow of a small hill, stands something resembling a redoubt called cruckaun a chaupeen.

Ballyhahil. O'Tahill's Town. The property of **Lord Clare.**

Ballykennedy North. The property of **Trinity College**. Nothing remarkable in this townland.

Ballykennedy South. The property of Samuel **Dickson,** Esq.

Ballynaroogabeg. Town of the Defeat (Little). The property of Thos. Alex. **Odell**, Esq.

Ballynaroogamore North. Town of the Defeat (Big). The property of Thos. Alex. **Odell,** Esq.

Ballynaroogamore South. The property of **Lord Clare.**

Carhoomore. Great Quarter. The property of Revd. Henry **Hart.**

Clouncagh. The property of Lord Clare and Thos. A. **O'Dell,** Esq. of Odellville. Here are two R.C. chapels, St. Patrick's Well, Sunday's Well and Lady's Well.

Gortnacreha Lower. Garden or Field of the Plunder. The property of Matthew **Scanlan,** Esq. Names in this townland Oughanskaw and Brook Lodge.

Gortnacreeha Upper. Property of the Hon. Wandersford **Butler**.

Gurteen East. Gurteen: the Little Field, Gort or Garden a.k.a. Cahirighane and Gurteencahirane. The property of Thos. Alex. **Odell,** Esq.

Gurteen West. The property of **Lord Clare**. There is a smithy at the cross roads. To the SW stands 'Laught Paudrick'

Kilnamona. Church of (at or in) the Bog. The property of Hamon **Massy**, Esq. A minor. There is a small lough called 'Lough a Guole.'

Teernahella. District of the Elbow or Angle. The property of **Lord Clare**.

Teerveena. Mainy's District. The property of the Reverend Ed. **Jeffries**.

Glebe of Clouncagh, # 1. The property of Christopher **Delmege**, Esq., Castle Park near Limerick. Bounded by Gurteen E., Clouncagh, Ballykennedy S. and Ballybeggaan. All under tillage and pasture.

Glebe of Clouncagh, # 2. A small circular glebe near the ruins of Clouncagh Church. Property of C. **Delmege**, Esq.

St. Patrick's Well. Townland of Clouncagh. A large holy well at which stations are performed on Saturday nights. It is celebrated for curing blindness. **Sunday's Well. Lady's Well.** A holy well so called in the townland of Clouncagh. *(It is not clear if these three names refer to the one well, but it appears that they do. C.K.)*

Clouncagh Church. In the Glebe of Clouncagh, # 2. An old church in ruins with a burial ground.

Oughanskaw. River of the Shadow. A small river flowing into the Deel.

Ballinarooga Castle. The ruins of an old castle in the townland of Ballynaroogamore South.

Brook Lodge. A neat house, one story high, with offices and a plantation. The residence of John **Mason**, Esq. In the townland of Gortnacreeha Lower.

Laught Paudrick. Patrick's Monument. In Gurteen West townland. A remarkable stone surrounded by brushwood.

Cruckaun a Chaupeen. Hillock of the Cap. In Ballybeggaan townland. A redoubt on the brow of a small hill.

Lough a Guole. Lough of the Coal. In Kilnamona parish (?). A small lough with an island in it.

Ballyno Bridge. Newtown Bridge. Between Ballyno and Gortnacreha Lower. A bridge on the road leading to Brook Lodge over the Aughanskaw river.

PART II

Early 19th Century Records.

Civil registration of marriages did not begin until April, 1845 and applied only to non-Catholics. In 1864, civil registration of births, deaths and marriages became compulsory for everyone. With the loss of the censii from 1800 - 1900, genealogical information from this early 19th century period is at a premium. The following series of records were researched as found and are reproduced here, in their limited format, in the hope that they may be of interest to most people and of specific benefit to some. As well as genealogical based records I have included some information on trade statistics which are of interest to the region.

1792-1870. The Vestry Book of Ballingarry.

The old vestry book for Ballingarry is on microfilm in the National Archives. The Rev. Hamilton quoted from it in his book but attached is a chronological record of what I consider are the events of the Vestry in the time period covered by it. The Vestry was an assembly of parishioners who met for the dispatch of parochial business and took it's name from the meeting room - the vestry of the church. By law however all the officers of the committee had to be members of the Church of Ireland. There was a select vestry which dealt with church affairs and a general vestry which dealt with parish affairs. The churchwardens appointed were responsible for parish finances. Those present at the various vestry meetings were generally the same with a slight change in personnel over the years. As I want to name everyone who was recorded as being in Ballingarry I will not repeat the same names.

1792.
Tuesday, April 10th. Present were: William King, Batt Mara, Geo. Sheehy, Allexr. Odell (churchwarden); George Massy (churchwarden) and John Graves, Minister.

Monday, April 16th. At the vestry meeting the following expenditure was agreed: Parish Clerk, £10. Sexton, £03. Bread & Wine, £00-13-04. Registrar, £05-05-00. Pair of stocks, £00-10-00. New vestry book, £00-05-05. Fees for making collection, £3. Panes of glass wanting in the windows, £00-15-00. Keeping roof in repair by John Phair, £02-00-00; in addition to money laid in at former vestries for a bell. Repairing two seats near the door, repairing window sashes & church door, £03-16-03. It was decided that the widow of the sexton (deceased, not named) be appointed to act in his place. The sum of £30-07-01 to be applotted by Mr. David Fitzgerald and Mr. Patrick Mason.

1793.
Tuesday, April 2. Michael Scanlan, junr and Mr. Miles Monkton appointed churchwardens. Among those present were Patrick Mara and Thomas Odell.

April 8. It was resolved 'to make up a deficiency in money laid out on a bell and carriage of it from Dublin, £03-01-03. Making five perches of a sewer to carry off the water from the church yard and gravelling the ground. Also, "church gates, piers and a good padlock."

April 19. Jeffrey Foote present among others.

1794.
April 18. Voted money to families whose husbands served in the County of Limerick Royal Militia. To Mary Cronin, wife of Darby Cronin (had one child) and to Mary Cronin, wife of John Cronin (had one child). Also wife of John Cregan (had four children, all under ten). Also wife of Thomas Fitzmaurice (had three children). Present were Anthony Parker, Michael Monkton & others.

April 23. Present were Robert Odell, Nicholas Monkton, John Lonegan, Richard Odell & others. Applotted 1s-6$^1/_2$d per 100 acres for four months provisions for two militiamen's wives and children.

April 25. Present were Michael Fitzgibbon, William Massy and others.

June 25. Examined whether Margaret Leddin, wife of John Leddin serving in the County of Limerick Royal Militia be entitled to financial support during her husband's absence whilst called out into actual service. It was decided she was not entitled to anything. Present were Richard Standish, Michael Lane and others.

1795.
April 7. Resolved that the ground formerly occupied by Mr. Tuthill's seat be granted to Thomas Odell, esq. for a seat. Reference was made to extraordinary trouble in collecting last year's cess (tax).

1796.
March 9. Hugh Cox and Aleck Odell appointed churchwardens. Resolved for sending down to Limerick town a foundling child thirteen shillings. Present were James Purcell and others.

1797.
April 18. George Massy of Glenwilliam and Hugh Cox of Ballinoe appointed churchwardens. Resolved that Denis Bowen would collect the cess (tax). That Hugh and John Cox become a security for the said Dennis Bowen whilst collecting and paying in said cess. Edward Lloyd and Nicholas Monkton be appointed to applot said sum on parish.
May 16. Resolved it is agreed to give ground vacant near the Communion Table to George Massy to build a seat on. Present were John Airey and others.

1798.
April 10. George Massy and John Cox of Ballinoe appointed churchwardens. Reference was made to re-building north wall of the Church. Among those present was Dobbyn Casey, John Lenegan and others.

1799.
March 26. Present were Michael Fitzgerald, Jnr. and others.

1800.
April 15. George Massy and Henry Odell appointed churchwardens.

1801.
April 7. George Massy and William J. Harte of Coolruss appointed churchwardens. Among those present was John Hardin.

1802.
April 20. George Massy and George Monkton appointed churchwardens. Aid to re-build church, £151-10-04.

June 5. Pursuant to directions of the Bishop of Limerick for the maintenance of foundling children the following persons are hereby appointed overseers of deserted children in said parish for the ensuing year, viz Thomas Lenegan, John Monkton and William Sperin all resident in said parish and that a sum of £5 only be raised for the maintenance of one foundling already in the care of said parish since October last and that the sum of £5 pounds sterling as a fund to provide for any other foundlings that may herein after be in said parish.

1803.
April 11. Voted towards re-building of church, £202. Present were Thomas A. Odell and others.
May 12. Present were George Hamilton and others.
Sept.19. At the request of the Deputy Governors held at Ballingarry, viz. Charles Conyers, Michael Scanlan, Brandish Plummer and William Lock for the purpose of levying £109-4-0 county cess (tax) to give eight men to serve in the army of the reserve being the quota of said army to be raised for said parish.
Sep. 29. Present were James Purcell, Joseph Benson, John Sullivan, John Hederman, George Manning and others. As there were no churchwardens for Kilfinny it was agreed to applot same which they did. John Cox of Mount Cox and William Sullivan of Ballingarry were appointed to applot the sum of £136-10-00, with Patrick Hanan of Kilfinny and William Sullivan of Ballingarry applotting Kilfinny.

1804.
April 3. Among those present were Mick Hanlon.
May 1. Among those present was Richard Stephenson.

1805.
April 16. Present were Edward Murphy Rice, W.N.Crips, and others.
June 8. One foundling removed to the nursery at Shannon Grove. Appointed overseers of deserted children were John Lonegan, parish clerk: William Sperin and Thomas Lonegal all parishioners. Present were Edmond Crips and others.
April 4. To Kate Roach for looking after a foundling, £ 4-00-00. To James Mingane for painting, £12-00-00. To John Mooney, £ 6-06-00. To John Neville, £16-00-00. To Thomas O'Brien for Ironworks, £10-00-00.

1807.
Apr. 4. Resolved that a Protestant clerk be found to act as a schoolmaster.
Nov. 11. At a meeting on Nov 2 of the Deputy Governors held in Ballingarry it was agreed that Kilfinny and Bruree would come under parish control of Ballingarry and that parish quotas for militia would be as follows - Ballingarry, 10; Bruree, 6 and Kilfinny, 2 . Cess tax was applotted to pay for above.

1811.
June 18. Vestry Meeting. Southwell Ryan and others.

1818.
Apr 4. Vestry Meeting. Thomas Odell of Ashborough and Thomas Odell of Odelville be appointed to applot the cess tax.

1820.
May 4. Adjourned as a mark of respect on the death of Revd. John Graves.
Jul 17. Minister, W. Maunsell present.

1821.
Apr. 24. Minister Edward Grime present.

1824.
Apr 20. To James Connell, £4 for painting and glazing the church. To Connor Scanlan, £2-11-00 for Ironworks.

1825.
Jun 4. David Fitzgerald of Fort Lodge and others.

1826.
Jun 4. Special Vestry Meeting. Present were: William Cox, John Crokers, clk., Thomas Gibbings, vicar, George Massy, W. T. Monson, John, Thomas and Robert D. Odell, Thomas Odell, junr. and John Tuthill. *This was the meeting that agreed the Tithes*. The Revd. Gibbings was on behalf of Mrs Graves. See Part III, the section dealing with the tithes.

1827.
Apr 17. To Thomas Mitchell £2-16-00 for timber used in repair of church roof. Robert D. Odell of Fortwilliam and William Odell of Ballingarry tithe applotters.

1834.
Present were W.Barry, D. Power, Anthony Lebiep, Timothy Costelloe, Thomas Spearing and others.

1835.
Michael Brown and Thomas Bernard Odell appointed Churchwardens.

1837.
Mar 28. Michael R. Graves of Woodstock Cottage and others.

1841.
Present were Crone Odell, Wm. Ring, Alexr. Ryan, John Ryan, James L. Patterson, Michael Hickie, George Ryan and others.

1842.
William Hamo de Massy of Glenwilliam and James William Gubbins of Clouncagh appointed churchwardens.

1844.
Apr 9. Richard Power of Fortwilliam and Thomas Odell of Cottage appointed churchwardens. Note - Michael Casey has obtained a licence from the Revd. George G. Gubbins to erect a fount stone over the remains of his ancestors in Shanavoha Church. This 20th day April, 1844. G.G.G., vicar. Present were Sandy Ryan, John Quilty and others.

1845.
Present at the Easter vestry meeting were William Alexander, Michael O'Brien, Alexander and Thomas Bryan, John Dalton, parishioners, and the churchwardens D. D. Power and Richard Standish of Frankfort.

1847.
Apr 5. Dawson Hunt of Odelville and D. D. Power of Ashborough appointed churchwardens. Also present was Henry Ryan.

1848.
May 3. Frederick Massy of Ballingarry appointed churchwarden with James D. Gubbins of Clouncagh. Also present were John Brown, Parish clerk and others.

1850.
Apr 2. Present was Thomas Browne and others.

1851.
Present were Mr. Higinbotham, clk., William Jones and others.

1853.
Mar 28. John Courtney Llock of Glenwilliam appointed churchwarden with D. D. Power of Ashborough. Also present was William Denny. It was unanimously resolved that the 3rd pew from the pulpit be appointed to Mrs.Crone Odell who paid £5 toward the repair of the church.

1854.
Apr 17. Francis Odell of Liskinnitt and Thomas W. Wilkinson of St. Oswald's appointed churchwardens.

1855.
Joseph Gubbins of Kilbeg House and D. D. Power of Ashborough churchwardens. Edward Cowans, clk.

1857.
Apr 6. Thomas Sharpe, John Mason and others.

1858.
Apr 6. Also present was George Russell.

1859.
Apr 25. Colonel Jones, Kilmore House churchwarden.

1860.
Apr 10.
Michael Henry Cotter, vicar.

1862.
The following certificate is recorded in the book; 'I certify that four family burial portions of land viz. that part of the addition made to Ballingarry Churchyard nearest to the western wall of said addition, have been granted and sold by me to the following parties: John Cox, Esqr. of Ballyneale: John Neville, Esqr., Civil Engineer, Dundalk; Captain Wilkinson, St. Oswalds and Mr. Frederick Massy of Ballingarry. John Cox, Esq. vault lies on the southside of Mr. Neville's, which is on the southside of Captain Wilkinson's, whose vault is on the southside of Mr. Fredr. Massy. Each burial ground contains about fourteen square feet and by the powers vested in me I make the abovesaid plots of land to the respective parties. G.G.Gubbings. April 21, 1862.

1863.
Vestry meeting. John Airey and others.

1865.
Apr 17. Edward Atkinson donated land to enlarge the burial ground. Edward Le Geare churchwarden with E. Atkinson, Glenwilliam.

1868.
Apr 13. Mr. William Shine of Lisamota and Michael Scanlan of Ballyknockane, churchwardens.

1869.
Mar 29. Grady F. Conyers of Liskinnitt and Edward Morony of Odleville appointed churchwardens. General Jones a synodsman.

1870.
Apr. 18. Present were:

Bouchier, Joseph,	Cox, Robert	Cox, William
Crawford, Henry	Mick, Peter	Morony, Edward
Patterson, James	Shine, William	Switzer, Arthur
Townley, Charles and	Wilkinson, Captain.	

The subsequent vestry book is missing and cannot be located.

1811-1830. Local Historical Incidents.

These are snippets of local interest I found when I was researching the Limerick Evening Post.
There are also a few items for this time period from the National Archives.

1811.
Weds., Oct. 30. To Be Let - For such term as may be agreed on. Knight-Street Mills, near Ballingarry which are situated in the Centre of a fine Corn country contiguous to Rathkeale, Charleville and Croom and is well supplied with a sufficiency of water in all Seasons. Immediate possession will be given. Applications to be made to **John Neville**, Architect, Mount-Trenchard, Shanagolden or Kilcool near Rathkeale: or Mr. **Simon Flannedy**, Ballingarry either of whom will close with a solvent tenant when the value is offered. On Nov 13, 1811 the same advertisment as above appeared with the addition ... NB - **Gullivan's Lot**, adjoining the Mill, is to be let, from the 25th March next.

1812.
Sat. June 27. County Limerick. **Samuel Dickson, John Mullane** and **Edward Shehy**. To be sold on Thursday, the 4th of June next, at the New Court House, at one o'clock in the afternoon, the defendants interests in the lands of Ballynoe and Ballyanrahan, by me under the executions in these Causes. Dated 26 May, 1812. Gerald **Blennerhassett,** Sheriff. Note: The above sale is adjourned to Monday 29th inst. Dated 24th June, 1812. G. Blennerhassett, Sheriff.

1812.
Sat. 18th April. To the Gentlemen Clergy & Freeholders of the County of Limerick. A General canvas having commenced in our county, I trust my being obliged to attend my duty in Parliament will plead my excuse for not immediately paying my personal respects - I shall take the first opportunity of soliciting a continuance of that confidence which you have placed in me for five successive elections & have the honor to be, with the greatest respect and gratitude, your faithful humble servant **William O'Dell,** The Grove, April 8, 1812.

1812.
Sat. July 18. The Co. Limerick Grand Jury List.

Blennerhassett, John	**Bruce,** George E.
de Burgho, Sir John; Bart.	**Conyers**, Charles
Creagh, John	**Creed**, Charles
Crips, Edward	**Evans,** Eyre
Fitzgibbon, Thomas G.	**Foreman,** M. P.
Forsbury, George	**Glentworth**, The Rt. Hon. Lord
Gubbins, Joseph	**Harding,** Sam.
Lloyd, Rickard	**Lyons,** James
Massy, James	**Massy,** John
Odell, William	**Ryves,** William
Smyth, William	**Studdert**, John
Tuthill, George	

1813.
Weds. Jan 6. To Be Let. From 25th March, 1813. The farm of Ballynerogy, containing about thirty acres, now in the occupation of **Hayes** and partners. That small farm of Clonneagh, containing 11 acres, now occupied by **Thomas Bourke**. These two farms are situated near the Town of

Ballingarry in the barony of Upper Connello. Proposals etc. to the Rt. Hon. Earl of Clare, Mount Shannon or to **Stephen Dickson**, Esq., Georges St., Limerick. Dated: Dec. 29, 1812.

Jan 23. This contains an extract from the Cork Southern Reporter drawing attention to the upsurge in the exports of potatoes. It called for the export of potatoes to be banned in view of the fact it is the staple diet of so many people and putting the poor people at risk of starvation.

Oct 2. Twenty Guineas Reward. Whereas on Friday night, the 17th inst. a bright black mare, four years old and about 15 hands high: one of the fore feet white to nearly the knee, and the two hind over the fetlocks; ball-faced, switch tailed and trimmed rather short: was stolen out of my stable with a bridle and a saddle. I will pay 5 guineas reward to any person giving such information as may recover her and 20 guineas for mare and thief on prosecution. **David Edward Fitzgerald,** Echo Lodge, Ballingarry.

1814.

March 2. To be sold at Odelville the thining of the plantations consisting of Ash, Elm, Fir, Beech, Birch etc. The ash and elm are very gross. Terms half cash and half approved bills for remainder. Odelville, 28 Feb, 1814.

1818.

February. Statement of Evidence of **Stephen Childerhose**, Kilbeg who swore .... "..that on the night of Friday, February 6th, 1818 he was having supper with his family. Between 7-8pm a stranger called to the house and inquired for **Mrs. Fitzgerald** as he had a message for her. When **Mrs. Fitzgerald** was called the stranger asked the distance to Ballingarry. He stated he had come from Limerick. He declined the offer of refreshments and when about to leave a party of about twelve men rushed into the house armed with pitchforks and wattles and attacked **George Switzer** and **Darby Jordan** who were seated at the table. He gives a graphic account of his own beating and how he eventually escaped into another room and hid in a cupboard. He heard the assailants drag **George Switzer** out into the yard. They returned looking for him but the maid swore he had escaped in the confusion. They stole a pistol belonging to George Switzer and then left. They heard **George Switzer** groaning in the yard. He was brought into the house bleeding profusely. He died at 5.00pm on the 7th February, 1818. *(SOC ref. 1963/9 Nat. Arch.)*

October. Glenwilliam, Ballingarry. **George Massy** wrote - On 29th October at Upper Cross, Castletown Conyers, a Constable **Robert Gorman** was murdered by person or persons unknown. Constable Gorman was the man responsible for the arrest of the 'notorious **James Ryan'**. A reward of £500 had been offered for Ryan's arrest and he was found guilty and executed. (No details are given). He also arrested a Mr. **P. Riordan,** also found guilty and executed. (No details given). Mr. Massey requested approval for the offer of a reward for the apprehension of the murderers. This was approved, ref. 1959/26, and offer published in the Limerick Chronicle. *(S.O.C. Papers)*

Saturday, July 18, 1829. The house of **John Dwyer,** esq., of Liskennett, near Croom, was attacked by a numerous party at an early hour on Wednesday morning. The family roused from their beds by the smashing of the front windows prepared to resist the burglars, but the assailants, aware of the circumstances did not persevere in the attack, having retired after destroying 52 panes of glass in the house. The inmates, however, remained on the watch to day-light, when **M. Dwyer** opened the hall-door and found chalked thereon a Rockite notice, a literal copy of which is annexed :

Sir,

You may thank the hura **Tom Odel** for what is done its not for that purpose I khem here but to kill you and your family you wore well regarded in this place only for your son John the Brunswicker now dont neglect this warning I have left you.' After this followed a demand to discharge a watchman named **Costelloe.** This outrage is supposed to have been done in consequence of Mr. Dwyer, jnr., having given shelter to **Alexander Odell**, Esq., the brother of the gentleman engaged in the late duel, on the night of Saturday last, when several men were stoning the friends of **T. Odell** they could meet. *(Limerick Chronicle)*

1829.

Saturday, 12 December. Edward Fitz-Gerald, Esq., of Ballingarry in this county was Monday last sworn in as one of the Attornies of His Majesty's Court of Exchequer in Ireland and also admitted a member of the Honorable Society of King's Inns.

1830.

William Cox, Esq., of Ballinoe, High Sheriff of the County.

1806 - 1845. Births, Deaths and Marriages.

These are genealogical extracts from the Limerick Evening Post and elsewhere.

1806.
July 5. Marriage. In Quebec. Thomas Bateman **Lloyd**, aged 25, to Elizabeth **Hill,** (18) a widow. Witnesses: John ***Gondie*** & James ***Fitzgibbon***.

1812.
Sat. Jan 18. Died. On Monday at her house in William Street, **Mrs. Scanlon**, widow of Michael Scanlon, Esq., late of Ballynaha, in this county - her death is sincerely and deservedly lamented by her numerous family and by all who had the pleasure of her acquaintance.

Sept. 5. Marriage. At Croagh Church on Thursday last, **James Griffin** of Golden House, County Limerick to **Anna Brown**, 3rd daughter of Henry, of Deansfort, Co. Limerick.

Weds. Dec 9. Died. Sunday evening last at Mount Brown in this county, sincerely and deservedly lamented by her family and friends, **Mrs. Brown**, wife of John Brown, Esq.

1813.
Apr. 14. Birth. On Thursday night last, (Apr. 8th) a son. The Lady of George Gough **Gubbin,** Esq., of Maidstown.

May 29. Birth. At his father's seat, The Grove, the Lady of Thomas **Odell**, Esq., Commissioner of Excise, of a daughter.

1814.
Sat. June 25. Marriage. At the seat of her brother **Richard Taylor**, Esq., Hollypark, of this county (by special licence). **Thomas D'Arcy Evans** of Knockaderry, Esq., to **Bradazon Taylor**, daughter of the late Richard, Esq.

Sat. Jul 23. Birth. The Lady of Captain **Robert O'Dell,** Co. Limerick, of a son.

Sat. Jul 23. Ordained. In Limerick as a Priest, **William Edward Lloyd.**

Sept. 10. Died. On Monday morning at the Grove, **Mrs. Odell,** wife to Lieut. Colonel William O'Dell, M.P. for this county and one of the Lords of the Treasury. The death of this truly amiable lady is a source of the deepest affliction to a kind husband, her numerous children and an extensive highly respectable circle of relatives and friends. To the poor she was a constant benefactress, and the recollection of her benevolent and amiable qualities will long live in the memory of all who knew her. Her remains were interred on Wednesday last in Ballingarry.

1814.
Sat. Sept. 10. Died. In Cork on Sunday last, **Sir Hugh Massy** of Glenwillee, Co. Limerick, late Captain, 35th Regiment of Foot.

Weds. Nov. 16. Died. On Saturday night at his seat, Coolruss, **William Johnstone Harte**, Esq., the only son of Sir Richard Harte.

1845.
Grand Jury. John Switzer, and that he on 20th Sept., 10th late King, at Ballingarry, Co. Limerick did marry one **Mary Hodgens** and he had for his wife, and that whilst he was so married he on the 12th November, 8th Queen at Ballycahane, Co. Limerick feloniously and unlawfully did marry one **Honora McMahon**, and to her was married, the said Margaret, his former wife, being then alive against peace, etc. No details of trial.

1807 - 1846. Grand Jury Records.

Local Government in Ireland is Anglo-Norman in origin. What is known as the Norman conquest of Ireland took from 1169 to 1250. The Normans ignored the native Irish tribal tradition and arbitrarily divided the country into baronies. These were later shired and eventually became counties. The word shire is a very old term denoting a land division and from which has sprung the name Sheriff. A system of local government based on the Sheriff was put in place. He in turn had duties and responsibilities via the Grand Jury system. As the King's judges travelled on circuit it was decided that certain other functions would be dealt with at the court sitting. The system was that the Sheriff would summon twenty three of the largest landowners in the county to meet the judges and carry out some public administration duties as well as jury service. They dealt mostly with the building and repair of roads, bridges, pipes and gullets, quay walls, the erection and maintenance of courthouses and gaols and other similar type functions and in raising the finance for these works. This finance was raised by way of a tax called the county cess, levied on occupiers of land. During the 1760,s it was decided to put repair of the roads out to contract. A system was devised whereby anyone could present to the Grand Jury a certificate, attested by a Justice of the Peace, stating that works were necessary and the estimated cost. Hence the word presentment. As there was not the necessary check system in place this led to widespread abuse. This led to the Survey of the Roads of Ballingarry, 1814. (See below). The Grand Jury system was abolished in 1898.

For a better understanding of the Grand Jury system see 'An Overview of the Development of Local Government in Ireland' by Brian Donnelly, Archivist, National Archives and published in Irish Archives, Autumn 1996. The above introduction is taken in part from that article with the kind permission of Mr. Donnelly.

The work of the Grand Juries is published in book form but the various books are scattered in various archives. They are divided into Spring and Summer Sessions and the work of each session is dealt with by barony. They are important now as a census substitute. The following list of names is taken from the Grand Jury books held in the County Limerick Library and deal, in the main, with road repairs and maintenance. The book format is to give names of contractors without addresses, outline the work to be done and by describing where the work was to be done help to identify where people lived. I found these books difficult to research as I found the details in many cases not to be very specific. As the records refer to the barony it is possible that some of the names are from outside the locality. However, by comparison with the rest of the people details in this book it is possible to be almost certain that most of these people lived and worked in the area covered by this book. Also it is not too clear sometimes whether the name is owner of the house or land. Extracts are re-produced here for what they are worth. In any cases of doubt or difficulty the original books should be consulted.

1807

Barry, M.	Ballyvologue, house	Barry, J.	Killoughty, house
Burns, Thomas	Coolruss	Calinan, J.	Killatal, land
Chamberlaine, W.	Grenagh	Coleman, J.	Killattal
Collins, J.	Odelville, house	Cronnin, J.	Ballingarry, house
Daly, James	Knockferna, house	Enright, M.	Killattal
Fitzgerald, John	Ballingarry, house	Fitzgerald, W.	Lisamota, house
Fleming, W.	Caherhennessy, house	Gill, William	Ballingarry, house

Noonan, Dave	Capininghane, house	Hammond, J.	Cahirhenessy, house
Hayes, M.	Cappinihane, house	Hayes, R.	Killattal
Kean, D.	Ballyelan, land	Long, C.	Cappinihane, land
Lyons, John	Ballynaha, house	Miniter, T.	Gurteen, house
O'Donnell, J.	Ballyscanlan	Quaid, M.	Ballykennedy, house
Ranaghan, E.	Knockforan, house	Rose, F.	Kallattal
Scanlan, J.	Downes, house.		

Contractors mentioned were :

Barry, D.	Coftley, T.	Collins, P.	Conyers, C.
Cox, W.	Crips, E.,	Cull, H.	Dickson, S.
Fitzgerald, D.	Fitzgerald, E.	Foley, J.	Glarney, P.
Graves, Rev. J.	Hanrahan, J.	Healy, P.	Hederman, W.
Heffernan, P.	Houlihan, J; (Senr. & Junr)		Humphreys, J.
Hunt, John	Lanagan, T,	Massy, G.	Murphy, A.
Naish, F.	Odell, A.	O'Dell, T.A.	O'Grady, Jas.
O'Grady, S.	Quaid, T.	Shanahan J.	Sheehy, H.
Sperin, J.			

To T. A. Odell & F. Rose to repair road between the end of C. Odell's dry wall, Ballingarry and the little bridge near Cahernessy, 10 perches.

To **William Chamberlaine** of Grenagh in said parish for prosecuting to conviction **Thomas Burns** of Coolruss in said parish for illegally cutting and taking away one ash tree from and off the lands of Grenagh aforesaid, £5.

John **Sperin,** Keeper of the Bridewell, Ballingarry. William **Sperin**, Sub-constable. Half year's salary, £2..

1808

Carroll, J.: Coolruss, land.	Carmody, E : Kilmihill, house.
Casey, Dobbyn.: No details.	Enright, T.: Ballyelan, house.
Fitzgerald, M.: Gortnacrehy, land.	Fitzgerald, W.: Lisamota, house.
Fleming, W.: Caherhennessy, house.	Geoghegan, E.: Gortnacrehy, land.
Gibbons, R.: Ballinrura.	Gorman, P.: Lisamota, house.
Gorman, Widow: Ballygrennan, house.	Hanrahan, D.: Gortrou, house.
Harrold, P.: no further details.	Hartigan, P.: Lisamota, house.
Hayes, M.: Ballyguilebeg, house.	Keary, J.: Ballynaha, land.

Keily, Henry: Ballynaha, house.
Magrath, Thomas: Ballynaha, land.
McCarthy, William: Clonregan, house.
McGrath, Thomas: Ballynaha, land.
Morissy, James: Kilmihil, house.
Murphy, John: Ballinrura
Quaid, E.: Ballyhahil, house.
Ryves, Richard: Ballykevan, house.
Schollands, James: Crossroads, Fairplace, Ballingarry, house.
Tuomy, Denis: Gortrou, house.

Kennedy, Timothy: Ballyteague, land.
McCarthy, D.: Kilmihill, house.
McEnerney, James; Ballyelan, house.
Moran, P.: Doroclogh, house.
Murphy, Darby: Kilmikill Cross, house.
O'Shea, Timothy: Lisduane.
Quinlivan, Mr.: Caherhennessy, house.

Wallace, William: Lisduane.

Contractors mentioned were:
Collins, M.; Graves, J.; Kenny, J.; Monckton, G. and Odell, W. M.

1810
Daniel Geran, Thomas Odell and **M. Scanlan** for repairing Bridewell and Sessions Room, Ballingarry, £80-00

M. Hannon, Richard Hayes and **Thomas Odell** to lower 21 perches of the hill of Knight - Street in Ballingarry between Mr. Graves's wall at the Fair-Field and Doneen's new house at the cross of Ballingarry, £42.

D. O'Callaghan, G. Massy and **Thomas McMahon** to build an arch over the water-course on the road from Ballingarry to Charleville, £10.

Daniel Callaghan and **Daniel Kennelly** for having repaired or re-built the lintern which lately fell on the lands of Gortnacrehy.

John Sperin, half years salary as Bridewell Keeper, £2-10-00

Thomas Lonegan, A. Murphy and **T. Odell** to repair the road leading through the street of Ballingarry between the bridge and Kitt's forge.

Henry Sheehy and **T. Odell** to repair road from cross of Pound Lane to house of **John Leo.**

Fitzgerald, E. and **Moore M.** - from **John Leo's** house to house of **Terence O'Brien**, Lisamota

Other names mentioned were
O'Brien, Patrick: Kilmichael, house.
Coffee, Edmond: Cloncagh, house.
Crimmin, John: Ballynoe, house.
Downey, C.: Ballyelan, house.
Fitzgerald, John: Ballynoe, house.
Hannon, John; Killatall, land.

Cantillion, William: Ballykavane, house.
Condon, John: Doonsclonlara, land.
Cronan, Thomas: Glinwiliam, house.
Dunn, Denis: Lisamota, house.
Hannan, John; Ballynashig, land.
Hayes, E.: Gortroe, house.

Horan, Maurice: Frankford, house.
Houlihan, John: Ballyneal, house.
O'Keeffe, Daniel: Glinwilliam, house.
Shanahan, William: Gortroe, house.
Simon, John: Kilmore, house.
Tierney, Darby: Ballyelan, house.

Houlihan, E.: Gurteen, house.
Houlihan, John: Killatell, house.
Neil, Denis: Gortnacrehy, house.
Shaughnessy, Michael: Ballyneal, house.
Sullivan, Daniel: Killatell, house.
Trehy, John: Ballyneal, house.

Contractors mentioned were:

Ahern, Connor	Casey, D.	Crips, E.	Dorgan, P.	Dunworth, James
Hanrahan, James	Healy, B.	Healy, M.	Kenelly, Denis	Liston, M.
Nash, R.	Odell, William	O'Grady, G.T.	O'Grady, M.	Riordan, Dan
Quaid, Tim.				

1811

Burns, Thomas: Doroclogh, house.
Costeloe, Edmond: Ballyellan, house.
Goolde, William: Ballingarry, house.
Hayes, Daniel: Doroclogh, house.
Keeffe, Daniel: Liskennett, house.
Long, Thomas: Gurteen, house.
McIniry, Michael: Liskennett, house.
Ryan, Widow: Ballyelan, house.
Shields, William: Ballyvologue, house.

O'Brien, M.: Gurtnacrehy Upper, house.
Dore, David: Ballyvologue, house.
Hays, William: Ballyguile, land.
Keane, Michael: Ballynoe, house.
Liston, Michael: Gurtnacrehy Upper, house.
McIniry, John: Ballyelan, house.
Norris, John: Ballingarry, house.
Sheehy, John: Ballygrennan, house.
Trehy, John: Ballyneal, house.

Contractors mentioned were

Pat Hiffernan, Pat Mahiny, Edmond Hays and Thomas O'Brien in the Liskennett area. Matt Scanlan in the Dollas / Kilmacow area.

1813.

Barron, John	Ballinleeny, house	Burns, Thomas	Dorroclogh, house
Comba, Patrick	Derawlin, house	Carroll, Owen	Drewscourt, house
Clifford, John	Lisduane, land	Coleman, Daniel	Ballyelan, house
Collins, Patrick	Ballyelan, house	Connell, James	Knockfeerena, house
Crowley, Thomas	Coolruss, house	Cull, John	Lisduane, house
Fitzgibbon, Gerald	Kilmore, house	Fitzgerald, Gerald	Ballinleeny, land
Garvey, John	Ballygrennan, house	Gorman, Thomas	Killatell, land
Graddy, Corn.	Grinagh, house	Griffin, Patrick	Ballingarry, house
Hannan, John	Killattal, land	Hayes, Denis	Ballinleeny, house
Hehir, Pat	Clounregan, house	Hickey, Patrick	Cappanihane, house

Keane, Nicholas	Ballynoe, house	Kennedy, Patrick	Ballyellan, house
Long, Thomas	Gurthrue, house	Lynch, Edmond	Liskennett, house
McAuliffe, John	The Downes, house		
McCan, William	the cross of Ballingarry, house		
McEniry, John	Ballyelan, house	Ryan, John	Gurthrue, house
Ryan, William	Clouncagh, house	Sullivan, John	Ballynaha, house
Sweeny, John	Ballyneale, house	Towhill, Johanna	Knockfeerena, house
Trassy, Thomas	Ballykennedy, house	Welsh, Marks	Kilmihill, house

Contractors mentioned were

Ahern, John	Beham, James	Costelloe, Timothy	Day, Pat
Dineen, John	Downy, Michael	Finaghty, John	Fitzgerald, David
Glorney, John	Greaves, John	Harte, William Johnson	
Hayes, John	Lenegan, Thomas	Mason, Edward	Nunan, Jeremiah
Nunan, Michael	Odell, Thomas	O'Grady, James	Quill, Maurice
Scanlan, Michael	Sheehy, Henry	Sheehy, Richard	Tracy, Tim
Tierney, E.	Trehy, Denis	Trehy, Michael	Walker, Francis

In these records reference is made to the south end of Doosclonlara orchard and the pond at Gurteen.

1843. Summer Assizes, Upper Connelloe.

We present that £247-10- 00 be raised on said Barony and paid to **Henry Harte** to make 330 perches of a new line road from Ballingarry to Dromcollogher between **Michael Hennessy's** house at Ballyahill and the cross of Clounfrasteen, to be raised by three instalments of £82-10-00 each, the first instalment at this Assizes.

1845. Presentment Book, Upper Connelloe.

(Nat Arch ref 1D-42-109)

Coolruss area — Thomas Long and David Walsh
Morenane area — Edmund Houlihan
Ballingarry area: Francis Burton, John Casey, James Donovan, Thomas Fitzgerald, David Hannigan, David Landey, Matthew O'Brien and John Walsh.
Gurteen area — John Lyons and Michael O'Brien
Clouncagh area — James and Michael Hickey
Lisduane area — Patrick Mahony and William Wallace

1846. Implements Bill for Smith and Repair Work.
(Nat Arch ref 1D-42-109)

Smith	Lisduane	Cornelius O'Brien
Smith	Clouncagh	James Fitzgerald
Wheelbarrows	Liskinnitt	John Noonan
Wheelbarrows	Clouncagh	Michael Fitzgerald
Handles	Lisduane	Maurice Roche

1814. A Survey of the Roads of the Barony of Conelloe Upper.

One of the many duties the Grand Juries had to deal with were the building and maintenance of roads. Because of the absence of a proper roads survey it was possible to engage in widespread fraud in tendering for road repairs by describing the same stretch of road in different ways. On 26 July, 1813 a meeting of the landholders of Newcastle, Monegea, Killeedy, Castlemahon and Abbeyfeale was held in Newcastle. The purpose of the meeting was to protest at the waste of the high County Cess Tax they were paying in the roadworks repairs scheme and called for an end to the apparent abuses. On Weds. September 8th, 1813 the following notice appeard in the Limerick Evening Post. A meeting of such Gentlemen of the Barony of Upper Connello who wish to enter into an Association for preventing Frauds heretofore practised on the County Grand Juries and the Public in applying for presentments and accounting for the repairs of roads in that Barony, is requested at Ballingarry on Monday the 13th Sept. inst. at which time a Plan of Survey will be laid before them calculated to assist the above purpose which it is proposed shall be made and Printed by a Voluntary Subscription. On 25 Sept. a similar meeting to that called for above was advertised in the L.E.P. and a list of names was published:

Carte, Edward	Casey, Dobyn	Cox, John	Conyers, Charles
Evans, Thomas D.	Fetherston, Robert	Furlong, Joseph	Furlong, Thomas
Grave, J.: Clk.	Leake, George	Lloyd, Edward	Nash, Edward: Clk.
Massy, George	McCarthy, Denis	Monckton, George	Odell, Thomas
Odell, Thomas A.	Parker, Robert	Scanlan, Michael	Sheehy, Bryan
Sheehy, Edward	Shelton, John	Upton, John	

In the same edition of the paper was a long article complaining of the widespread abuse of the presentments system. On the 6th October, 1813 a report of a meeting re the Roads Survey held in Ballingarry on Oct. 2, 1813 appeared in the Limerick Evening Post. The chairman was Thomas O'Dell.

There were various resolutions passed with a view to making the system foolproof and a committee to oversee this was appointed, as follows :

Carte, Edward; Newcastle	Conyers, Charles; Castletown
Furlong, Joseph; Monegea	Furlong, Thomas; Abbeyfeale
Langford, James; Drumcolligher	Lloyd, Edward; Mahoonagh
Nash, Revd. E.; Brury	Massy, George; Ballingarry
O'Dell, Revd. William B.; Killaholehan	O'Dell, Thomas A.; Knockaderry
Scanlan, Michael; Kilpenny	Sheehy, Edward; Killeedy
Shelton, John; Kilmeedy	

It was also resolved that the thanks of this meeting are eminently due and hereby given to **Edward Carte,** Esq., for his independent and spirited exertions in the suppression of road jobbing. Signed, By Order: Thomas **O'Dell**. Subsequent to the above meetings the roads were surveyed and a copy of the survey, including map, is in the National Library. It is a small book. *Ref.No.IR 94144 L 2.* Before he details the survey, **Edward Carte** writes an explanatory preface.

A Survey of the Public Roads In the Barony of Upper Connolloe, County of Limerick. Divided by parishes and townlands. Projected and arranged by Edward Carte, Esq, of Newcastle, in said county, in the year 1813. Surveyed by David Landers and John Minihan.

To The Public. It has appeared that at least one-third of the money granted for the Repair of Roads has been paid for Presentments doubly and trebly (and sometimes more) which has occurred for want of known or fixed landmarks as boundaries; the object of the following Survey is to prevent more than one Presentment being granted for the repair of the same part of any road, by giving a Schedule which shall contain all the particulars necessary for filling the Affidavits, viz., one fixed description of the direction of each line of Road from one Town to another, with the correct number of perches in each Townland. He then goes on to outline the problems he hopes to resolve and further states: 'Houses are generally taken as landmarks, yet as there is not any restriction on those applying for Presentments, a large stone, a bush, a gap or any other object which presents itself, is frequently used." He also states "the survey is classified in parishes divided by townlands which afford certain and permanent landmarks and that each line of road when begun is measured to its extremity within the parish to which it belongs, and the several branches left and right and also the turns from them until all is measured.'
Edward Carte. Newcastle, Jan 1, 1814.

The Survey is written in the following format. Figures in brackets are perches.
Road from Kilmeedy to Ballingarry.
No. 1. Ballykevan (216). Between the bounds of Ballyhahill and the bounds of Frankfort.
From Bruree to Ballingarry.
No. 23. Ballynoe (252). Between the cross in Ballynoe (as in No. 21) and the Ballyneal bridge.
Road from Ballingarry to Bruree.
No. 45. Grenagh (235). Between the bounds of Grenagh and the bounds of Coolrus.
The nett effect of this was that each stretch of road could now be described only in one agreed format thus eliminating duplicate contracts. In the Limerick Evening Post, Sat. July 30, 1814 there was an extensive article deploring the widespread practice of 'road-jobbing'. Mr. Carte's book was favourably reviewed and recommended as the way for other baronies to end road-jobbing forever.

The construction of roads seems to have been of great importance in Ireland in the early 19th century. In **1828** the following report, (adapted by me) was made by **Richard Griffith**, taken from records in the Genealogical Office *(Ref GOM 623).* It gives an interesting insight into the effect roads and their construction were having in rural Ireland. I could not find any account dealing specifically with the Ballingarry region.

My Lord,

Herewith I have the honour to submit to you a General Statement of the amount expended by me on the Public Works in the Southern District of Ireland during the year **1828** and to describe the progress that has been made towards the completion of the several roads commenced since **1823.** The Southern District comprehends the counties of Cork, Limerick and Kerry: and the Public Roads which I have commenced in it, by order of the Irish Government, have been confined to mountainous and uncultivated tracts, hitherto inaccessible or nearly so, and which, in periods of disturbance, have been the rendezvous and asylum of rebels, murderers and robbers. He gives details of the roads in the making which are all in the Abbeyfeale area and writes on:

At the commencement of the works, the people flocked to them from all quarters seeking employment at any rate which might be offered. Their general appearance bespoke extreme poverty. Their looks were haggard and their clothing wretched. They rarely possessed any tools or implements of husbandry beyond a small ill-made spade, and as might be expected under such circumstances nearly the whole face of the country was in unimproved and in a state of nature. Since the completion of the roads, rapid strides have been made towards cultivation and improvement; upwards of sixty new lime-kilns have been built for the purpose of burning lime for agriculture within the last two years. Carts, ploughs and harrows of superior construction, and other agricultural implements have become common. New houses of a better class have been built, or are building, in the vicinity of the new roads, and this country, has become perfectly tranquil and exhibits a scene of industry and exertion at once pleasing and remarkable.

1802-1850.
The following miscellany of records give an insight into various aspects of life in Ballingarry, Granagh and Clouncagh region as well as Limerick in the early part of the 19th century.

National Imports 1802 - 1821.

Drapery	49,692,058 yds.	Raw Sugar	6,089,175 cwts.
Refined Sugar	490,315 cwts.	Tea	66,847,251 lbs.
Coals	10,897,970 tons.	Iron	5,530,682 cwts.
Tobacco	116,112,836 lbs.	Cotton Yarn	19,995,350 yds.
Flax Seed	934,049 h.hds.	Cotton Wool	538,542 cwts.
Timber	490,245 tons.	Hats	1,387,209 (No.)
Hides (undressed)	450,031 (No.)	Hops	400,701 cwts.
Hosiery	7,995,640 pcs.	Oak-Bark	2,550,853 barrels.
Barilla	2,182,060 cwts.		

National Exports 1802-1821.

Linens	832,403,860 yds.	Butter	7,915,949 lbs.
Pork	2,565,403 brls.	Wheat	4,223,782 brls.
Meal & Flour	1,686,948 cwts.	Barley	1,842,993 brls.
Candles	205,958 cwts.	Hogs	687,569 No.
Oats	16,112,142 brls.	Spirits	10,349,752 gals.
Bacon Flitches	6,248,527 No.	Soap	19,506 cwts
Horned Cattle	747,815 No.	Lard	313,867 cwts..
Copper Ore	30,243 tons.	Feathers	106,307 cwts.
Kelp	64,731 tons.		

Reference Nat. Lib. P 1417.

Value of Exports of Provisions from Limerick Port for the year ended April 30, 1814.

8,802	Tierces	Beef	@	180s each	=	£ 79,218-00-00
4,579	Barrels	Beef	@	120s each	=	£ 27,474-00-00
9,163	Tierces	Pork	@	230s each	=	£ 104,974-10-00
19,650	Barrels	Pork	@	140s each	=	£ 137,550-00-00
15,892	Flitches	Bacon	@	55s each	=	£ 44,703-00-00
17,001	Hundred Wt.	Butter	@	120s each	=	£ 102,006-00-00
840	Hundred Wt.	Lard	@	100s each	=	£ 4,230-00-00
65,751	Barrels	Wheat	@	50s each	=	£ 164,377-10-00
62,370	Barrels	Barley	@	28s each	=	£ 87,348-00-00
141,955	Barrels	Oats	@	20s each	=	£ 141,955-00-00
16,577	Hundred Wt.	Flour	@	30s each	=	£ 24,805-10-00
19,008	Hundred Wt.	Oatmeal	@	20s each	=	£ 19,008-00-00
6,540	Hundred Wt.	Bread	@	33s each	=	£ 10,791-00-00

Published in the Limerick Evening Post, Sat. May 5, 1814.

Return of the number of electors who polled at the contested elections in Ireland since 1805 together with the names of the candidates for whom they respectively voted and the numbers for each candidate. *Ref GO M 623, Nat. Lib.*

1806	Colonel O'Dell, 851.	Hon. W. Quin, 628.	William.T. Monsell, 224.
1818	Col. Fitzgibbon, 2,476.	Hon. W. Quin, 1,721.	Capt. O'Grady, 1,450.
1820	Col. Fitzgibbon, 4,186. Walter O'Grady, 1,921.	Capt. O'Grady, 3,334.	Sir A.D.V. Hunt, 2,928.
1826	Col. Fitzgibbon, 4,539.	Thomas Lloyd, 3,054.	Capt. O'Grady, 2,462.

Arms seized by Geo. Massy	**1807**	**1808**	**1809**
Muskets	3	3	5
Fowling Pieces	2	–	–
Pistols	2	3	2
Bayonets	2	–	–
Carbines	–	1	3
Musket Barrels	–	2	–

Names Who Registered Their Trees.

1812	Hunt	John	Ballynash
1817	Monsell	Wm. Thomas	Tervoe
1829	Browne	Henry & Francis	Danesfort

(Circuit Court Records, Nat. Arch.)

1817.

Persons registered as freeholder - distinguishing the value of the freehold and the right under which registered. *(Ref.GOM 623.)*

Number 23. Number 32 in registry book. Name of Freeholder: Odell; Thomas, Esq., Ballingarry, Co.Limerick. Freehold: houses and tenements at Brunswick St. and John St. Value of Freehold, £50. Date of Registry: Affid. swo. before Bar. Smith at Sum. Ass.1817 and read at adj. sessions 21 Oct., 1817

1822.
Names of Magistrates in the County from Ballingarry area:

Brown	Henry	Deansforth
Harte	Sir Richard	Coolruss
Massy	George	Glenwilliam
Odell	Thomas A.	Odellville
Odell	Thomas	Ballingarry
Odell	Rev. Wm. B.	Altaville ?
Scanlan	Michael	Ballinahaha (Deceased)
Waller	John	Castletown
Westropp	Rev. T	Ballyscanlan.

Circuit Court Records, National Archives

1822.
Names of Magistrates, Ballingarry area, entitled to receive the Statutes.

Dickson, S	Evans, Eyre	Gubbins, Joseph
Lloyd, Rev. R.	Lloyd, Thomas	Massy, George
Massy, William	Maunsell, George M.	Odell, J. A.
Odell, Colonel Thomas	Odell, Rev. W. B.	O'Grady, Darby
Tuthill, John	Waller, B.	

Circuit Court Records, National Archives

1829.
Registry of Freeholders :

No. 71. Thomas Connor, Ballingarry: house & land: Townland of Ballingarry: £20.

No. 84. James O'Connell, Ballingarry: house & land: Townland of Ballingarry: £20.

Limerick Chronicle Sat, July 11, 1829

Names of People who Registered their Arms.
(Circuit Court Records, Nat. Arch.)

1825
Browne	Pierce	Deansfort	6 Guns
Switzer	Nathan	Ballinlina	2 Muskets
Teskey	Jacob	Ballinlina	1 Gun

1834
Power	Daniel D.	Ashboro	2 Guns and 2 cases Pistols.

1835
Carmody	Daniel	Ballygrennan	1 Gun
Odell	William	Fortwilliam	2 Guns; 1 rifle and 1 case Pistols.

1836
Brown, Henry	Ballynahaha	2 Guns and 3 Pistols
Cox, John	Ballyneale	1 Gun, 1 Pistol and 1 case Pistols
Fizzle, Jacob	Ballyagran	1 Gun, 1 Pistol and 1 Sword
Massy, William	Glenwilliam	8 Guns, 4 Pistols, 6 Swords and 1 Blunderbuss
Scanlan, Hugh	Kilbeg	2 Guns, 3 Pistols and 1 Blunderbuss
Scanlan, Mat	Ballynahaha	2 Guns and 1 case Pistols
Scanlan, William	Ballyknockane	4 Guns, 1 Pistol and 1 Sword
Walsh, Edward	Ballyroe	2 Guns and 1 case Pistols

1837
Brown, William; Fortwilliam. Cox, Mr.; Ballynoe. Donohoe, Mr.; Rossmore. Greaves, Richard D.; Woodstock. Lloyd, Edward; Heathfield. Shelton, J. W.; Rossmore
No details of arms were given for 1837.

1831.
Court Case. Thomas Coleman, Kilatal V Connor Quinlan, Kilatal. Witness for Coleman - Mr. William Houlihan, late of Ballyscanlan. No further details.

1831.
December. Patrick Tierney, Kilbeg. A teacher.
Pound Keepers registered for Ballingary area.
1838, William Odell. **1843,** William White, Knockfierna. **1844-1849,** Patrick and Michael Barrett. **1850.** Frederick Massy
(Circuit Court Records, Nat. Arch.)

PART III

The Tithes Records

Tithes Applotment For The Parish Of Ballingarry, 1826.

The tithes were a Church tax on one's annual income and date back to the Middle Ages. After the Reformation **(Martin Luther 1483-1546)** they were designated to the upkeep of the Established Church. In the case of Ireland this developed into the upkeep of the Church of Ireland and led to widespread dissaffection with this by all nor. Church of Ireland people. Initially the responsibility of supplying a priest for the people was with a monastery who received the tithes. The tithes were divided between the two. The vicarial tithes, about one third, went to the priest, the remainder, the rectorial tithes, went to the monastery. It was a source of income to own the rectorial tithes and after the monasteries were suppressed by **Henry VIII** in 1536 and 1539 the ownership of the rectorial tithes passed on to lay persons. This was called impropriation of the tithes. In 1826 Ballingarry and Granagh and in 1833 Clouncagh were applotted for tithes. This record of named peoples in their place in their time is very important due to the loss of the censii.

It is the first big genealogy record for the early 19th century and it is fortunate that they have survived. What follows is a sequential series of records beginning with the vestry meeting of 1826 setting the tithe amount (money); an example of a Tithe Commissioner's oath; details of the people of Granagh / Ballingarry parish in the tithe applotment and the tithe applotment for Clouncagh. There is details of a court case disputing the rate of tithes, the decision and finally the amended list of tithe payers showing their initial applotment and subsequent reduction. *These records, under the control of the National Archives, were accessd at the Gilbert Library Ref. Film 65, sub ref 17/81,*

1826.
Aug. 5. We, **John S. Brown,** jr., and **Michael Lynch**, Commissioners duly appointed and sworn under and by virtue of an Act passed in the fourth year of the reign of King George the Fourth entitled 'An Act to Provide for the Establishing of Compositions for Tithes in Ireland for a limited time. Do certify that at a Vestry duly held on the 24th day of July in the year one thousand eight hundred and twenty six in the parish Church of Ballingarry in the County of and Diocese of Limerick for the purpose of carrying the provisions of the above Act into effect in said parish, it was agreed on by the Parishioners and accepted by the Vicar and Lay Impropriator that the sum of nine hundred pounds should be the Composition for the Vicarial and Rectorial Tithes of said Parish by the year for the term of twenty one years from the first day of November next. Dated this 5th day of August, 1826. John S. Brown, jr., and Michael Lynch: Commissioners. *(According to Rev Hamilton's 'Records of Ballingarry' this meeting was chaired by John Tuthill of Kilmore House.)*

This an example of a Tithe Commissioner's oath.
Oath of Commissioner to be taken before any Justice of the Peace of any County in which the Parish shall be situate, in which such Commissioner shall be appointed to act.
I, Philip F. **Drought**, 5, South Frederick St. in the county of City of Dublin do swear that I will faithfully, impartially and honestly, according to the best of my skill and ability, execute and perform the Powers and Authorities vested and reposed in me as a Commissioner in the Parish of Clouncagh by virtue of an Act passed in the Fourth Year of the Reign of King George the Fourth, entituled 'An Act to provide for the establishing of Composition for Tithes in Ireland for a limited time,' and by virtue of an act passed in the Second and Third Years of the Reign of His Majesty King William the Fourth entituled 'An Act to amend Three Acts passed respectively in the Fourth, Fifth and in the Seventh and Eight Years of the Reign of His late Majesty King George the Fourth, providing for the establishing of Compositions for Tithes in Ireland, and to make such Compositions 'permanent' according to the Directions of the said Acts,

and according to equity and good conscience, and without favour or affection, prejudice or malice, to any Person or Persons whomsoever. So help me God.
Sworn before me this 31 Day of August, 1833. **T. I. Vokes**.

Composition of Tithes of the Parish Of Ballingarry.

The Vicarial Payable to Rev. Thomas Gibbings and Rectorial to Mrs. Catharine Ann Graves. Acres - 16,219-02-05. Composition - £300. Mrs.Graves, £600. Total - £900 British. Nine hundred pounds (£900) per annum from 1st Nov., 1826 for 21 years. Lodged the 7th day of August, 1826 in the Registry office of the Deoc.of Limerick. Flor. Bryan McMahon; Regrs. Francis Hill, Apparitor.

We the Revd. Thomas **Gibbings,** vicar of the Parish of Ballingarry and Mrs Catherine Ann **Graves**, Impropriator of said Parish do nominate and appoint John S. **Browne,** esq., junr. of Mount Browne in the County of Limerick to be Commissioner on our part in said parish under the provisions of the Late Acts for the Compositions of Tithes in Ireland -- given under .. of July 1826, signed Thos. **Gibbings.** On behalf of Mrs Catherine Ann **Graves** - signed, Thos. R. **Graves.**

The records of the tithes composition give the following information in respect of each individual = 1) A sequential number. 2) Lands where situate, divided into ploughlands and sub-denominations, usually Commons. 3) Occupiers names. 4) Number of acres, Statute measure. 5)Value per acre. 6)Total value. 7)Composition per acre. 8)Total amount of composition and observations.

Townlands Index of the Tithes Composition Records for Granagh / Ballingarry 1826.

Ballinaha	Ballinaha Commons	Ballinarogy
Ballinlyny	Ballinoe	Balliroe Odell
Balliroe Odell Commons	Ballycavin	Ballyelane
Ballyelane Commons	Ballygrinnan	Ballygrinnan Commons
Ballyguile Beg	Ballyguile Tagil	Ballynashig
Ballyneale	Ballynockane	Ballyrow Nash
Ballyrow Nash Commons	Ballyvologue	Bantabee
Caherhenessy	Caherhenessy Commons	Clounregan
Clountemple	Coolrus	Dolas Lower

Doorlasbeg	Doroclough	Downs
Everground	Frankford	Glenwilliam
Granagh	Graugebeg	Graugueacurra
Gurteen	Hoaresfield	Kilbeg
Killougta	Kilmacneerla	Kilmacow
Kilmichael	Kilmichael Commons	Kilmihill
Kilmore	Kilshanabbey	Kingsland
Knightstreet	Lisamote	Lisavarra
Lisduane	Lisduff	Liskinnitt
Nightstreet	Rylanes	Woodstock

Please note that these records were made in long hand and it is sometimes difficult to decipher the handwriting. Every effort has been made to be accurate but in any case of doubt the original records should be consulted. Frequently, the same name is repeated in a townland. I have not repeated these names. In the actual records the names are not in alphabetical order but I have arranged them thus for ease of reference.

Coolrus

Barron, John	Barry, Edmond	Barry, Nicholas	Burke, James
Burke, Richard	Burns, Daniel	Burns, James	Burns, John
Burns, Patrick	Burns, Widow	Carroll, John	Carroll, Widow
Connell, Cath(erine)	Connell, John	Cronan, Thomas	Dillane, Thomas
Dillane, Widow	Dundon, James	Dunworth, James	Dunworth, Michael
Fitzgerald, Widow	Galligan, Michael	Gready, John	Guare, Widow
Hart, Richard	Harte, James	Healy, Patrick	Kane, Darby
Kane, Maurice	Kirriwan, Michael	Long, John	Lynch, James
Lyons, John	Martin, Bridget	Mahon, Martin	Mahony, Darby
McNamara, John	Minahan, James	O' Brien, John	O Brien, Timothy
O'Donnell, John	O'Donnell, Robt. D.	Regan, John	Sullivan, Michael
Twomey, John			

Kingsland

Guiry, Maurice	Noonan, Daniel	Quinn, Michael	Webb, John

Ballinlyny

Blake, Thomas	Burns, Edward	Cahill, Laurence	Callaghan, Thomas
Carroll, Richard	Coghlan, William	Coply, John	Daly, William
Fitzgerald, Maurice	Fitzgibbon, David	Fitzgibbon, J'miah	Fitzgibbon, Widow

Gready, William	Hartnett, Thomas	Kenny, John	Keys, John
Lynch, Thomas, jnr.	Lyston, Patrick	Madden, James	Maher, Martin
Martin, Widow	Moran, James	Mullins, Daniel	Noonan, John
Noonan, Timothy	Regan, James	Shanahan, John	Sheehan, Conner
Sheehan, Patrick	Sheehan, Timothy	Sheehy, Edmond	Shiely, Daniel
Walsh, John	Walsh, David	White, Thomas	

Kilmore

Dineen, James	Falvy, David	Graddy, Conner	Graddy, John
Houlehan, Jeremiah	McCarthy, Ml. jnr.	McMahon, Michael	McMahon, Ml., jnr.
McMahon, Thomas	Minahan, Michael	Noonan, Timothy	Tuthill, John

Granagh

Keyes, John	Lynch, Michael	Lynch, Thomas, jnr.	Lyons, William

Doorlasbeg

Callaghan, Michael	Cummins, John	Graddy, John	McCarthy, John
McMahon, Thomas	McNamara, Jas, sr.	McNamara, Jas, jnr.	McNamara, Patrick
Morissy, James	Morissy, John	Morissy, Patrick	Phillips, Richard
Shiels, David			

Liskinnit

Brown, David	Burns, John	Carmody, Edmond	Dwyer, John
Gready, John	Keating, James	Reeves, Patrick	Sheahan, John

Graugueacurra

Barry, Widow	Bennett, David	Dixon, Stephen	Doyle, Edmond
Kelly, Patrick	Kilbridge, John	McCarthy, John	McMahon, Ml. & Prtnrs.
O'Brien, Darby	Quinn, Michael	Rierdan, John,	Rierdan, Michael
Rierdan, Patrick	Scanlon, Michael	Sheahan, Daniel,	Shiels, Thomas
Shiely, Thomas	White, Michael		

Lisduane

Bermingham, Patk.	Biggane, Patrick	Cull, James	Duane, John
Gorman, James	Gorman, John	Gorman, John & Prtrns	Hynes, John
Kinnane, John	Lynch, Thomas	Mahony, William	Mason, Miles
Mason, Walker J.	McCarthy, Rev. C.	McCarthy, Michael	Morrison, Edmond
Nash, Edmond	Quinn, John	Shea, Denis	Wallace, William

Graugebeg

Casey, William	Clifford, John	Culnane, Wm. & Ptnrs	Fitzpatrick, Patrick
Kelly, William & Co.	Lee, John	Lee, William	Masterson, John
Sheehan, David			

Dolas Lower

Cavanagh, Ellen	Gready, Henry	Gready, John	Hayes, Patrick
Keeffe, Edmond	Lynch, Marks	Morrissy, Patrick	Power, John
Shea, Patrick			

Everground

Hickey, James   Sullivan, David

Lisduff

Dea, Catherine	Dea, Denis	Dea, Hanora	Dea, James
Fooly, William	Kilbridge, Michael	Lyston, Richard	Mahony, Denis
Storin, William			

Kilmacaneerla

Ahern, John	Ahern, Thomas	Burns, Edmond	Cagney, Patrick
Connors, James*	Peppard, Robert	Rierdan, Daniel	Shea, Thomas

* *could be Conmey / Conway ?*

Bantabee

Barry, James	Bennett, William	Burke, John	Costello, Michael
Halleron, Michael	Kilbridge, Michael	Lynch, George	Moran, John
Neligan, Timothy	O'Brien, Thomas	Scanlan, Michael	White, Michael

Kilmacow

Barry, James, snr.	Barry, James, jnr.	Collins, John	Connell, Timothy
Hayes, James	O'Brien, Thomas	Power, Samuel D.	Shaughnessy, David
Sheehy, Maurice			

Ballinahaha

Carey, Edmund (Hill)	Carey, Edward	Carey, John & Co.	Carey, Thomas & Co.
Deneely, Own	Duane, Timothy	Kennedy, Edmond	Mahony, Thomas
O'Brien, Daniel	O'Brien, Thos. Wm.	O'Brien, Thos. (Firm)	Riedy, John & Co.
Scanlon, William	Sheahan, Simon & Co.		Sullivan, Daniel

Ballinahaha Commons

Carey, Edward	Donohoe, Ml. & Co.	Doyle, James	Halloran, Timothy
Lynch, George			

Ballyknockane
Scanlan, William, esq.

Kilbeg
Dee, Widow	Scanlan, Hugh	Sexton, Widow

Lisavarra
Cowhy, Thomas	Cronan, Corn.& Co.	Kilbridge, Michael	Sexton, Widow

Caherhennessy
Bowen, John & Co.	Fitzgerald, Edmond	Fitzgerald, Edward	Fleming, John
Gorman, John	Gready, James	Hannon, John	Hanrahan, John
Hartigan, Richard	Hogan, Denis	Jirdon, Darby	Kane, Michael
Kiely, Henry	Lee, Widow	Leo, John	McCarthy, William
Morrissy, Denis	O'Brien, William	Odell, William	O'Gready, Mr. James
Quinlivan, Michael	Regan, Darby	Roche, Richard	Scanlon, John
Sperin, John	Sullivan, Edmond	Walsh, Thomas	

Note - William Odell is shown as a Counsellor.

Caherhennessy Commons
Culnane, William	Hanly, James	Kane, Michael	Kiely, Henry
Lee, Widow	Morrissy, Denis	Roche, Richard	

Ballyrow Nash
Carroll, John & Prtrns	Hart, Widow	Keating, Patk & Prtrns	Murphy, Michael
Sullivan, James	Treehy, Michael		

Ballyrow Nash Commons
Carroll, John & Partners		Hart, Widow & Partners
Murphy, Michael	Sullivan, James	Sullivan, John

Balliroe Odell
Connell, Patrick	McCarthy, Rev.C.	Moore, Thomas	Odell, Robert D.
Rierdon, John			

Balliroe Odell Commons
Coghlan, William	Dore, David	Dunn, William	Hartigan, Richard
Kelly, Widow	Kiely, Patrick	Madden, Timothy	Roche, James
Sullivan, James	Wolf, Richard		

Woodstock
Fitzgerald, Edmond	Odell, Robert D.

Lisamote

Buckly, John	Condon, John, snr.	Condon, John, jnr.	Conway, James
Cronan, Timothy	Crimmin, Own	Duane, Timothy	Hallinan, Thomas
Hanrahan, James	Hogan, Conner	Hogan, John	Hogan, Michael
Hogan, Patrick, snr.	Hogan, Patrick, jnr.	Kennedy, Michael	Kilbridge, James
Lynch, William	Madigan, Denis	Madigan, Timothy	McCarthy, Michael
McCarthy, William	O'Brien, Terence	Odell, Robert D.	Regan, John
Scanlon, William	Shanahan, John	Sheehy, Henry	Sullivan, John
Sullivan, Thomas			

Kilshanabbey

Hannon, Patrick

Rylanes

Croker, Revd. John   O'Dell, Thomas

Nightstreet

Allen, James	Collins, John	Cox, John,	Dinneen, Jeremiah
Dunworth, David	Dunworth, Wm.	Fitzgerald, W. Thos.	Gibbings, Rev.Thos.
McNamara, John	O Dell, Thomas	Rierdon, Thomas	Sperin, John.
Sperin, William.			

Knightstreet

Baggott, Michael	Burke, Michael	Collins, John	Condon, John
Connors, Thomas	Cronan, Michael	Devany, John	Dinneen, Jeremiah
Dinneen, John	Duane, Thomas	Egan, Stephen	Egan, Thomas
Farrell, Moll	Faulkner, James	Flanady, Simon (Mill)	Gibbings, Rev.Thos.
Gorman, John	Graves, Mrs C. A.	Hogan, Timothy	Hurly, Denis
Lynch, Doctor	Madigan, Michael	McCann, John	Meade, Patrick
Quinn, James	Russell, Garrett	Scanlon, Connor	Scanlon, John
Slatery, Johannah	Sperin, John	Sullivan, Own	

Clountemple

Alby, Nicholas	Barry, Patrick	Boyle, William	Burke, Michael
Carmody, Denis	Carroll, John	Cavanagh, Denis	Cavanagh, Michael
Clifford, James	Clifford, John	Coleman, Daniel	Condon, John
Connell, James	Connell, Jas. glazier	Connell, Jas. skinr.	Conners, Thos. G.
Cox, John	Crotty, John	Curtin, John	Davern, Matthew
Dowling, Edmund	Duane, Patrick	Duane, Thos. snr.	Duane, Thos. Jnr.
Duhig, Thomas	Dunworth, Michael	Fanning, Richard	Fitzgerald, Edward

Fitzgerald, James	Flanagan, John	Gill, William	Gleeson, Thomas
Gready, John	Griffin, Thomas	Hannon, John	Hannon, Patrick
Hoare, Mrs	Hogan, Phillip	Houlehan, John	Hurly, Denis
Kelly, David	Kelly, Denis	Kelly, Patrick	Kett, Patrick
Leary, Margaret	Leary, Patrick	Naughton, Widow	Nevill, John
O'Brien, Michael	O'Brien, Thomas	O'Brien, William	O'Dell, William
O'Donnell, John	Preston, George	Roche, Eliza	Ryan, Hugh
Scanlon, John	Shanahan, James	Shanahan, John	Sheehy, George
Shine, John.	Sperin, John	Sperin, William	Twohill, Daniel
Walker, Thomas	White, William		

Killoughta

Barry, James	Barry, Martin	Shaughnessy, David	Shaughnessy, Patrick

Ballyvologue

Dore, David	Duane, John	Duane, Thomas	Fitzpatrick, Edmund
Kiely, Morty	Mahony, Widow	Power, William	

BallyguileTagil

Bennett, Thomas	Cangny, Edmond	Curtin, Michael	Houlehan, William
Noonan, James	Noonan, John	Noonan, Michael, (hill)	Scully, John
Scully, Thomas	Sullivan, Conner		

Downs

Carmody, John	Hannon, John	Power, Patrick	Sheehy, Henry

Ballinarogy

Cangny, John	Fitzgerald, David	Fitzgerald, Patrick	Fitzgibbon, Thomas
Gorman, John	Hanrahan, James	Kenny, Patrick	Massy, George
McMahon, Michael	Odell, Thomas A.	Odell, Major	* Odells, Thos. Steward

* This could be read as the property of T. Odell's steward.

Ballycavin

Gready, Patrick	Massy, George	Wigmore, John

Frankford

Costello, Edmond	Dillane, John	Enright, Timothy	Gore, Patrick
Hanly, Daniel	Hanly, Thomas	Hanrahan, Patrick	Hestin, Conner
Massy, George	Peppard, John	Riedy, William	Standish, John
Quaid, David			

Hoaresfield,
Meade, W. Patt.

Clounregan
Brusnahan, Connor
Connell, James, skinr.
Cullinane, Michael
Hogan, John (Denis)
Meade, W. Patt.
Twohill, John
Burns, Redmond
Costello, Tim
Fitzgerald, James
Hurly, Denis
Mooney, Mary
Carroll, Widow
Cronan, Daniel
Hayes, Widow
Lynch, Thomas
Rawley, James
Collins, James
Cronan, Patrick
Hogan, David
McCann, Darby
Twohill, Ellen

Gurteen
Barrett, Patrick
Casey, William
Falahee, Patrick
Molony, Matt
Walsh, Michael
Blake, James
Connell, James, glazr.
Gleeson, Thomas
Murphy, Denis
Blake, Michael
Conners, Thomas
Gready, John
O Dell, Thomas,
Burke, Michael
Falahee, Edmond
Madigan, Michael
Twohill, John

Ballygrinnan
Beggane, Timothy
Curtin, Patrick
Dixon, Stephen,
Feehene, Widow
Hederman, John
Kelly, William
Power, William
Taylor, Edmond
Carmody, Daniel
Curtin, Patrick, jnr.
Dea, Thomas
Gorman, Jeremiah
Houlehan, Denis
Morissy, Michael
Ranahan, Edmond
Costello, James
Curtin, Timothy
Dore, David
Hannon, Michael
Houlehan, James
McEniry, Edmond
Roche, William
Coleman, John, snr.
Dinneen, Patrick
Enright, Michael
Hannon, Widow
Houlehan, John
Power, James
Quinlivan, Edmond

Ballygrinnan Commons
Broderick, Daniel
Burns, David
Costello, James
Dore, John
Kilbridge, Thomas
McGlinn, Michael
Moylan, Widow
Sheehy, Darby
Treecy, Edmond
Broderick, Thomas
Burns, John
Costello, Michael
Feheen, Widow
Lee, John
McGrath, Jeremiah
Ranahan, Edmond
Sheehy, John
White, Eustace
Beggane, Maurice
Carmody, Daniel
Curtin, Patrick
Fitzpatrick, Thomas
Lewis, David
McGrath, Lewis
Roche, William
Sullivan, Ellen
White, Nicholas
Burke, Peggy
Casey, William
Dinneen, Patrick
Jackson, Widow
McEniry, Patrick
McGrath, Thomas
Russell, George
Treacy, David
White, William, snr.

Note - *William White - Pound Keeper.*

Ballynashig
Hannon, John	Hannon, William	Power, Samuel D.	Sullivan, Widow

Ballyguilebeg
Clifford, Robert	Clifford, William	Hayes, William, snr.	Hayes, William, jnr.
Hayes, Wm. David	Neile, Widow		

Ballyelane
Carmody, Conner	Carmody, Edmond	Carney, Widow	Collins, Patrick
Costello, Daniel	Costello, James	Curtin, Timothy	Downy, Michael
Duane, Patrick	Hanrahan, Daniel	Hartigan, John	Hartigan, Patrick
McCarthy, Patrick	McEniry, Michael	Noonan, David	Noonan, Edmond
Noonan, Michael	Regan, Conner	Regan, Darby	Regan, Maurice
Regan, Michael	Regan, Thomas	Reidy, James	Riedy, David
Riedy, John	Roche, Michael	Roche, Toby	Taylor, John

Ballyelane Commons
Barry, Garrett	Casey, Betty	Collins, Matthew	Cronan, Denis
Cronan, Own	Cullinane, Anty.	Flanidy, Edmond	Hanly, Edmond
Hanly, Michael	Hartigan, Patrick	Keating, Patrick	Keeffe, Patrick
McCarthy, Bridget	McEniry, David	Noonan, Edmond	Ranihan, Peter
Regan, Conner	Regan, Darby	Regan, Michael	Regan, Patrick
Reidy, James	Roche, Batt	Sheehy, Edmond	

Ballyneale
Casey, Andrew	Casey, Gerald	Casey, Patrick	Casey, Thomas
Collins, Michael	Cowhy, Edmond	Cox, John,	Donohoe, Daniel
Donohoe, Jeffrey	Donohoe, J. & Prtnrs	Donohoe, Thomas	Dore, James
Harrington, Maurice	Massy, George	Regan, Daniel	Riedy, Edmond
Rierdon, James	Ryall, John	Scully, Maurice	Walsh, John

Kilmihill
Dunworth, David	Dunworth, James	Leeny, Maurice	McAuliff, John
McCarthy, Daniel	Scollard, Edmond	Scollard, William	

Kilmichael
Barrett, Edmond	Burns, Edmond	Burns, John	Cullinane, Patrick
Connell, James, skinr.	Dunworth, Peter	Dunworth, Widow	Foren, Edmond
Keeffe, Thomas	Mortane, John	O'Brien, John	Odell, William
O'Donnell, Michael	Regan, John	Reidy, William	Reidy, William smith
Scollard, Patrick	Wring, Michael		

Kilmichael Commons

Connell, Jas., snr.	Connell, Jas., jnr.	Cullinane, Anty.	Cullinane, Patrick
Dore, David	Fitzgerald, Alby & Prts.		Hannon, Widow
O'Brien, Michael	Scollard, Thomas		

Glenwilliam

Corree, John	Cowhey, Denis	Crimmin	Curtin, Patrick
Duggin, Michael	Harrold, Patrick	Harrold, Paul	Henessy
Massy, George, esq.			

Note: Crimmin & Hennessy partners. No Christian names given.

Doroclough

Blake, Edmond	Blake, Val	Burns, Patrick	Cangny, Daniel
Carroll, John	Carroll, William	Collins, Michael	Connell, Widow
Cox, William,	Cullinane, D. & Prts.	Curtin, John	Flanidy, Ed. & Prtrs.
Flinn, James & Prtns.	Gleeson, Patrick	Hanly, Matt	Hanly, Michael
Hanly, Patrick	Hanly, William	Hannon, James	Kennelly, Daniel
Kilbridge, Edmond	Morisson, Robert	O'Donnell, Thomas	Quinn, Patk (John)
Quinn, Timothy	Scanlon, Edmond	Scanlon, Michael	Wall, Mathew

Ballinoe

Ahern, John	Blake, William	Bowen, Thomas	Burns, Patrick
Cahill, Thomas	Ceary, John	Collins, Own	Cowhey, James
Cox, William,	Cullinane, Patrick	Cullinane, William	Donohoe, Michael
Dorgan, Denis	Fitzgerald, James	Glourney, Patrick	Gorman, Patrick
Hannon, Thomas	Hayes, Maurice	Houlehan, William	Leary, James
Leary, Wm. & Prtnrs.	Maher & Neale	Murphy, John & Prtns	
Scully, Michael	Supple, Pierce	Treacy, John	Walsh, David

Applotted on 16,219 acres-2 roods-5 perches-25 $^{1}/_{4}$ yards, statute measure. The Commissioners were John Southwell Brown, junr. and Michael Lynch, esqrs.

Tithe Composition Of Clouncagh, 1833.

Philip F. Drought was the Commissioner appointed for composing the tithes for Clouncagh.

Titheable Land	4,331 Acres - 01 Roods - 38 Perches
Untitheable Land	36 Acres - 00 Roods - 13 Perches
Rectorial,	Nil
Vicarial,	£ 85 - 00 - 00
Lay Impropriator,	£ 170 - 00 - 00
Total	£ 255 - 00 - 00

Townlands Index of the Tithes Composition Records for Clouncagh, 1833.

Ballybeggane, Ballyhahill, Ballykennedy, Ballykennedy North, Ballynarougymore, Carumore, Clouncagh, Gortnacrehy Lower, Gortnacrehy Upper, Gurteencaherane, Killnemona, Teernahilla, Tiervena

The tithe form for Clouncagh differed from that of Ballingarry. It gave greater details of rent, lands, etc. However I am reproducing townlands and occupiers only.

Gortnacrehy Lower

Coffee, James	Cregan, James	Fenoughty, John	Fitzgerald, James
Frawley, James	Gibbings, Mrs.	Hamond, Edmond	Hamond, John
Keeffe, Daniel	Leahy, Thomas	Massy, H. M.	Quaid, David
Quaid, Tim	Scanlan, Michael	Scanlan, Mr.	Sullivan, Patrick
Tierney, John			

Gortnacrehy Upper

Connors, James	Furlong, James	Hearlihy, Richard	Lawlee, John
Liston, Michael	O'Brien, Michael	O'Brien, Patrick	O'Neil, Denis
Ryan, Widow	Scanlan, James		

Carumore

Barry, David	Coleman, Corn. D.	Coleman, Darby	Coleman, John
Culhane, Thomas	Culhane, William	Daniher, Patrick	Hanly, John
Kennelly, Patrick	O'Neil, Daniel	O'Neil, Henry	O'Neil, Thomas
Power, John			

Ballyhahill

Bennett, William*	Fitzgibbon, James	Hamond, Patrick	Hennessy, Widow & Co.
O'Dell, Henry	O'Dell, Richard	O'Dell, Robert	O'Dell, William
Sheehan, Thomas	Sheehy, Patrick		

* Difficult to be sure about this name - could be Bumilly ?

Teernahilla

Costoloe, John	Eary, George	Falahee, John	Hamond, Thomas
Hanly, John	Hanrahan, Patrick	Leo, Denis	Mullane, John
Quaid, John	Sheahan, Simon	Sheehan, Edmond	Sullivan, Laurence
Wall, Richard			

Ballynarougymore

Carroll, Edmond	Condon, David	Costoloe, John	Costoloe, Richard
Fitzgerald, John	Fitzgerald, Mrs.	Fitzgerald, Widow	Flanagan, Maurice
Gilburn, Robert	Hamond, Patrick	Hanrahan, John	Moylan, James
Quaid, Edmond	Quaid, Martin	Quaid, Mrs.	Quaid, Thomas
Quaid, Jeremiah	Ryan, Mrs.	Treacy, James	Treacy, Thomas

Clouncagh

Baggott, Edmond	Baggott, James	Clare, Lord	Dineen, Michael
Eary, Michael	Egan, Jeremiah	Egan, John	Fitzgibbon, John
Hanrahan, Patrick	Healey, Batt	Hearlihy, Tim	Hickey, James
Houlihan, Martin	Jourdan, Edmond	Nash, Frank	Nash, Richard
O'Dell, Thomas	Smith, Henry		

Gurteencaherane

Barnawell, John	Boyce, Darby	Cronin, Michael	Cullinan, Rev. John
Dineen, Michael	Enright, John	Enright, Michael	Fitzgerald, William
Fitzpatrick, Edmund	Hickey, William	Houlihan, Martin	Kennedy, William
Lyons, William	Noonan, John	Noonan, Patrick	O'Dell, Alexander
O'Dell, William	Quaid, Andrew	Quaid, Tim	

Ballykennedy

Costolo, Mrs.	Fitzpatrick, Edmond	Treacy, Timothy	Quaid, George

Ballykennedy North

Neil, Timothy   Power, Mrs.

Ballybeggane

Rahally, John

Killnemona

Flaherty, Denis

Tiervena,

Quaid, John

Order diminishing the amount of Tithe Rent charge as within payable in the Parish of Ballingarry in the Division of Rathkeale and County of Limerick, 1889.

Jonas Blackall and Son, Solrs.,
93, George Street, Limerick and
9, North Great George's Street, Dublin
County of Limerick.
Division of Rathkeale.
To Wit

By the Justices assigned to keep the peace in and for the County of Limerick at a General Sessions of the Peace holden at Rathkeale in and for the Division of Rathkeale in the said County of Limerick on the 3rd day of October 1889

WHEREAS by certificate in writing dated 5th August 1826 signed by **John S. Browne** junior and **Michael Lynch** Commissioners duly appointed under the Act 4th George IV C 99 it was certified that at a vestry duly held on the 24th day of July 1826 in the Parish Church of Ballingarry in the county of Limerick it was agreed on by the parishioners and accepted by the Vicar and Lay Impropriator that the sum of £900 should be the composition for the Vicarial and Rectorial Tithes of the said parish by the year for the term of 21 years from the first day of November then next

And whereas due notice in writing having been first affixed at the times and in the manner directed by the Statutes in such case made and provided signed by **Edmond Moroney, Thomas Fosberry, James O'Shaughnessy** and **Michael Scanlan** (four owners or occupiers of land in the said parish of Ballingarry charged with payment of £3 or upwards each in respect of such composition) of an application on behalf of them the said **Edmond Moroney, Thomas Fosberry, James O'Shaughnessy** and **Michael Scanlan** to the Justices of the Peace of the county of Limerick assembled at Quarter Sessions held at Rathkeale on the 13th day of June 1889 to have the Tithes Composition and Tithe Rent Charges in such parish varied and for that purpose to have the average price of wheat for the 7 years preceding the year 1826 and for the 7 years preceding the year 1889 inquired of and ascertained in Order that the Composition for Tithes and Tithe Rent Charges in the said parish of Ballingarry might be varied and diminished for the ensuing seven years in proportion to such average price

And whereas said application having come on for hearing at Rathkeale on the said 13th day of June 1889 and Mr **Wood G. Jefferson** instructed by Messrs. Jonas Blackall and Son having appeared of counsel for the said Tithe rent payers in support of said application and **Messrs. Sellors and Fitt** having appeared on behalf of the persons entitled to the Impropriate Tithe Rent Charge in said Parish and the said Notice of Application and Certificate and that the said **Edmond Moroney Thomas Fosberry James O'Shaughnessy** and **Michael Scanlan** were entitled to make such application having been proved the said Justices granted the application and referred it to Mr **James Green Barry** to ascertain from the Dublin Gazette the average price of wheat for the 7 years preceding 1st November 1826 and for the 7 years preceding 13th June 1889 and make his report to the Clerk of the Peace and adjourned the application to the next sessions

And whereas the said **James Green Barry** duly made his report in writing Now we the said Justices do ascertain from the said Dublin Gazette that the average price of wheat for the seven years preceding the 1st day of November 1826 was one pound ten shillings and seven pence three farthings per barrel of twenty stone and that the average price of wheat for the seven years preceding the thirteenth day of June 1889 was eighteen shillings and ten pence three farthings per barrel of twenty stone as aforesaid and we do accordingly order and adjudge that the amount of the said Composition for Tithes and Tithe Rent Charge in lieu thereof in the said parish of Ballingarry in the Division of Rathkeale and County of Limerick aforesaid other than such rent charges as became vested in the Commissioners of Church Temporalities in Ireland shall be diminished for the seven years next ensuing the first day of November 1889 in the proportion that the said sum of one pound ten shillings and seven pence three farthings bears to the said sum of eighteen shillings and ten pence three farthings and that the applotment of such Composition be amended accordingly and we do further order and adjudge that the said **Edmond Moroney Thomas Fosberry James O'Shaughnessy** and **Michael Scanlan** the applicants do pay to the said **James Green Barry** the sum of fifteen pounds and fifteen shillings as and for his costs and expenses of said arbitration and report and that the said applicants and the persons entitled to the Impropriate Tithe Rent Charge in said parish do respectively abide their own costs of the said application and all proceedings had thereunder. Dated 3rd day of October 1889. Chairman: **T. W. Purcell.** Clerk of the Crown: **John Elland**.

PARISH OF BALLINGARRY.

Calculation showing reduction in Tithe Rent Charge payable to the Lay Impropriator of the said parish pursuant to order made at October Quarter Sessions on the 3rd October **1889.** (Pounds/shillings/pence.)

No.	Townslands	Tithe-Rent Payers	From	To
1	Coolrus	Anne **Harte**	32-00-06$^1/_2$	19-14-11
2	Kingsland	Anna C.**Tuthill**	06-15-06	04-03-06$^1/_2$
3	Ballinleena: part of	James **Gardiner**	09-04-10	05-13-11$^1/_2$
4	Ballinleena: part of	Eleanor L. **Goodwin**	08-06-06	05-02-08
5	Ballinleena: part of	Reps.Rev.E. **Coen**	11-04-06	06-18-05
6	Kilmore Demesne	Reps Rev.Carew S. **O'Grady**	04-16-08	02-19-07
7	Granah	J. **O'Shaughnessy**, M.D.	10-19-00	06-15-00
8	Doorlas Beg	E. J. **Massy**	04-08-05	02-14-06
9	Liskennett/Ballykevin	**Trinity College Dublin**	19-03-02	11-16-03
10	Kilmacanearla; part of	Colonel **McAdam**	03-18-00	02-08-01
11	Kilmacanearla; part of	Colonel **McAdam**	08-19-08	05-10-09
12	Graigacurra	Stephen D. **Biggs**	17-16-04	10-19-08$^1/_2$
13	Killoughty/Ballyvologe	Stephen D. **Biggs**	12-05-00	07-11-01
14	Lisduane: part of	Mrs. **Braddell**	04-16-01	02-19-03
15	Lisduane: part of	Edmond **Moroney**	04-16-01	02-19-03
16	Lisduane: part of	F. **Willington**	05-09-01	03-07-03
17	Lisduane: part of	James **O'Shaughnessy**, M.D	03-17-00	02-07-05$^1/_2$
18	Kilmacow: part of	Assignees of W. **Power**	14-09-07	08-18-06$^1/_2$
19	Bantabuys	H.A.R. **Pigott**	10-11-00	06-10-01
20	Kilshane Abbey	H.A.R. **Pigott**	46-05-06	28-10-08
21	Ballinaha	H.A.R. **Pigott**	12-14-00	07-16-07
22	Caherhennessy and Ballyroe (Odell)	G.T. **Peacocke**	10-07-09	06-08-01
23	Rylanes/Clontemple: part of	G.T. **Peacocke**	04-10-00	02-15-06
24	Knightstreet; part of	G.T. **Peacocke**	02-03-09	01-06-11$^1/_2$
25	Knightstreet; part of	G.T. **Peacocke**	01-16-00	01-02-02
26	Lisamota	Captain **Bateson**	014-14-01	09-01-04

27	Rylanes / Clontemple; part of	Thomas D. **Atkinson**	01-16-00	01-02-02
28	Clonregan / Gurteen	Thomas D. **Atkinson**	10-13-10	06-11-10
29	Rylanes; part of	Thomas D. **Atkinson**	00-09-08	00-05-11$^{1}/_{2}$
30 /				
35	Ballyroe Nash	Illegible or blank.		
36	The Downes	Robert O'Brien **Furlong**	06-08-07$^{1}/_{2}$	03-19-03$^{1}/_{2}$
37	Ballynockane	Michael **Scanlan**	05-16-04	03-11-09
38	Kilbeg	Michael **Scanlan**	03-18-05	02-08-04
39	Kilmihill	Revd L.C.**Warren**	07-11-06	04-13-05
40	Ashboro	Mrs Kate **Power**	03-06-05	02-00-11
41	Ballinarouga: part of	Captain **Wilkinson**	02-05-01	01-07-09$^{1}/_{2}$
42	Ballinarouga: part of	Edmund **Moroney**	05-16-00	03-11-06
43	Ballyguileataggle	Thomas **Fosbery**	12-13-07	07-16-04
44	Glenwilliam	T.D. **Atkinson**	11-08-04	07-00-09$^{1}/_{2}$
45	Derryclogh: part of	T.D. **Atkinson**	02-01-08	01-05-08
46	Ballyelan	J.O'Grady **Delmege**	15-06-03	09-08-10
47	Ballyneale	J.G.M. **Beresford**	14-03-06	08-14-09$^{1}/_{2}$
48	Ballynoe	William **Cox**	22-04-08	13-14-02
49	Derryclogh: part of	William **Cox**	00-19-04	00-11-11
50	Derryclogh: part of	Peter **Bourke**	01-10-01	00-18-06$^{1}/_{2}$
51	Ballynafrompa	Edward **Mason**	00-17-06	00-10-09$^{1}/_{2}$
52	Graigue Beg / Ballyguile	Messrs. **Conyers**	07-05-08	04-09-10
53	Ballenaguile / Dollas	Lord **Langford**	03-16-03	02-07-00
54	Lisavara	Earl of **Dunraven**	03-17-00	02-07-05$^{1}/_{2}$
55	Knockfierna Commons/ Kilbeg	J.S. **Peppard**	02-16-08	01-14-11
56	Frankfort	Major W. **White**	10-11-10	06-10-07
57	Ballykevin	Marchesa della **Rochella**	04-05-01	02-12-05$^{1}/_{2}$
	Totals		£448-00-04	£276-08-07
	There is an addition of		£ 03-02-00	--- --- ---
	Totals		£451-02-04	£276-08-07

I certify that the above calculations of Tithe Rent Charge to be paid in pursuance of the above mentioned order are correct. Dated this 28th day of April, 1890. **James G.Barry**, Arbitrator.

PART IV

The People and the Land.

Prior to the Famine years of 1845-1850 the population of Ireland increased rapidly. This explosion of population was a cause of concern to the British Government. They instituted several investigations into the life of the poor people and the use of land. In this section there are two reports. The first, dating from early in the 19th century was in a question and answer format and I have reproduced it here in script form. It is unclear who completed the form but most likely a local C. of I. clergyman. This is followed by a synopsis of the evidence given to the Devon Commission.

The Commission appointed by His Majesty to Inquire into the State of the Poor in Ireland.

Most of this survey was destroyed but the full return for Oldcastle Parish, Co. Meath exists. This is an agricultural / rural small community so comparison with Ballingarry would be fair. The following is a summary of this survey and gives an incisive insight into how the rural poor survived in pre-Famine Ireland.

The average rent is 30 shillings per acre; no difference being shown between arable and pasture. The labourers are maintained in idleness by means of the wives and children going out to beg during the want of employment. Ordinary diet of potatoes and salt with occasionally a little buttermilk. Wages in Summer are 10 pence a day, without diet; 8 pence with diet. In the winter the rates are 8 pence and 6 pence accordingly. Unemployment is highest in January, February, July and August. Women and children are employed in Winter in clearing the land of stones; in Spring in dropping potatoes; in harvest in binding and stooking. Wages of women are 6 pence a day; of boys 4 pence. They are seldom employed above six weeks in the year. The average yearly income of a labourer is given as follows: Wages, £10. Profit on pig, £1-10-00. We do not think a man has a profit on his con acre allowing for rent, seed and labour. Annual expenditure of a labourer for food is as follows: Potatoes and Oatmeal, £6-10-00. Salt, two shillings and buttermilk fifteen shillings. Many are not able to afford even this. The landlords of cottages and cabins are generally of the lower sort: the wealthier landlords provide houses for their labourers. Rent for cabins without a garden is seven shillings a year. Rent for cabins with a garden of half a rood is thirty shillings to two pounds. The cabins are built of mud. There is no furniture but a few stools, very few bedsteads, the covering wretched and they sleep on beds of straw. **Napier** the landlord has for years increased the comfort of this class by distributing blankets and clothing at half price.

Con acre prevails 'very much' in my parish. Rent is £4 to £8 per acre for manured ground: sometimes free to tenants who will put out their own manure. The con-acre crop is a remunerating one. If it fails it is not unusual for the farmer to give an abatement - the principle benefit in a corn crop is the manure and straw for feeding cows.

There are twenty public houses and there are as many more unlicensed for the sale of poteen. There was a great deal of illicit distillation last year and it still prevails, but not to the same extent as it has been checked by the Revenue Police. There are 217 old and infirm people. They are supported by the piety of their families. Others by begging; some entirely: some occasionally. People have their own areas when going to beg. About 100 beggars receive alms after Market Day. On other occasions, alms are usually given in food. To our certain knowledge we know of only one case of a deserted child. None (children) have perished through neglect to our knowledge. No person we know of has died of destitution in the last three years.
Ref. GOM 10214, Genealogical Office, Nat.Library.

The Devon Commission, 1844.

In the early part of the 19th century the British Government were concerned about the rising population in Ireland and the poor state of agriculture in the country. As the population increased more and more people crowded on to the land. They had nowhere else to go. There was no industrial revolution to attract the surplus population into the cities. Ignoring this fact the British Government urged landlords to make their estates efficient by 'rationalising' the numbers of tenants. Of course this meant that with the best will in the world, some tenants were going to lose. The Government did many investigations into the state of affairs and one of these was the Devon Commission. This is the background to the clash between Archdeacon Fitzgerald and John Cox of Ballynoe. In 1820-21 the Government gave financial assistance to people to emigrate to Canada. This is the emigration scheme referred to by Archdeacon Fitzgerald. What follows is an abbreviated version of their evidence to the Commission. The evidence of the Devon Commission is in question and answer format but I have reproduced the excerpts in prose form. *Nat. Lib. Ref. Part II; IR 333 0941 D4.*

Evidence taken before Her Majesty's Commissioners Of Inquiry into the state of the Law and Practice in respect of the Occupation of Land in Ireland given at Newcastle, Aug., 28, 1844.

List of Witnesses :

Lloyd	Edward	Heathfield
Fitzgerald	Rev. Michael	Ballingarry
Quade	Maurice	Ballykennedy
Cox	John, jnr.	Ballyneale
Cox	William	Ballynoe
Coll	Rev. Thomas	Newcastle
Christie	John	Adare
Fosberry	George	Curraghbridge, Adare
Harnett	Michael	Droumtrasna O'Brien
Hayes	Patrick	Abbeyfeale
Locke	Rev. John	Newcastle

Evidence given by Archdeacon Michael Fitzgerald, Parish Priest of Ballingarry.

I reside in Ballingarry. I am the only person from that electoral division. I represent one of the largest electoral divisions in the union. One of the evils which press most heavily on the agricultural class in my neighbourhood (and I make no doubt, generally in Ireland) is the want of capital. The want places it utterly out of their power to stock their grass lands or cultivate their tillage lands to the best advantage. This want is not only a physical but a moral drawback and obstacle, in the disheartening difficulty and despondency which attend on it. The profits of perhaps five out of six of the farms in this district are diminished to an extent seldom short of thirty per cent from want of capital. There are in this parish about 250 occupiers of land rated under the poor law to £30 value, and about as many more rated from £30 downwards to £5 or £6. I am persuaded, and I am now on oath, that out of these 500 there are fully 400 who, putting their interest in the land out of sight, may be fairly called insolvents: that is to say that if their liabilities were to be satisfied on the spot, with all their effects above ground, they would go forth into the world as naked as they came into it. This state of things leads to a system of shifting and borrowing as best they can (or buying on time at enormous prices): in fact the life of many is a warfare - a hopeless and endless struggle against ever-growing embarrassments; and I need not say that such a struggle must, in an economical as well as a moral point of view, be attended with the worst effects. The want of capital is indeed miserably felt: but I know of no remedy for the evil: that is for wiser heads than mine.

With respect to excessive and exorbitant rents I believe this district is, in about two-thirds of it's extent, not worse off than other parts of Ireland. The two-thirds alluded to are the property of noblemen and other persons of large property; and I believe it is generally found that proprietors of large property (say £1,000 a year or upward) are by no means so exorbitant in their demands, or so harsh in their enforcement of them, as the poorer class of landlords (whether owners in fee or perpetual leases) at small head rents. Therefore exorbitant rents are not so much the rule as the exception in this district. But the exceptions are not few, and there are acreable rents forty, fifty or ninty per cent above the tithe composition value, struck in 1827 when prices were higher than at present. Such rents of course it is impossible to pay; arrears accumulate, and these unpaid rents are made a pretext for turning out these wretched people; levelling their cabins and making their fields the pasture range of the sheep and black cattle of the landlord. It is true that many of the landlords in this minor grade are themselves overburdened with debt; but it is certainly against this class, more than against the higher grade, that legislative protection is necessary. Gentlemen of narrowed incomes are generally found rapacious in their demands and disposed too often to exercise the rights with as little regard as may be to the duties of property.

This, which I am now coming to, is the particular thing I wish to call attention to. The **Ecclesiastical Commissioners**, who hold certain see lands in this district, acted with great harshness on a recent occasion in preferring a middleman to the occupying tenants, who were industrious, honest and solvent, and who would have deemed themselves lucky if they get the fields they and their fathers had tilled at a rent even beyond that given by the middleman, who had no previous connexion whatever with the land. The rent of these ill-used men was nearly doubled on the coming in of the middleman. Some were put out: the farms were, as it were, shuffled up, and cut out into parallellograms; strangers were introduced into the hamlet, and all, besides holding at a rack-rent, hold at will; with the comfortable prospect of making way for the middleman or his son, at no distant date.

The middleman in question was introduced, I believe, to save themselves trouble. **Mr. Knox** sought to save himself trouble by it, though the tenants were all perfectly solvent and of good character. The tenants held about twenty to twenty five plantation acres each: very comfortable farmers. Only three were dispossessed. Then there was another place he was clearing and he brought the tenants in there that he was clearing out elsewhere, and he doubled the rents upon them. **Mr. Nash** formerly held these lands under the Ecclesiastical Commissioners. It was on the expiration of his lease and ejectment for non-payment of rent. I mention also, that for twenty years no agrarian outrage was committed; no attempt at assassination took place in the parish; though there were very many agrarian grievances; and on that occasion I have reason particularly to know, there was a plot of assassination projected, which did not take place. This was against the middleman, **John Cox**.

Another party I may name residing in Limerick, happening to the misfortune of the poor, to become the proprietor by purchase of a large townland called Ballyneale turned out a number of thriving, honest and industrious tenants whose fathers had been born on the land. The tenants were encouraged to propose and then the land was given at their offer, principally to a person previously unconnected with the farm, and with the obligation as he alleges of turning out every single tenant. It is but justice to say he went through harsh duty with as much lenity as the case admitted: but great suffering resulted and many families were thrown on the world. The middleman alluded to in both cases was **John Cox.** He resides in Ballyneale. He was the younger son of a gentleman and quite penniless 'til he got in at the expense of these poor people.

In Castletown, and in the different parishes about there, greater hardship was done than in my parish by the manner of the letting of lands: but all the land was let to this middle man at a lump rent. This was an arrangement with him. The occupiers had an opportunity of proposing, and I believe they did propose and they got into law about it. Within these few years past, upon the property of certain other gentlemen, hundreds of acres previously occupied by tenants have been taken into demesne. Great misery has resulted in some cases. In some instances the tenants expelled succeeded in obtaining settlements elsewhere: some were driven into some neighbouring town, to pick up subsistence as best they could; some were reduced to the greatest misery; and those persons deemed themselves fortunate who were retained as workmen, with lots of land at exorbitant rents; but in many cases, gentlemen of this class do not allow their workmen potato land. I have heard and fully believe that some gentlemen sell their wretched workmen potatoes from their own stores, or procure for them on credit, in both cases at double the market price, so that the wretched workman who has nominally 8d or 6d a day (the 6d in money and the 8d in kind) is by this truck system robbed of half his hire.

I am obliged to say that I believe the rights of property have been often exercised of late years in this district with extreme harshness and with a seeming recklessness as to any suffering that might ensue. I am prepared to give instances if required. (None were given.) No gratuity was given to the tenant as a result of the demesne being increased, except the remission of the arrears of rent and which it was impossible for them to pay. The system was, the people were removed from good land; they were removed by degrees; they were removed from the low land higher up the hills and removed from where their fathers had been fifty years before and at last they were either turned out of the place entirely, or sent up to the top of the hill, where they got an acre at £4 which was not worth £1. I am prepared to give instances. The system has been going on for years and it is not yet complete. The name of this gentleman who is most remarkable for this consolidation and hardship is **William Cox,** Esq. of Ballinoe. Ballingarry is the post-town. He has turned out over twenty or thirty families to my knowledge in that way within a period of seven or eight years. Several of them were turned out very lately. My curate went to attend a poor man dying in a cabin and the land was ploughed up to the very house and they had left a rough sort of avenue to the place. My curate told me that the poor man's anxiety was lest he should not be dead by a certain day on which day it was appointed that the house should be levelled. There are now beautiful fields and pastures there but those beautiful fields are the sepulchres of the poor. In point of fact the house of the man I referred to was levelled. The name of the man was **Houlahan.**

He then goes on to make an extensive submission as to how things could be made fairer between landlords and tenants. He makes one prescient point: that in all cases of loss of animals by disease that the landlord should allow half the loss in the rent payable, and he says 'it is a question whether some such provision ought not to extend to the failure of potatoes when the failure is extensive, as this casualty has in many cases of late years rendered tenants insolvent in this part of the country.' He further states 'the agricultural hireling in Ireland is a miserable slave, toiling and starving on 6d or 8d the day and with no prospect (after enduring the wet and cold of winter when rheumatism and old age set in) but to close his days in the workhouse. The landlord farmer, I honestly confess, appears to me to be one of the worst enemies the poor have in Ireland.'

He encourages a policy of aid-assisted emigration to Canada for the poor and unemployed. He concludes - 'In 1822 every person (who emigrated to Canada) got a piece of land and I believe a cow and the accounts that came over were very flattering and the people were anxious to avail themselves of it. He goes on to say - 'The evil is the immense over-population; they are pushing each other off their stools. Half of the labourers in my parish are idle; they are working at 6d a day, which I never knew before; and they do not get the good diet they got before. They used to get milk: but employment is not to be had.' This concluded his evidence to the Commission.

Note - *Demesne - Land possessed or occupied by the owner himself. In modern terms land immediately attached to a mansion.*

Evidence of William Cox of Ballynoe.
He refuted most of the allegations made against him by Archdeacon Fitzgerald. He explained in great detail the many problems he had. He had been threatened by **Captain Rock**. He admitted ejecting **John Tracy**. Some of the evidence of Archdeacon Fitzgerald was read to him and he refuted it. He stated that the old man who was waiting for death was over 90 years old and that the house was still standing and inhabited by the old man's son and daughter. He stated that he had other things to do rather than go about "harrassing and hampering the people which, I venture to say, I have not done." He says he is on very good terms with his tenants and travels day and night unarmed and unmolested. In 1826 he came to live at home. In 1827 he dispossessed 5 tenants but got them farms on **Mr. Hart's** place in Coorass. He explains that there was a lot of overcrowding on his estate. He concludes by saying 'there would be very little talk about the necessity of having lands divided except that it is perferctly evident it lessens the revenue of the Roman Catholic clergy having land taken up by the proprietor.' He also states 'I can recollect when my labourers had not shoes or stockings or a coat, and now they go to prayers as respectably clad as the farmers, and I think they are more comfortable.'

Evidence of John Cox of Ballyneale.
He stated that he held the lands - 300 to 400 acres - under the **Ecclesiastical Commission**, part of the estate of the See of Ossory on a 21 year lease. The previous lessees were 'persons of the name of **Nash-Ryland and Nash**.' The Ecclesiastical Commissioners evicted the Nash interest and put up the lands to public competition by public advertisement. He goes on to state that he had difficulty in getting physical possession of his land as many tenants had proposed to the Ecclesiastical Commission to take their own lands. In their disappointment at being denied this, they refused to acknowledge **John Cox** as landlord. He found the farms (of the tenants) were in a zig-zag direction whose boundaries were difficult to trace. He reorganised the estate into more orderly strips of land and claimed that no one was left short in the re-organised farms. He complained about a resident occupier named **Hartnett** who had 46 acres. He refused a new arrangement with Cox and was ejected. The farm is now occupied by another. He stated that the tenants felt very strongly that they should get the land themselves without any intermediate landlord. He refuted Archdeacon Fitzgerald's allegations and states that **Mr.**

William Cox was forced to evict 20 tenants over 18 years. He claimed that William and he "give a vast deal of employment." He also stated that "the poor are in a very deplorable state certainly." He also said that he had to eject two brothers named **Casey**. He further declared that he had let two farms to two Roman Catholic priests (un-named).

Evidence of Edward Lloyd of Heathfield.

He stated that he was a member of the Board of Guardians, a landed proprietor living on the estate of Sergeant Warren of Dublin "but I hold it under a lease in perpetuity." He had nearly 400 acres mountain and 260 acres arable land in his own occupation. His evidence was sympathetic to the plight of the poor and tenantry and stated; 'Latterly the failure of the potato crop, and the disease among the cattle, have reduced many of the tenants to circumstances of great poverty, who were formerly comfortable. The small tenantry are very miserable and the labourer is in a wretched state.' Several times he refers to the disease in animals and failure of potato crop. He stated that "the tenant ..... hold their land too high (rent) and have no capital and are not able to improve the land. If they improve it for a while they will be likely to tear it to pieces afterwards or they will marry their children and divide their lot. Sub-dividing is carried to a great extent, particularly among the children on their marriage. He also stated that the good landlords - **Colonel White** and **Sergeant Warren** - had assisted the tenants in building houses in my neighbourhood. He gives his opinion that "I do not think a man ought to be employed as an agent except he is a man of honour and feeling and judgement who could go among the tenants and see if a man had a crop fail or stock died and allow him for the loss of stock or crop for they have nothing to support them but out of their little bit of land which they take at the full value. He stated that he could employ for 6d a day but paid 8d per day. He also stated that in respect of younger children at the death of their parents become paupers almost invariably except the farming class who sub-divide their farm.

Evidence of Maurice Quade of Ballykennedy.

He stated he resided in Ballykennedy and he is a farmer. He has about 100 acres and another farm elsewhere (not specified). He stated he was acquainted with the Cloncagh Electoral Division on which he was able to give evidence. He stated his land was principally grazing, taken by private contract on an acreable rent. He stated many farms in Cloncagh were without lease and their occupiers were anxious to get a lease. Though the past three years had been bad the tenants would take their holdings at the past rents. He claimed this had a bad effect as no one wanted to improve their holding without a lease. Allowances for improvements by Lord Clare are one and a half pence to two pence ($1^1/_2$d - 2d) per perch sod-draining and three pence to four pence (3d-4d) for stone drains, which is considered very little. Subletting was rare. Conacre is charged at £6 - £10. Coarse land is one guinea to £2-10-00 a quarter. That is sometimes the fallow but ley is generally for £6 - £10 per acre. It is paid in cash or labour. Wages were not paid in cash as there was usually a house or something against it. The rent paid by the small tenants is greater than the big farmer. He suggested changes to the law on the sale of corn. When they went to market they were obliged to pay toll, porterage and beamage. With butter they pay custom and toll. They also pay weighouse fees. He complained the Grand Jury cess was very high and oppressive. He went on to suggest changes to the dates of the gale days. That concluded his evidence.

Note: The evidence given to the Commission by the above parties was roughly in proportion to the extracts I made.

PART V

Griffith's Valuation

Griffith's Valuation, 1852. The Primary Valuation Of Tenements.

The second big genealogical record of the 19th century is The Primary Valuation Of Tenements. Early in the 19th century it was decided that a form of taxation based on property would be levied on the people. Once this was decided, a valuation of every house and tenement in the country was undertaken. The official name for this survey is **The Primary Valuation Of Tenements**.

This huge project was supervised and brought to a successful conclusion by the Commissioner of Valuation, **Sir Richard Griffith**, (1784-1878). Thus the survey is universally referred to as **Griffith's Valuation.** The project began in 1848 and concluded in 1864. In respect of each entry in the survey the following details are given:

1) A map reference showing location of property.

2) Townland and Occupier.

3) Immediate Lessor.

4) Description of Tenement: house: house & garden, etc.

5) Area.

6) Net annual value of Land,

7) Net annual value of Buildings and

8) Total.

General Valuation of Rateable Property in Ireland under the Act 9 & 10 Victoria cap 110. County of Limerick. Barony of Upper Connello. Ballingarry. Union of Croom. Primary Valuation. Dated at the General Valuation Office: No. 2 Fitzwilliam Place, Dublin this 10th day February, 1852.

Townlands Index.

Ballyelan	Ballygrennan	Ballyguileataggle	Ballyguilebeg
Ballykevan East	Ballykevan West	Ballyknockane	Ballynahaha
Ballynarougabeg E.	Ballinarougabeg W.	Ballynashig	Ballyneale
Ballynoe	Ballyroe East	Ballyroe West	Ballyvologe
Caherhenesy	Cloonregan	Cloontemple	

Town Of Ballingarry: Cloontemple

Cool Lane Nt.	Cool Lane St.	Main Street	New Road
Pound Street	Sparr Street	The Mall	Town Field
Turrett St.	Well Lane		
Commons	Coolrus	Dollas	Doorlus
Downs	Durraclogh	Frankfort	Glenwilliam
Gorteen	Graigacarragh	Graigbeg	Granagh
Kilbeg East	Kilbeg West	Killoughty	Kilmacanearla Nth
Kilmacanearla St.	Kilmacow	Kilmihill	Kilmore
Kilmore Demesne	Kilshane	Kingsland	Knightstreet

Town of Ballingarry: Knightstreet

Castle Street	Downs Road	Echo Lane	Main Street (part of)
The Mall	Sparr Street (part of)		
Lisduane	Lisduff	Liskennett East	Liskennett West
Lissamota	Lissavarra	Morenane	Rylanes

Town of Ballingarry: Rylanes

Turrett Street (part of)
Woodstock

*The following are the townlands and occupiers as listed in the Valuation. These records were made in long hand and it is sometimes difficult to decipher the hand writing. I have tried to be as accurate as possible but in any case of doubt the original records should be consulted. Frequently the same name is repeated in a townland but I have listed each name only once. In the actual record of the valuation the names are not in alphabetical order. For ease of reference I have done so. The names listed are shown as having a house and property or just property. I have used the star * to denote property only. All other names have a minimum of a house in the townland. In a small number of cases it was impossible to decipher the names.*

Ballyelan

Cahill, James	Carmody, Patrick	Collins, Mary	Collins, Patrick
Donohoe, Alice	Hartigan, James	Hartigan., Patrick*	Lynch, Johanna
Noonan, David	Noonan, Edmond	Noonan, Michael	Nealon, Michael
O'Grady, James	Ready, David	Ready, James	Ready, John
Ready, Patrick	Regan, Cornelius	Regan, Maurice jnr.	Roche, Margaret
Taylor, John			

Ballygrennan

Barry, David*	Biggane, Timothy	Carmody, Mary	Carmody, Patrick
Dore, David	Dore, Edmond	Hannon, John	Hederman, John
Lynch, Johanna*	Mangan, Michael	McEnery, David	Moncton, James
Moncton, John*	Moncton, Patrick	Moran, Bridget	Neligan, Michael
O'Brien, Daniel	Pigott, John	Power, William	Ready, Francis

Note: Here is a burial ground.

Ballyguileataggle

Bennett, Maurice	Court of Chancery*	Clifford, Patrick	Cox, Robert
Cullinane, William	Curtin, Edmund	Curtin, Michael	Houlihan, Paul
Noonan, Edmond	Noonan, James*	Noonan, Michael	Noonan, Thomas

Ballyguilebeg

Conyers, Revd. E. J.   Hanly, Honora

Ballykevan East

Ahern, James	Cronin, Michael	Glorney, John	Irwin, Edmond

Ballykevan West

Earl of Clare	O'Dell, Crone	Grady, John	Kennedy, Patrick

Patrick Kennedy lives in the Gate Lodge.

Ballyknockane

Hall, Robert	Hacman, William*	Scanlan, William *(inc. Gate Lodge)*

Ballynahaha

Bennett, David	Cagney, John	Cagney, Michael	Carey, Bridget
Carey, Mary	Carey, Michael	Carey, Thomas	Donnelly, Deborah
Donohoe, Michael	Drew, William	Hannon, William	Hickey, William
Kennedy, John	Lynch, Patrick	Murphy, Margaret	O'Brien, John
O'Brien, Thomas	O'Brien, William	Scanlan, William	

Ballynaroogabeg East

Cotteral, Catherine	McCarthy, Patrick	Power, Daniel D.

Ballynaroogabeg West
Connery, Mary	Donohue, William	Fitzgerald, John	Fitzgerald, Mary
Hennessy, Bridget	Kiely, John	O'Dell, John	O'Dell, Thomas H.

Ballynashig
Hannon, John	Hannon, Michael	Power, Samuel	Quinn, Jeremiah
Sullivan, Edmond			

Ballyneale
Cox, John	Cox, Robert	Cox, William*	Donohue, John
Hannon, Honoria	Hayes, Patrick	Massy, Hon. John*	O'Brien, John
Regan, Patrick	Trehy John		

Ballynoe
Anderson, William	Bowen, Mary	Cahill, Thomas	Carey, John
Cox, William	Dea, John	Gorman, John	Hallinan, John
Hannon, William	Hayes, Denis	Kilbridge, Margaret	Leacy, Catherine
Leary, Mary	Leary, William	Maher, John	Morrison, Robert
Morrissey, Denis	Murphy, John	Murphy, Patrick	Murphy, Sonia
Neil, Patrick	Neil, Thomas	Reasy, Robert	Reardon, Alice
Scully, Michael	Shannahan, James	Walsh, Margaret	

Notes. Here is a Constabulary Force, Police Barracks and yard. John Dea and Sonia Murphy are shown living in gate lodges. There is also a pound, Patrick Neil.

Ballyroe East
Ecclesiastical Commissioners*		Donohoe, John	Hartnett, Timothy
Keating, John	Murphy, Patrick	Sullivan, James*	Trehy, Michael

Ballyroe West
Boyce, Patrick*	Daly, Mary	Daly, Martin	Casey, Mary
Casey, Patrick	Hartigan, Patrick*	Hayes, Johanna	Hurley, Patrick*
Roche, Johanna	Moore, Thomas	Ready, Thomas*	

Ballyvaloge
Biggs, Stephen D.	Downes, John	Fitzgerald, Thomas*	Fitzpatrick, Thomas
Grady, Mary	Kelly, Mary	Kiely, Edmond	Mahoney, James
Mahoney, Mary	Reardon, Cornelius	Regan, Catherine	Sheahan, Maurice
Walsh, Patrick			

Caherhennessy
Bourke, James*	Bowen, Callaghan	Bowen, Edmond*	Bowen, John
Boyce, Patrick	Brownrick, John*	Cagney, Patrick	Cain, Patrick

RECORDS OF BALLINGARRY, GRANAGH AND CLOUNCAGH, 1800 - 1900 – COUNTY LIMERICK

Casey, Patrick*	Egan, Mary	Feehan, Catherine*	Fleming, John
Hallinan, Edmond*	Hayes, James	Hayes, Johanna*	Kelly, Matthew
Lee, Bridget	Leo, Bridget	Leo, Patrick	O'Connell, Maurice*
O'Dell, John*	O'Dell, Robert*	O'Dell, William	O'Grady, Bridget
O'Grady, James	Quinlan, William	Regan, Thomas	Russell, James
Walsh, Edmond			

Note: John Brownrick is shown having 2 roods and 30 perches Waste and Water.

Cloonregan

Collins, James	Fitzgerald, Edward*	Keeffe, John	Keeffe, Thomas*
Mara, Timothy	Meade, Patrick *	O'Donnell, Patrick	Ready, Thomas

Cloontemple

Brien, Johanna	Hanrahan, Mary*	Maxwell, Robert*	O'Dell, William*
Ready, Thomas			

Here is a gravel pit and waste, William O'Dell.

Cloontemple - Town of Ballingarry - Main Street.

Airy, Robert	Blake, Michael	Brown, Jeremiah*	Carmody, Denis*
Casey, Patrick	Costelloe, Michael	Cox, John	Culhane, Catherine
Davern, Timothy	Donahy, Daniel	Doohy, Maurice	Downes, John
Fenaghty, Patrick	Fitzgerald, Thomas	Fleming, Margaret	Frehy, Mary Anne
Gubbins, Rev. G. G.	Hayes, Alice	Hayes, John	Hore, James
Hurley, Patrick	Keating, John	Kennedy, Mary	Madigan, Anne
Malowney, Michael	Mara, John	McMahon, Patrick	Mulcahy, Timothy
Naughton, John	O'Connell, Thomas	O'Dell, William	O'Donnell, Catherine
O'Donnell, John*	O'Donnell, Mary A.	O'Donnell, Patrick	O'Grady, John
?? Grady, Roger	O'Regan, Michael	Quaide, John	Regan, Daniel
Regan, Timothy	Ronihan, Henry	Sheehy, Deborah	Sweeney, Roger
Toohill, John	Toomy, Mary	Tracey, Edmond	Walsh, Michael

Notes. *Here is a Church and graveyard, Rev.G.G. Gubbins. Also John O'Donnell is shown as 'Reps. Of.'*

Sparr Street

Ahern, Johanna	Coleman, Mary	Connors, Mary	Cronan, Patrick
Crowe, Michael	Duhig, Thomas	Fanning, Johanna	Gill, Honoria
Hanrahan, John	Hayes, Catherine	Hayes, Richard	Healy, Cornelius
Hogan, Margaret	Jordan, Jeremiah	Keating, John*	Keeffe, Johanna
Kelly, Timothy	Sullivan, Eugene	Treacy, Edmond*	

Note. *Three names are undecipherable.*

Cool Lane South

Creedon, Matthew	Cronan, John	Fitzpatrick, Richard	Garen, John
Hogan, John	Kelly, Ellen	Mahony, Catherine	O'Brien, Edmond
Russell, Thomas			

Pound Street

Ahern, William	Bowen, Edmond	Casey, Patrick*	Connell, Mary
Connelly, James	Connors, Jeremiah*	Connors, Mary	Crotty, Denis
Culhane, Patrick	Curten, Timothy	Davern, Michael	Dolan, Thomas
Dunne, Eugene	Dunne, John	Dunne, Patrick	Fitzgerald, Mary
Guiry, Michael	Hannon, Edmond*	Hannon, Edward	Hannon, John
Hannon, Michael	Hartigan, William	Jordan, Ellen*	Kelly, David*
Lane, David*	Massy, Frederick	McCarthy, Denis	Meade, John
Moncton, George	Mullins, John	Murphy, John	Power, Daniel D.*
Russell, George	Ryan, Honoria	Stokes, Henry	Sullivan, John
Supple, John	Supple, John jr.	Sweeny, James	

Here is a pound, Fred Massy.

Wall Lane

Condon, Mary*	Downs, John*	Sullivan, Terence

New Road

Gubbins, Rev. G.G. *

Cool Lane North

Brien, Henry	Clifford, Patrick	Hurley, Margaret	O'Leary, Michael

Turrett Street

Downes, James	Fitzgerald, Edward	Flanedy, Michael	Gubbins, Rev. G. G.*
Houlihan, John	Liddy, Rev. Dan.*	Mone, James*	Noonan, William
O'Grady, James*			

Here is a National School House, office & yard, James Mone.

The Mall

Culhane, Johanna	Dillane, Roger	O'Brien, Michael	Sheehy, James
Sheehy, John*			

Townfield

There were no house owners in Townfield. The following held land only.

Ahern, William	Boyce, Patrick	Bowen, John	Carmody, Garrett
Condon, Mary	Connell, James	Donehy, James	Duhig, Thomas
Fanning, Johanna	Gill, Honoria	Greene, Robert	Hayes, Alice

Hogan, Michael	Hurley, Patrick	Keating, John	Kelly, Michael
Liddy, Rev. Dan.	Massy, Frederick	John, Mullins	Tracy, Edmond
Walsh, Michael			

Note: James O'Connell is listed as 'The Reps. Of' as is Michael Kelly.'

Common

The following are shown having at least a house in this area.

Barry, John	Barry, Michael	Biggane, Margaret	Bridgeman, Thomas
Broderick, Daniel	Burns, Margaret	Cagney, Alice	Cantillon, Alice
Carey, Geoffrey	Carey, John	Carey, Richard	Clancy, Thomas
Cronan, Eugene	Coghlan, Michael	Collins, Johanna	Costello, Daniel
Costello, Michael	Cowhey, Eliza	Culhinane, Patrick	Cullinane, William
Curtin, Margaret	Donohoe, Maurice	Dore, David	Dore, Edmund
Dore, John	Dore, Michael	Dore, Patrick	Downs, Cornelius
Downs, Honoria	Downs, James	Doyle, Margaret	Dwyer, Thomas
Fitzgibbon, John	Fitzpatrick, Thomas	Frawley, Mary	Gorman, James
Guiry, William	Hanly, Denis	Hanley, Honoria	Hannan, James
Hannon, Mary	Harnett, Edmund	Harte, Catherine	Hartigan, Mary
Hartigan, Patrick	Hawly, Denis	Hogan, William	Houlihan, Michael
Keating, Patrick	Keeffe, Michael	Keely, Margaret	Kennedy, Mary
Kirby, James	Kirby, Michael	Leary, Margaret	Linihan, Johanna
Liston, Bartholemew	Liston, John	Lyons, Philip	Madigan, Catherine
McCann, John	McCarthy, Michael	McGrath, Johanna	Meehan, James
Murphy, Margaret	Neligan, Catherine	O'Brien, James	Ready, James
Ready, Michael	Regan, Johanna	Regan, Michael	Regan, Thomas
Roche, Anastasia	Roche, Patrick	Roche, Thomas	Roche, William
Russell, William	Scanlan, Edmund	Shanahan, John	Shea, Redmond
Sullivan, Cornelius	Sullivan, James	Sullivan, John	Sullivan, Thomas
Tracy, Margaret	White, Honoria	White, Patrick	White, William

The following are shown having property other than houses.

Barry, Catherine	Bourke, James	Boyce, Patrick	Bridgeman, John
Cagney, John	Carey, Patrick	Carmody, Patrick	Casey, Patrick
Cavanagh, John	Connell, William	Costello, Patrick	Donohoe, Margaret
Donohoe, Michael	Dunworth, Catherine	Fitzgerald, Edmund	Gorman, Johanna
Grady, Michael	Gubbins, Rev.G.G.	Hannan, John	Hannan, Michael
Hartigan, John	Hederman, John	Hurley, Patrick	Keating, John
Kiely, Bridget	Liddy, Rev. D.	Morrissy, Honoria	Murphy, Patrick
Noonan, David	Noonan, Edmund	Noonan, Michael	O'Brien, Daniel

| O'Brien, Edward | O'Brien, John | O'Connell, John | Regan, Mary |
| Regan, Michael, jnr. | Scanlon, William | | |

Notes. *Here is a school house, Johanna Gorman. A school house and garden, Honoria Morrissy. A school house and offices, Rev. G. G. Gubbins. A Constabulary Force, Police Barracks, office and garden. Commonage area of 198 acres - 03 roods - 38 perches. Michael Grady and Catherine Dunworth are each shown having land (incld. road).*

Coolrus

Ahern, Patrick	Barry, Edmund	Bourke, John	Brown, Catherine
Burke, Ellen	Burke, James	Burns, Daniel	Burns, James, jnr
Burns, Patrick	Cahill, Honoria	Carroll, Honoria	Carroll, John
Carroll, Martin	Cuthbert, Patrick	Daly, Jeremiah	Dillon, Thomas
Guare, Patrick	Guare, William	Hanrahan, Patrick	Kielly, John
Hederman, Thomas	Houlihan, Denis	Leahy, John	Long, Maurice
Lynch, James	Lyons, John	Lyons, Patrick	Maher, William
Mahony, Jeremiah	Martin, William	McCauliffe, John	McNamara, John
O'Brien, Cornelius	O'Brien, Ellen	O'Brien, James	O'Donnell, Robert
O'Donnell, Thomas	Quinlivan, Michael	Sheehan, John	Shiely, Thomas

Notes. *Here is a Tuck Mill and land, John Carroll. James Lynch is living in Gate Lodge*

Dollas

Grady, John	Hayes, John	Kavanagh, Daniel	Kavanagh, James
Leary, Daniel	Lynch, Thomas	Lynch, Timothy*	Martin, Richard
McCarthy, Catherine	Power, Michael	Shea, Denis	Whelan, Timothy

Doorlus

Callaghan, Daniel	Cummins, John	Kennedy, Catherine	Lawley, Thomas
McMahon, Thomas	McNamara, William	Morrissy, Bridget	Morrissy, James
Morrissy, John	Morrissey, Thomas*	Sheily, Denis	Storeen, Mary

Downs

| Casey, John | Furlong, Alfred | Hannan, James | Hannan, John * |
| Hannan, Patrick | Twohill, James | | |

Durraclogh

Ahern, John	Blake, Valentine	Carey, John	Carroll, John
Carroll, John, jnr.	Collins, Margaret	Curtin, Bridget	Donohoe, Cornelius
Donohoe, Michael	Flannady, William	Fitzgerald, Ellen	Hanly, Bartholemew
Hanly, Mary	Hannan, Jeremiah	Hayes, Denis *	Kenneally, Catherine

RECORDS OF BALLINGARRY, GRANAGH AND CLOUNCAGH, 1800 - 1900 – COUNTY LIMERICK

Kenneally, Patrick   Kennedy, John   Kilbridge, Edmund   Morrison, Patrick
Murphy, Michael   O'Donnell, Thomas   Quinn, Michael   Sexton, Edmund
William, Sheily

Frankfort
Cronan, Thomas   Kelly, Patrick   Massy, William H. de   Regan, John
White, John
Note - Reps of Massy, W. H. de

Glenwilliam
Connell, William   Cowley, Denis   Harrold, Patrick   Hennessy, Timothy
Kielly, Mary   Massy, Mary Anne   William, Ready
Notes. Here is a forge, William Ready and thirty acres mountain, Denis Cowley. The Court of Chancery is shown having 456 acres - 03 roods - 10 perches.

Gorteen
Bourke, Patrick   Casey, Patrick   Grady, Michael   Ready, Thomas
Warren, S.*
Reps. Of S. Warren.

Graigacurragh
Barry, David   Bennett, David   Biggs, Stephen D.* Carmody, Edmond
Carmody, Mary   Hartigan, John*   Holmes, John   McEniry, Edmund
McMahon, John   Power, Maurice   Reardon, John   White, Michael
Sheehy, John   Sheily, Thomas   Walsh, Patrick   Walsh, John
Walsh, David

Graigbeg
Conyers, Rev. Ed.   Lee, William

Granagh
Bray, Mary   Burns, Michael   Connolly, Thomas   Howard, Johannna
Kennedy, Patrick   Lee, Michael   Liddy, Rev. D.*   Lynch, Ellen
Lynch, James   Lyons, Catherine   Lyons, James   Mahon, William
Murphy, John   Noonan, Edmund   O'Brien, James   Russell, Patrick
Rourke, John   White, Michael
Notes. *Here is an R.C. Chapel and yard, Rev. D. Liddy. Old Church yard and burial ground.*

Kilbeg East
Peppard, John

Kilbeg West

Connors, Margaret
O'Brien, John
Sullivan, Michael
Enright, Thomas
Scanlan, Eliz.W.
Lillis, John
Scanlan, Sarah
Lillis, Patrick
Sheehan, Anne

Killoughty

Biggs, Samuel D.*

Kilmacanearla North

Ahern, John
Cagney, John
Donohoe, William
Reardon, Thomas
Ahern, Thomas
Connors, Edmond
Kerr, Edmond
Shea, John
Burns, Daniel
Connors, Philip
O'Shea, James
White, James
Cagney, Cornelius
Conway, Patrick
O'Shea, Timothy*

Kilmacanearla South

Peppard, John

Kilmacow

Barry, David M.
Bridgeman, Ml.
Costello, Michael
Hogan, Edmond
Moncton, Eleanor
O'Donnell, Eliz
Ruddle, Catherine
White, Thomas.
Barry, James
Cane, Patrick
Hartigan, Patrick
Lillis, Michael
Moran, Jeremiah
Power, William D.
Scanlan, Michael
Bennett, Jeremiah
Connell, Honoria
Hickey, Honoria
Lynch, William
Neligan, John
Purcell, Patrick
Shanahan, Laurence
Burke, Patrick
Conway, John
Hickey, Thomas
McMahon, Michael
O'Brien, Thomas
Reardon, Michael
Storan, James

Notes. *Here is a graveyard. Here is a forge, John Conway. Here also is a Constabulary Force and Police Barracks.*

Kilmihill

Browne, Jeremiah
Dunworth, Ellen
Harold, Edmond
McEnerny, John
Sheehy, Patrick
Casey, John
Dunworth, Peter
Keeffe, Thomas
O'Brien, John
Clifford, Robert
Egan, John
Leary, Edmund
O'Donnell, John
Donohoe, John
Hannan, Patrick
Murtain, Michael
Power, Danl. D.*

Kilmore

Callaghan, Ml.
Carroll, Michael
Dooly, Edmond
Feehan, Timothy
Callaghan, Thomas
Collopy, Timothy
Doolan, Margaret
Feehan, Edmond
Callaghan, Thos. jnr.
Condon, John
Falvey, David
Fitzgerald, Edmund
Carroll, Margaret
Dineen, Michael
Falvey, Michael
Fitzgerald, Michael

Fitzgibbon, Edmund	Fitzgibbon, Thomas	Goolde, William	Grady, Catherine
Grady, Mary	Grady, Patrick	Harnett, Anne	Hayes, Thomas
Hedderman, Patrick	Houlahan, Jeremiah	Houlahan, Michael	Jones, Col. Wm.*
Kenny, Bridget	Kenny, Edmond	Lyons, Ellen	Lyons, John
Madden, James	Mahoney, Thomas	McEniry, James	McMahon, Mary
McNamara, William	Moncton, Margaret	Moncton, Michael	Morressy, Edmund
Noonan, Denis	Noonan, Mary	Reeves, Johanna	Shea, John
Shea, Margaret	Shealy, David	Sheehan, Margaret	Sheehy, James
Walsh, David

Notes. *Here is a National School House, Michael Monckton. A mill, Michael Houlahan.*

Kilmore Demesne
Jones, Col. William   Morrissey, Edmond (Gate Lodge)   Morrissey, James

Kilshane
Carmody, Garrett

Kingsland
Cronin, Catherine   Hederman, John

Knightstreet
Fitzgerald, Edward   Liddy, Rev. D.   Massy, Frederick

These are land owners only
Costello, Michael	Dineen, Jeremiah	Fitzgerald, Thomas	Houragan, Daniel
Houragan, Patrick	O'Connell, John	O'Dell, Robert	Ready, Thomas
Roche, Maurice

Main Street - Town of Ballingarry - part of Knightstreet.
Alexander, Mary	Bourke, James	Boyce, Patrick	Browne, John*
Condon, Mary	Connell, Michael	Costello, David	Cavanagh, John
Chapman, Mary	Copps, Mary	Culm, Richard	Culhane, John
Cullinane, William	Delaney, James	Dineen, Jeremiah	Donovan, William
Downs, Michael	Gubbins, Rev.G.G.	Hanrahan, James	Hearlihy, David
Hurley, Philip	Hurley, William	Jones, William	Jordan, James
Kelly, Denis	Kelly, Jane	Madigan, Eugene	Madigan, Nicholas
McCarthy, Bridget	McCarthy, Thomas	Meade, Patrick	Mitchell, Thomas
Morrosy, Patrick	O'Brien, Michael	O'Connell, John	O'Dell, Margaret
O'Grady, Anne	Quinlan, Michael	Ready, Ellen	Reddy, Ellen
Roche, Maurice	Russell, Garrett	Ryan, Michael	Scanlan, Eliza

Scanlan, Thomas	Sheehan, John	Sullivan, Samuel	Tracey, Mary
Tracy, Thomas	Scollard, Thomas	Walsh, Michael	

Notes. *Here is a Parochial School House and yard, John Browne. Ball-Court and garden, John Dineen. Fair Field and land, Thomas McCarthy. A Constabulary Force, Police Barrack, office and yard. Petit Sessions House and Bridewell, Co. Limerick Grand Jury.*

Echo Lane

Condon, John	Connor, Mary	Connors, Mary, jnr.	Copps, Joseph
Gubbins, Rev.G.G.*	Hammond, Catherine	Hanrahan, Hanoria	Kelly, John
Liddy, Rev.Dan.*	O'Brien, William*	Reardon, James	Scanlan, Cornelius*
Scanlan, Jeremiah	Sheehy, John	Sheehy, Mary	Sullivan, Patrick
Wynne, Michael			

Note. *Here is a Forge, Joseph Copps.*

Castle Street

Carey, Geoffrey	Donohoe, Geoffrey	Donohoe, Patrick	Egan, Margaret
Houlahan, Thomas	O'Dell, Robert	Russell, Garrett*	

Notes. *Here is an Auxiliary Poor House, offices & garden, Poor Law Guardians. A forge, Patrick Donohoe.*

Downs Road

Ahern, James	Ahern, John	Burns, Alice	Cain, Margaret
Cantillon, Patrick P.	Carmody, Denis	Cathoral, Francis	Connors, Michael
Cronan, Ellen	Curtin, Mary	Devaney, John	Dineen, James
Dineen, John	Dineen, Margaret	Dolan, Patrick	Downs, Patrick
Dunson, James	Hayes, John	Hennessy, Michael	Hearlihy, Jeremiah
Hogan, Catherine	Hogan, James	Joyce, Mary	O'Donnell, James
Reardon, Jeremiah	Tuohill, Margaret	Walsh, James	Walsh, Michael *
Wall, Edmund			

Sparr Street

Boyle, William	Burns, Daniel	Connell, John	Cregan, James
Curtin, Bartholomew	Dineen, Jeremiah	Donohoe, Thomas	Dungan, Johanna
Dunworth, David	Guiry, Michael	Hickey, Thomas	Howard, James
Kelly, John	Leary, Jeremiah	Lyons, Anne	O'Farrell, John
Sullivan, Thomas			

Lisduane

Ahern, Patrick	Bennett, David	Biggs, Stephen*	Burke, David
Cagney, Edmond	Dorgan, Denis	Dunne, John	Fitzgerald, John

Gorman, John	Gorman, Thomas	Heffernan, James	Hore, Thomas
Hynes, James	Lee, Michael	Lynch, Thomas	Lynch, John
Lyons, Catherine	Maher, John	Mahony, Patrick, snr.	Mahoney, Patrick, jnr.
Mason, John	Mason, Myles*	Mason, Margaret	McCarty, Michael
Murphy, Mary	O'Brien, Thomas	Quirk, John	Reardon, Denis
Ryan, James	Shea, Catherine	Shea, Timothy	Wallace, Johanna
Webb, James	Whelan, John		

Lisduff

Dea, Margaret	Enright, Patrick	Foley, Gibbon	Garvin, David
Hickey, John	Keith, James	Lahive, Eleanor	McMahon, Denis
Quinn, Daniel*	Storen, James	Storen, Mary	

Liskennett East

| Galvin, Jeremiah* | Hare, John | Keeffe, John | Lynch, Michael |
| McEniry, John (Gate Lodge) | | | Walker, Francis S. |

Liskennett West

Barry, George	Broderick, Thomas	Burns, Mary	Galvin, Jeremiah
Hartigan, John*	Heffernan, John C.*	Keys, Michael	McEniry, Michael
Raleigh, Jeremiah			

Lissamota

| Berns, Richard B. | Eyres, George W. |

Note. *There are eleven houses shown vacant in this townland*

Lissavarra

| Bridgeman, Margt. | Cronan, John | Cronan, Michael | Kiely, Edmund |
| Kiely, Patrick | Wynne, Maurice | Wynne, Michael | |

Morenane

Brown, Ellen	Brown, James	Brown, Patrick	Blake, Thomas
Cagney, Cornelius	Cronan, Thomas	Cullinane, Joseph	Cullinane, Michael
Fane, Timothy, jnr.	Frehy, David	Frehy, John	Hanrahan, Mary
Houlihan, Edmond	McMahon, John	Neil, Patrick	Noonan, James
Quinn, Lord George	Storin, John	Storin, Thomas	Storan, William

Note. *Here is a burial ground. The name Frehy could be read as TREHY.*

Rylanes

| Brownrick, John* | Crotty, Denis* | Gubbins, Revd.G G. | Liddy, Rev. Daniel* |
| Maxwell, Robert* | Quinlan, Michael* | Supple, John* | Walsh, Michael* |

Notes. *Here is a Hospital, offices and yards, Rev.G.G.Gubbins. A Roman Catholic Chapel and Yard, Rev. Daniel Liddy. A flour mill and yard, John Brownrick. An Auxiliary Workhouse, Robert Maxwell.*

Rylanes- Town of Ballingarry - Turrett Street

Broderick, Patrick	Cain, John	Cronan, Ellen	Curton, William
Fitzgerald, David	Hogan, John	Reardon, John	Walker, Thomas

Woodstock

Fitzgerald, John   Hanly, Michael   Power, Richard*   Smith, John

Note. *Here are a Flour Mill, pond and yard, John Smith.*

Parish of Clouncagh, 1852. Griffith's Valuation.

Townlands Index

Ballybeggane	Ballyhahil	Ballykennedy North
Ballykennedy South	Ballynaroogabeg	Ballynaroogamore North
Ballynaroogamore South	Carrowmore	Cloncagh
Gorteen East	Gorteen West	Gorteenacreeha Lower
Gorteenacreeha Upper	Kilnamona	Teernahilla
Teervena		

Ballybeggane

Fitzgerald, John*   Keating, Jeremiah   Kelly, William   Quaide, John

Ballyhahil

Ambrose, John	Barry, Mary	Earl of Clare*	Condon, Mary
Galvin, James	Hayes, Martin	Hennessy, Mary	Hennessy, Michael
Hennessy, Patrick	McCann, Michael	Mullane, Edmund	O'Dell, Richard
O'Dell, Robert	Shea, Mary (Harding)	Sullivan, Lawrence	

Ballykennedy North

Hickey, Eugene

Note. *The Ecclesiastical Commissioners own a mountain, 103 - 03 - 24.*

Ballykennedy South

Brown, Ellen	Costelloe, Patrick	Dixon, Capt. Sam*	Lynch, Ellen
Quaide, Elizabeth	Tracy, Mary		

Ballynaroogabeg

Fitzgerald, Thomas   Green, Robert   Kielly, Michael   O'Dell, Thomas*

Ballynarooogamore North

Blackeny, Valentine	Fitzgerald, Thomas	Moylan, John	O'Dell, John*
O'Dell, Thomas*	Power, John		

Ballynaroogamore South
Condon, Thomas	Earl of Clare*	Gilburn, Robert	Lyons, Patrick
Quaide, Edmund	Quaide, Jeremiah	Quaide, Martin	Quaide, Thomas
Sheehy, John			

Carrowmore
Barry, Daniel	Coleman, Bridget	Coleman, David*	Coleman, James, jnr.
Coleman, Jeremiah	John, Coleman	Coleman, John, jnr.	Coleman, Michael
Coleman, Patrick	Culhane, Honoria	Culhane, John	Culhane, William
Hanly, John	Kielly, Cornelius	Lee, John	McCann, Michael
Neill, Henry	O'Hara, Bridget	O'Neil, Eller	O'Neill, Daniel
O'Neill, Daniel, jnr.	O'Neill, Daniel (Henry)	O'Neill, Thomas	Sullivan, Thomas

Cloncagh
Airey, Thomas	Baggott, Edmund	Begley, John	Connell, Patrick
Dundon, Michael	Earl of Clare*	Egan, John*	Fitzgerald, John
Hanrahan, Michael*	Hartney, Catherine	Hickey, James	Jordan, David
Lyons, William	Mulcare, Bridget	Murphy, Margaret	O'Brien, Rev.Denis*
Quaide, Michael	Reardon, Johanna	Switzer, Jethro*	

Note. *Here is an R.C. Church and yard, Rev. Denis O'Brien. Here also is a graveyard.*

Gorteen East
Fitzpatrick, James	Frawley, Daniel	Kennedy, William	White, Col.Henry

Gorteen West
Condon, Mary	Hickey, Honoria	O'Brien, Rev. Denis

Gorteenacreeha Lower
Airy, Michael	Cregan, Daniel	Cregan, Patrick	Cregan, Thomas
Curtin, Johanna	Cregan, James	Fennaghty, John	Greene, Patrick
Green, Thomas	Hayes, Alice	Hennessy, Jeremiah	Hennessy, Michael
Keiffe, Margaret	Lahy, Catherine	Lyons, Eugene	Madden, David
Madden, David, jnr.	O'Brien, John	O'Kelly, David*	Quaide, David
Quaide, Maurice	Quaide, Timothy	Scanlan, Michael	Sheehan, John
Stokes, Michael	Sullivan, James	Tierney, John	

Gortnacreeha Upper
Brown, Margaret	Burns, Michael	Cain, James	Casey, Margaret
Cremins, Robert	Farrell, Michael	Hearlihy, John	Lalee, James
Liston, Michael	McGrath, Thomas	O'Brien, Eliza	O'Brien, Patrick
O'Neill, John	Ryan, Daniel	Scanlan, Cornelius	Tierney, Timothy
Walsh, John			

Kilnamona
Behan, James
Shine, Catherine

Behan, John
Walsh, Thomas

Kelly, Jeremiah

Quaide, Patrick

Teernahilla
Airy, Richard
Fitzgibbon, John
Sheehan, Edmund

Earl of Clare
Flynn, Daniel

Costello, Michael
Mullane, John

Costello, Patrick
Wall, Richard

Teervena
Dore, Patrick

Dore, Robert

Hennessy, Honoria

Quaide, Thomas

PART VI

The Censii

A census was taken on the first year of every decade from 1821 to 1911. What follows are excerpts taken from the various censii from 1821 to 1891. Unfortunately, the censii proper giving details of families, etc. have all been destroyed so we are left with the abstracts. Nevertheless, studying the data can give interesting insights into the way the Famine affected the parish. What follows are selected extracts from the Census records which I researched in the Gilbert Library. These records are under the control of the National Archives.

Census 1821. Preliminary Observations. Introduction.

As the Act of the 55th Geo. 111 has afforded the first opportunity of ascertaining the Population of Ireland the actual Enumeration of it's Inhabitants, carried on under the sanction of the Legislature, a Preliminary Statement of the principles on which this process has been conducted may be necessary, both to shew the propriety of having deviated, in some points, from the Plan which had been pursued in Great Britain, and adopted here, in the attempt at taking the Census in the years 1812 and 1813; and also for the purpose of proving the accuracy of the Result in the present instance: And as the following Return is, consequently, the first authentic Statement of the Actual Number of Souls in Ireland, it may also appear not uninteresting, to present a brief Sketch of the various attempts heretofore made to solve this great National Problem.

1672

The first attempt worthy of notice was that made by the celebrated **Sir William Petty.** The circumstances in which he stood, with respect to this country, gave him great local advantages towards the solution of a question, to the investigation of which his mental powers and habits of study peculiarly qualified him. He had superintended the great Territorial Survey of Ireland, instituted, during the Protectorate, for the distribution of Forfeited property *(This is the Cromwellian Plantation and this work by Petty is known as the Down Survey, 1654)* the importance and accuracy of which may be estimated from the consideration, that, though undertaken for a special and limited object, and therefore not pervading the whole country, it still, after a lapse of more than two centuries, continues to be the standard of reference, in the courts of Judicature, as to points of disputed property, and the only authentic source of information, as to the minuter subdivisions of the Land, as well as to many circumstances relating to local taxation. His estimate, taken in the year 1672, gives a Total of 1,100,000 Souls. (Note. In the course of his calculations to ascertain the actual number of the People, at the period at which they were made, Petty introduces another, as to the numbers living in Ireland previously to the Civil War of 1641 which, from a variety of ingenious suppositions, he estimates 1,466,000.) A previous conjecture was made by *(Fynes)* **Moryson,** who visited Ireland under **Lord Mountjoy,** at the close of the reign of **Elizabeth.** *(Eliz.I, 1558-1603).* This writer states that at the termination of the war which his patron had just brought to a successful issue, the total of Souls left did not exceed 700,000.

1695

The result of a subsequent attempt, made by **Captain South** in the year 1695, appears in the Transactions of the Royal Society of London. It is not easy, from the brief and unsatisfactory memoranda there given, to ascertain the value of the data on which his calculation rests. The total Number of Souls is stated by him at 1,034,102.

1712

Mr. Thomas Dobbs, in the second part of his Essay on the trade and improvement of Ireland, published in 1731, gives an account of the number of Houses in the years 1712, 1718, 1725, and 1726. The calculations on which they are formed, are taken from the Returns of the Hearth-

money Collectors; and give the following results, at an average of six Souls to a house.
1712 = 2,099,094. 1718 = 2,169,048. 1725 = 2,317,374 and 1726 = 2,309,106.

1731
In the year 1731, an Inquiry was instituted by order of the House of Lords of Ireland, for ascertaining the Population thereof, through the medium both of the Magistracy and of the Established Clergy. On reflecting on the state of Ireland at that period, when large tracts of the country were not subject to the jurisdiction of the former of those classes, or to the influence of the latter, the result of an inquiry made by either of them, when unsupported by the authority of an Act of the Legislature, must be deemed far from satisfactory. The Number of Souls is stated to have been 2,010,221.

1754
Hearth Money Collectors. Several subsequent attempts were made to ascertain the Population; all of which rest on the same basis as that just stated. Their Results are as follows.
1754 = 2,372,634. 1767 = 2,544,276. 1777 = 2,690,556 and 1785 = 2,845,932

1788
In 1788 an Inquiry was instituted by Mr. **Gervais Parker Bushe**, one of the Commissioners of the Revenue; the result of which is published in the Transactions of the Royal Irish Academy. Like the preceding attempts, it is founded on the Returns of the Hearth-money Collectors; and the details stated in Mr Bushe's Memoir prove, that he considered this basis to stand in need of much correction and amendment. The Total is computed by him to amount to 4,040,000.

1791
From a Return of the number of Hearths, made to the Irish House of Commons in 1791, the population is estimated at 4,206,612.

1792
In the subsequent year **Dr. Beaufort** published his Ecclesiastical Map of Ireland. The Memoir which accompanies it, affords a vague estimate of the Population of each county, averaged according to difference of local circumstances, at from 5 to 6 Souls to a house.
The Total thus amounts to 4,088,226.

1805
Major Newenham, in his inquiry into the progress and magnitude of the Population of Ireland, published in the year 1805, endeavours to correct the inaccuracies of the Hearth-money Returns, by a variety of ingenious calculations, formed on other bases. His corrected Estimate gives a Total of 5,395,456.

1812
In 1812 an Act passed for taking an account of the Population of Ireland, and of the Increase or Diminution thereof: it was chiefly copied from that of 1810 for Great Britain; to the provisions of which it adhered in all the practical details, more closely than the different circumstances of the two Islands would justify. At the expiration of two years employed in endeavouring to accomplish the object of the Legislature, it was found, on examining the Returns, that out of the forty Counties and Counties of Cities and Towns into which Ireland is divided, ten only furnished complete Returns; in four, no steps whatever were taken in pursuance of the Act; and those of the remaining twenty-six were inaccurate or defective. The Act therefore may be considered to have been wholly inoperative as to its main object, that of ascertaining the number of Souls by actual Enumeration. By the aid of comparitive calculations founded on previous inquiries and on the partial results of the Act, the amount of the Population in 1813 has been conjectured to be 5,937,856.

The failure of the Act of 1812 was due to differences in circumstances between Ireland and mainland Britain. In England the details of the census were entrusted to the Overseers of the Poor, a body familiar with dealing with the poor who were in good stead to collect the census. In Scotland the Parish Schoolmasters presented a body equally pervasive. In Ireland there were no Poor Laws nor a plentiful supply of Parish Schoolmasters and, it is stated 'from the limited quantity of instruction they are required to impart, also comparitively inferior in intellectual qualifications, no constituted body was to be found possessing all or even most of the requisites for this duty.' Hence the failure of the Act 1812. The Act of 1815 was another attempt to collect a proper census in the British Isles and the 28th May, 1821 was the commencement date. This Act laid down rules and regulations as to how the census was to be collected; forms filled in; vetting of Enumerators, etc. It also laid down the geographic areas to be collected. Pursuant to the Precept and Instructions, two Returns were made by the Assistant Barrister and Bench of Magistrates of each County of a city or town, at the first special Sessions held under the Act, in the month of January, 1821. The first List contained an account of all Sub-divisions of the country, according to which the local taxes are assessed and levied, and by which the Enumerators were to proceed in the Census. These divisions are generally uniform, proceeding from counties to baronies, parishes and townlands, etc.

The division of Ireland into Counties took place shortly after the Anglo-Norman Invasion. In 1211 **King John (1199-1216)** divided the whole of the country that then acknowledged his government into twelve counties in Leinster and Munster, in which little regard seems to have been paid to the ancient division of Ireland into five Provinces.

In Leinster he created Dublin; Meath; Uriell (now called Louth); Kildare; Catherlough (Carlow); Kilkenny and Wexford. These contained all the province of Leinster, except these territories following: Upper Ossory, inhabited by the Fitzpatricks; Leix which was inhabited by the Moores; Offaly which was inhabited by the O'Connors; Ely O'Carroll which was inhabited by the O'Carrolls; and some other territories which were inhabited by other Irish septs. Later in Leinster, the territories of Leix, Offaly and Ely O'Carrol and some others, were reduced into shire-ground in the time of **Queen Mary (1553-1558)** and then divided into two counties, the one called the Queen's County and the other the King's County. The county of Wicklow, which had hitherto been vaguely considered as part of the counties of Dublin and Carlow, was made into shire ground and formed into a separate county in the third year of **James I (1603-1625).** In Munster, King John created the counties of Waterford, Cork, Kerry, Limerick and Tipperary, which last mentioned five counties did contain the whole province. So likewise the provinces of Connaught and Ulster were divided into counties by a Statute of the 11th of Eliz. (1558-1603). Connaught was divided into seven counties; viz. Galway, Clare, Roscommon, Mayo, Sligo, Longford and Leitrim, but since that time Clare has been included in Munster, and Longford in Leinster. In like manner the province of Ulster was divided into nine counties: namely those of Down, Antrim, Tyrone, Ardmagh, Monaghan, Cavan, Fermanagh, Donegal and Londonderry. (Vide Harris's Hibernica, P2 F3 folio)

Baronies. The first Subdivision of Counties is into Baronies, corresponding in a great measure with that of Hundreds (or Cantreds) in England. The name derives from the sub-division of the conquered land among the Norman barons, hence barony. Other baronies appear to have been formed sucessively in consequence of the submissions of the Irish chiefs or captains who ruled over them; the territory of each constituting a Barony. This may account for the inequality in size between them and the manner in which parts of many are intermixed among each other in some cases.

Parishes. The next subdivision into Parishes is of much greater antiquity than that of Baronies. Originally it was purely Ecclesiastical, and was introduced among the civil subdivisions from motives of convenience. Some peculiar circumstances arising from this cause have produced much difficulty in the progress of the Census. The Civil and Ecclesiastical arrangements do not always correspond: Parishes are found to extend, not only into different Baronies, but into different Counties; and Townlands are sometimes attached to one Parish for the assessment of the County taxes, while with respect to Tithes and other Ecclesiastical contributions, they are considered as forming part of another. Antient unions or divisions of Parishes have increased this discrepancy; their names have also been frequently changed. The arrangement of Parishes by the Established Church, being in many cases different from that of the Roman Catholics, has also been the cause of considerable difficulties; as in many parts of the south-west of Ireland the latter arrangement has been adopted in various points of public business.

Townlands. The smallest subdivision of the country is that of Townlands. This name, however, is not universal throughout Ireland: some counties have adopted Ploughlands in lieu of it, each Ploughland being supposed to contain 120 acres; but as the quantity was taken by estimation, not by measurement, their extent varies considerably, even in the same county. Townlands in many instances have been sub-divided, and in many cases the name has been changed. Many names, now antiquated, were formerly used to designate the smaller sub-divisions of land in Ireland. The following are the most remarkable: A Gneeon (Gneeve) containing 5 acres, being 1/12th of a Plowland. A Gort, containing 6 acres. A Pottle containing 12 acres. A Ballyboe containing 16 acres (but in some parts 60 or 100 acres). A Poll (or Pole) containing 50 acres. A Cartron containing 60 acres (called also a Plowland). A Tagh (or Tate) containing 60 acres, English. A Ballybeatach containing 960 acres (being 16 Ballyboes of 60 acres each). The Plowland and the Gneeve are the only names noticed by the Enumerators as still in use in some parts of Ireland. The superficial Measures of Land now in use in Ireland are the Irish or plantation acre, the Cunningham acre and the English acre. The difference between these arises from the different lengths of the perch used as a standard in each: the Irish perch consisting of 21 feet, the Cunningham of 18.75 feet and the English of 16.5 feet. The preamble goes on to give details of how exactly the census was to be taken and makes the following observations on points of interest. 'It was evident that the filling up of the column of the Return which was to contain the Ages of the persons named in the preceding, must prove a point of much delicacy .... and that in so doing the greatest attention should be paid to the feelings of the parties concerned.' Also, the occupations of the people caused some concern. 'The principle occupations were those of Farmers, Labourers and Servants as most persons who earn the chief part of their subsistence as hired labourers hold also a small portion of land, and therefore in the common language of the country, are entitled to the name of Farmers. Neither was the distinction between Day-labourers and Out-door or Field-servants less difficult to be ascertained" The Enumerators were instructed 'to execute their duty in the mildest and most inoffensive manner; complying as far as could be with the feelings of the people and never having recourse to the law except in the most urgent necessity.' There are notes on what constitutes a family and among other points raised were - 'Strolling beggars were considered as forming distinct families and where met with on the road at a distance from their usual place of residence were entered as residing in the house in which they last lodged.' It also noted that 'every collection of contiguous Houses, if under twenty, was to be considered as a Hamlet; if more than twenty and not under any peculiar local jurisdiction a Village.' It also comments that in organising the data of the census 'in the classification of the Sexes no difficulty occurred.' Signed W. Shaw Mason, Record Tower, Dublin. 11 July,1823.

Censii Details.

The Baronies of County Limerick are Clanwilliam, Conello Lower, Conello Upper, Coonagh, Coshma, Costlea, Kenry, Owneybeg, Pubblebrien and

Small County. In respect of the 1821 and 1831 censii the Barony of Upper Connello is defined as follows :

1821	**1831**
Abbeyfeale Parish	Abbeyfeale Parish
Abbeyfeale Village	Abbeyfeale Town
Ballingarry Parish	Adare (Part of)
Ballingarry Town	Ballingarry Parish
Bruree (part of)	Ballingarry Town
Castletown	Bruree Parish (part of)
Killeedy	Bruree Village (part of)
Kilfenny	Castletown Parish
Killoholihane	Dromcoloher Town
Knockaderry	Clouncrew Parish
Mahoonogh	Croom Parish (part of)
Monegay	Drehidharsnie Parish (part of)
Newcastle Parish	Grange Parish
Newcastle Town	Kilfenny Parish
	Killeedy Parish
	Killololihane
	Knockaderry Parish
	Knockaderry Village
	Mahoonagh Parish
	Monagea Parish
	Newcastle Parish
	Newcastle Town

UPPER CONELLO. Census Abstracts		**1821**	**1831**
Houses Inhabited		7,221	7,817
Families		7,606	8,744
Uninhabited		178	100
Building		9	73
Males		22,359	26,303
Females		22,435	26,547
No. of Persons in Agriculture		8,111	6,683
No. in Trades, etc.		4,720	1,189
Other Occupations		3,491	872
Total number occupied		16,322	2,061
Pupils in Schools,	Males	2,443	-----
	Females	804	-----

Comparitive figures from the censii		1821		1831	
BALLINGARRY		**Parish**	**Town**	**Parish**	**Town**
Houses	Inhabited	852	272	938	254
	Families	890	298	1,000	302
	Uninhabited	20	9	10	14
	Building	Nil	Nil	3	8
Persons	Males	2,728	763	3,598	808
	Females	2,600	790	3,368	877
Mostly employed in Agriculture		726	54	846	73
Mostly employed in Trade / Manufacture/ Handicrafts		172	280	91	155
No. of persons occupied (other)		329	87	63	74
Total no. of persons occupied		1,227	421	–	–
Pupils in Schools	Males	120	238	–	--
	Females	Nil	Nil	–	--

Cloncagh is not separately listed in the 1821 and 1831 censii.

KNOCKADERRY		1821	1831	1831
		Parish	**Parish**	**Village**
Houses	Inhabited	528	345	57
	Familes	536	372	69
	Uninhabited	8	2	–
	Building	Nil	7	1
Persons	Males	1,666	1,161	168
	Females	1,662	1,212	183
Mostly employed in Agriculture		629	336	25
Mostly employed in Trade / Manufacture / Handicrafts		367	15	26
No. of persons occupied (other)		291	21	18
Total no. of persons occupied		1,287	--	--
Pupils in Schools	Males	197	--	--
	Females	56	--	--

In the 1821 census there is a note on the margin giving these figures for Knockaderry Village - Houses = 33. Inhabitants = 194. In this (Knockaderry) parish there is one male upwards of 100 years of age.

In the observations column of the 1821 abstract the following data is provided.

Parish	Houses	Inhabitants
Adare Town	130	853
Ballyegran Village	32	172
Dromcolloher Village	118	647
Killmeedy Village	26	136
Mahoonagh Village	32	157

The 1821 Census also gives the following snippets of information: In Castletown Parish there is a school partly instituted by Luke **White**, esq., who allows a house, with a quarter of an acre, and pays ten guineas yearly for the education of 10 boys: there are also 10 boys and 10 girls instructed in this school. There are two more schools, one of 22 boys and 5 girls, the other of 50 boys and 16 girls. Robert **Stevelly,** esq., allowing 20 guineas towards the support of the former and 10 guineas towards that of the latter. In Newcastle Parish there is a parochial school of 60 boys and 20 girls.

The Census of 1831 asked the number of Capitalists, Bankers, Professional and other Educated Men. The answer for Ballingarry was: in the Parish, 49 and in the town 47.

In 1841 the Population of Ireland is given as 8,175,124. The number of non-native born is given as 34,608.

Abstract from the Census, 1841.

BALLINGARRY			RURAL	TOWN
Males.	Heads of Families & children		2,795	702
	Visitors		508	91
	Servants		246	25
Females.	Heads of families & children		2,504	707
	Visitors		650	119
	Servants		286	46
Total Number Males & Females			6,989	1,690
Houses Inhabited		1st Class	13	7
		2nd Class	140	83
		3rd Class	378	118
		4th Class	501	81
Totals			1,032	289

Uninhabited		25	8
Building		Nil	3
Total Number of Houses		1,057	300
Families Residing in Houses	1st Class	13	7
	2nd Class	141	112
	3rd Class	385	144
	4th Class	522	95
Total		1,061	358

Note. There were three criteria for classifying houses - extent, as shown by the number of rooms; quality, as shown by the number of windows, and solidity or durability, as shown by building materials used. Numbers were allocated to each building under above criteria on a sliding scale and the total figure graded the house. A 4th class house was built principally of mud or other perishable material, having only one room and one window. A 3rd class house was better than a 4th class house, varying from one to four windows. A 2nd class house was what might be considered a good farm-house, having from five to nine rooms and windows. A 1st class house was any house better than the preceding.

Abstract from the Census 1841 - CLONCAGH PARISH.

Males.	Heads of Families & children		605
	Visitors		70
	Servants		50
Females.	Heads of families & children		524
	Visitors		85
	Servants		55
Total Number of Males and Females			1,389.
Houses Inhabited.		1st Class	—
		2nd Class	20
		3rd Class	48
		4th Class	146
Total			214
Families Residing in Houses		1st Class	—
		2nd Class	21
		3rd Class	50
		4th Class	157
Total			228

BALLINGARRY: Population figures taken from the various censii.

Townland	1841	1851	1861	1871	1881	1891
Ballyelan	274	108	97	76	61	54
Ballygrennan	286	132	118	111	116	102
Ballyguileataggle	119	79	50	53	58	46
Ballyguilebeg	73	17	10	5	3	1
Ballykevan East	25	29	14	4	4	12
Ballykevan West	41	23	21	18	23	6*
Ballyknockane	23	27	19	12	12	22
Ballynahaha	222	128	94	72	77	65
Ballynaroogabeg East	42	19	34	25	19	31
Ballynaroogabeg West	69	44	28	28	23	20
Ballynashig	27	27	19	21	20	5
Ballyneale	168	89	69	52	47	29*
Ballynoe	307	159	117	122	82	62
Ballyroe East	51	37	31	29	25	26
Ballyroe West	13	45	15	15	9	7
Ballyvologe	76	65	43	39	37	41
Caherhenesy	108	83	39	38	34	36
Cloonregan	72	26	31	23	27	28
Cloontemple	–	–	–	–	–	–
Common	629	464	331	253	197	155
Coolrus	444	257	257	180	155	129
Dollas	110	46	33	30	20	13
Doorlus	117	89	71	43	45	37
Downs	30	35	22	20	16	21
Derraclogh	242	145	100	93	94	86
Frankfort	153	52	51	35	28	25
Glenwilliam	202	49	75	59	78	52
Gorteen	30	11	14	11	12	14
Graigacurragh	191	103	78	94	82	69
Graigbeg	64	17	26	22	29	17
Granagh	138	77	87	69	69	57
Kilbeg East	18	4	8	7	8	6
Kilbeg West	52	60	45	24	17	25
Killoughty	57	13	13	14	5	6
Kilmacanearla North	166	95	101	55	43	34
Kilmacanearla South	7	12	3	--	--	--
Kilmacow	319	212	164	133	147	108
Kilmihil	214	107	79	59	67	67
Kilmore	508	346	243	175	159	143

Townland						
Kilmore Demesne	18	16	14	5	14	4
Kilshane	2	14	13	3	3	7
Kingsland	104	13	–	7	6	15
Knightstreet	16	–	–	–	–	–
Lisduane	319	177	89	66	40	61
Lisduff	74	50	41	28	19	19
Liskennett East	61	52	21	30	44	33
Liskennett West	77	24	54	34	27	15
Lissamota	282	--	60	61	63	42
Lissavarra	59	54	40	35	30	27
Morenane	278	149	119	102	74	81
Rylanes	–	68	18	–	61	–
Woodstock	12	22	6	9	19	13
Totals	6,989	3,970	3,125	2,499	2,348	1,974
Ballingarry Town	1,690	1,451	1,032	873	795	637
TOTALS	8,679	5,421	4,157	3,372	3,143	2,611

Census Note = * The decline is due to emigration and moving to other townlands. The figure for Rylanes includes 51 inmates in Fever Hospital. The total for 1851 does not include 906 persons in the Auxiliary workhouse.

CLONCAGH: Population figures taken from the various censii.

Townland	1841	1851	1861	1871	1881	1891
Ballybeggane	20	23	28	23	31	6*
Ballyhahil	139	90	87	73	67	68
Ballykennedy North	19	10	13	18	22	32
Ballykennedy South	58	33	34	42	39	21
Ballynarooga Beg	–	14	11	8	4	7
Ballynarooga More North	57	21	15	11	18	18
Ballynarooga More South	114	80	84	58	55	51
Carrowmore	139	137	110	88	83	68*
Cloncagh	120	92	78	79	68	59
Gorteen East	114	16	27	19	17	11
Gorteen West	41	20	25	20	6	15
Gorteenacreha Lower	247	143	74	59	56	63
Gorteenacreha Upper	163	102	100	98	87	59
Kilnamona	46	28	29	24	24	25
Teernahilla	93	53	59	53	39	33
Teervena	19	10	14	11	8	5
TOTALS	1,389	872	788	684	624	541

Note: * Ballybeggane - The decrease is attributed to removals to other townlands since 1881.
*Carrowmore - The decrease is attributed to emigration and removals since 1881.

BALLINGARRY: Houses Figures for parish taken from the various censii.

Townland	1841	1851	1861	1871	1881	1891
Ballyelan	40	18	16	12	11	10
Ballygrennan	36	19	20	19	19	14
Ballyguileataggle	14	11	9	8	8	5
Ballyguilebeg	12	2	1	1	1	1
Ballykevan East	5	4	3	1	1	2
Ballykevan West	5	4	3	3	3	1
Ballyknockane	2	3	3	3	3	3
Ballynahaha	31	20	18	13	16	12
Ballynaroogabeg East	7	3	6	5	6	6
Ballynaroogabeg West	11	9	4	5	4	3
Ballynashig	3	4	3	4	3	1
Ballyneale	21	10	8	8	9	4
Ballynoe	43	24	21	20	16	12
Ballyroe East	6	5	5	4	3	3
Ballyroe West	3	10	2	2	2	1
Ballyvologe	9	10	6	7	6	6
Caherhenesy	18	15	7	8	8	6
Cloonregan	11	4	5	6	4	4
Cloontemple	–	–	–	–	–	–
Common	121	87	83	63	50	42
Coolrus	68	42	36	36	31	29
Dollas	16	5	5	6	3	2
Doorlus	15	11	11	8	10	6
Downs	4	4	2	2	2	4
Durraclogh	37	25	18	17	18	15
Frankfort	24	9	7	5	6	4
Glenwilliam	29	11	16	14	14	8
Gorteen	4	2	2	2	2	2
Graigacurragh	24	15	13	13	14	14
Graigbeg	8	4	5	3	3	3
Granagh	22	15	19	15	15	10
Kilbeg East	2	1	1	1	1	1
Kilbeg West	7	9	9	6	6	6
Killoughty	9	2	2	2	2	1
Kilmacanearla North	18	13	13	8	7	6
Kilmacanearla South	1	2	1	–	–	–

Kilmacow	43	33	23	20	23	19
Kilmihil	34	18	12	12	11	10
Kilmore	81	51	45	34	30	27
Kilmore Demesne	3	3	3	2	2	1
Kilshane	1	1	1	1	1	1
Kingsland	15	2	–	1	1	3
Knightstreet	1	–	–	–	–	–
Lisduane	50	35	14	12	8	11
Lisduff	13	9	7	6	5	3
Liskennett East	8	8	4	7	9	5
Liskennett West	12	5	9	7	5	4
Lissamota	37	–	11	11	8	8
Lissavarra	5	8	7	7	7	5
Morenane	41	20	16	16	14	12
Rylanes	–	2	5	–	10	–
Woodstock	2	3	2	2	4	4
Totals	1,032	630	542	468	445	360
Ballingarry Town	289	252	248	227	196	163
Total of Parish	11,321	885	790	695	641	523

Note: The 1841, 1851 and 1891 figures are nett figures, excluding houses uninhabited or being built. To get the gross figures add, Parish/Town = 1841 - 25/11 1851 - 35/17 1891 - 29/44

The 1861, 1871 and 1881 are gross figures. To get the nett figures subtract, Parish/Town = 1861 - 12/23 1871 - 07/17 1881 - 18/09

CLONCAGH: Houses figures taken from the various censii.

Townland	1841	1851	1861	1871	1881	1891
Ballybeggane	2	3	5	4	5	1*
Ballyhahil	23	14	14	12	11	11
Ballykennedy North	3	3	4	5	5	7
Ballykennedy South	6	5	5	7	6	4
Ballynarooga Beg	–	2	2	1	1	1
Ballynarooga More North	8	4	3	3	3	3
Ballynarooga More South	15	9	9	8	9	8
Carrowmore	24	26	17	16	17	12*
Cloncagh	20	18	15	13	12	12
Gorteen East	19	3	5	3	3	3
Gorteen West	5	3	3	3	2	3

Gorteenacreha Lower	39	28	13	11	10	11
Gorteenacreha Upper	27	15	17	19	17	15
Kilnamona	7	6	7	7	7	7
Teernahilla	14	9	9	8	8	5
Teervena	2	4	4	3	2	1
TOTALS	214	152	132	123	118	104

Note: These are gross figures. For nett figures subtract 1841 - nil. 1851 - 6. 1861 - 1. 1871 - 1 1881 - 2 and 1891 - nil.

* Ballybeggane - The decrease is attributed to removals to other townlands since 1881.
*Carrowmore: The decrease is attributed to emigration and removals since 1881.

Census 1891. Education Figures, male / female.

	Ballingarry	Cloncagh
Read and Write	908 / 916	197 / 182
Read Only	61 / 77	15 / 22
Illiterate	321 / 328	63 / 62
Totals	1,290 / 1,321 = 2,611	275 / 266 = 541.

Census 1891. Ages Profile Figures, male / female.

Under 7	7 to 9	9 to 12	12 to 20	20 to 40	40 plus.
Ballingarry					
187 /167	42	70	87	83	269	266	289	316	416	419
Cloncagh					
51/38	12/16	22/10	46/50	68/78	76/74

Ballingarry = 2,611. Cloncagh = 541.

Emigration Statistics Taken from Slater's Directory, 1894.

From the date when the enumeration of emigrants commenced :

May	1, 1851 - March 31, 1861 =	434,338	left the Province (Munster).
April	1, 1861 - March 31, 1871 =	364,105	left the Province.
April	1, 1871 - March 31, 1881 =	181,370	left the Province.
April	1, 1881 - March 31, 1891 =	252,080	left the Province.
Total		1,171,893.	

PART VII

The Workhouses

Ballingarry Workhouse, 1848 and The Grove Workhouse, 1850.

As the Famine took its toll, the efforts to ameliorate the lot of those most affected were the same as elsewhere - the establishment of workhouses. There were two in Ballingarry. These articles were researched and written by Sr. Delia Curtin, Sisters of Mercy, Abbeyfeale. They were first published under the name Sr. Eucharia, her religious name, in 'Knockfierna Remembers 1847-1997; The Famine Years', produced by Cnoc Firinne Heritage & Folk Group. It is reproduced here by kind permission of Sr. Curtin and the Cnoc Firinne Heritage & Folklore Group.

The Ballingarry Workhouse, 1848.

The workhouse in Ballingarry was originally a one-storey coach house and stable attached to the Grove House. This house was built by the Odell family. In early 1850, it was decided by Croom Board of Guardians to extend this building rather than erect a new workhouse. Consequently, the roof was removed and another storey added. This is the ruin which stands at the present time. All workhouse buildings were intended to be durable but as cheaply built as possible. The walls were of limestone rubble masonry, the inside unplastered but whitewashed. The ground floors were of mortar and clay. The upper floors were of timber. There was a raised sleeping platform of timber along either side of a central well. The inmates slept on straw spread on the sleeping platform.

The atmosphere in the workhouse was grim and cheerless, despite most conscientious efforts by Boards of Guardians to provide food, bedding and clothing as adequate as their funds would allow. The bare necessities were considered sufficient. Their provision marked the thin line between life and death for many Irish people at a time when grinding poverty was widespread. Despite all their drawbacks, the Poor Law Unions achieved a remarkable success in forcing property owners to pay rates towards the upkeep of the less well-off. Many of the workhouses are still standing, among them are Newcastle West, Rathkeale and Ballingarry. They are indeed a tribute to the standard of workmanship at that time.

When the Boards of Guardians were abolished in 1923, a massive record of their eighty five year administration was left in volumes of Board Minutes. These numbered 3,100 volumes. We can only admire the scrupulous attention paid to details of expenditure and income in these records. Browsing through these records is a most interesting exercise - but a demanding one. How and when was the workhouse system established in Ireland? To answer that question, we must go back in time to the year 1838. Ireland had no Government of its own. Its laws were enacted by the Parliament of Great Britain. Trade laws left the country poverty - stricken. The staple diet was the humble potato. If there was no land there was no food. So, landless or evicted people had no hope of survival.

In 1838 the Parliament of Great Britain passed an Act 'for the more effectual relief of the destitute poor in Ireland.' Poor Law Commissioners were appointed in London. They devised a plan for administering relief in Ireland. By mid - 1841, Ireland had been divided into 130 administrative districts known as Poor Law Unions. Each district or Union had its workhouse. A Board of Guardians - consisting of Justices of the Peace and members elected by the ratepayers of the Union - was responsibe for the administration of each workhouse. A Poor Rate was levied in each Union. A rate collector was appointed by the Board of Guardians.

Limerick County was initially divided into four Unions: Limerick Union, Rathkeale Union, Newcastle West Union and Kilmallock Union.

Newcastle West Union was declared in December 1838. It comprised the following electoral divisions: Abbeyfeale, Ardagh, Ballingarry, Castletown, Clonneagh, Dromcollogher, Killagholehane, Killeedy, Kilmeedy, Mahoonagh, Monagay, Newcastle and Rathronan.

A new workhouse, with accommodation for 550 was in operation in

Newcastle West from March,1841. The meetings of the Board of Guardians were held weekly. At each meeting, the clerk presented: The Register Book, The Weekly Relief List, The Provision Check Account and the Provision, Receipt and Consumption Account. The books of the Poor Rate collectors were also produced examined and authenticated. From detailed records of Board meetings, we find that relatively unimportant points raised and discussed give us valuable historic information. "Resolved unanimously that the conduct of our Matron, **Mrs. Burne,** from the opening of the Workhouse in March 1841, deserves our unqualified approbation in every particular. That we mainly attribute to her exertions the successful working of the System in this house, especially at its commencement, being the first rural workhouse opened in Ireland". *(Minutes of meeting of 22nd of October, 1844.)*

As early as 26th June, 1843 people endeavoured to find accommodation in the Newcastle West Workhouse. "Number of applicants admitted, 6. Number of applicants rejected, 22." *(Minutes of meeting 13th June, 1843.)*

Various cost - cutting measures were being introduced at subsequent meetings. "Mr. **George Roche** gives notice that, on this day fortnight, he will move that the services of the following three paid subordinate officers of the Union be dispensed with from September 29th next, viz. **William Leahy**, cook, **Mary Fitzgibbon**, laundress and **Honora Histon**, Infirm Ward attendant. Ordered that the Master and Matron do apply the services of pauper inmates from henceforth in discharge of the duties heretofore exclusively performed by those officers who will nevertheless assist as usual until discharged". *(Minutes of meeting 4th July, 1843.)* A high standard of cleanliness was maintained in these workhouses. "Ordered that 40 lbs. of soap weekly to be used only at present for washing". "Ordered that no soap be used in future for washing the rooms of the workhouse". *(Minutes of Board Meetings 29th of August, 1843).*

Further cost-cutting measures were also being introduced at successive Board Meetings. "The Assistant Commissioner, **Mr. Burke**, suggested to the Board the use of molasses and water with stirabout for breakfast, and gruel with potatoes for dinner instead of milk, whereby the cost of maintenance per head per week in some of the Unions under his charge had been reduced to one shilling, and stated that the paupers, after some time, and especially the children, seemed to be well pleased with the substitution of molasses for new milk, which also received the sanction of the Medical Officer".

The annual salary of the workhouse officers was discussed and determined by the Board of Guardians. The most important position was that of Clerk of Union. "Mr. **Michael Leahy** will on Tuesday next give notice for that day fortnight that the salaries of the undermentioned officers be fixed at:

The Clerk of the Union, £55. Master of the Workhouse, £35. Physician of the Workhouse, £40.

Matron of the Workhouse, £20. Apothecary, £20. Schoolmistress, £10. Schoolmaster, £15.

Hospital Nurse, £10. Porter £10.

(Board of Meeting of Tuesday, 26th September, 1843).

A number of Justices of Peace were appointed as ex-officio Guardians of the Union:

(Monday, 2nd October, 1843.)

Cox, William, Ballynoe, Ballingarry. **Furlong**, Alfred, The Castle, Newcastle. **Roche,** Thomas, Castleview, Newcastle. **Massey**, Eyre, Glenduff Castle, Dromcollogher. **Muskerry,** Lord, Springfield Castle, Dromcollogher. **Sheehy**, Bryan, Mayne House, Newcastle (Monagay). **Shelton**, John W., Rossmore, Ballingarry.

The Board of Guardians was comprised of approximately 22 people. Familiar names in West Limerick appear among those "declared by the Returning Officer on 21st of March, 1844 as duly elected Guardians for the several Electoral Divisions of Newcastle Union."

Name of Guardian	Residence	Electoral Division
William Smith O'Brien	Cahermoyle	Ardagh
John Cox. jnr.	Ballyneale	Ballingarry
Daniel D. Power	Odelville	Ballingarry
William Hamo de Massey	Glenwilliam Castle	Ballingarry
Edward Lloyd	Heathfield	Castletown

By 30th March, 1848 famine had taken it's toll in West Limerick, and Ballingarry area in particular was causing concern. An excerpt from the Minutes of 30th March, 1848 states "with reference to **Captain Narwell's** report in which he states that fever and other disease are prevalent in the Ballingarry districts of Newcastle Union."

A letter from the Central Board of Health dated the 28th March, 1848 requested the Guardians to write in the accompanying form a nomination of the Medical Officer whom the Guardians would recommend for the appointment under the Temporary Fever Acts in Ballingarry district.

"A tender from the Rev. **Mr. Gubbins** offering a house in Ballingarry for use as a Temporary Fever Hospital at a rent of £50.00 per annum was laid before the Guardians and ordered that the Rev. Mr. Gubbins tender be forwarded to the Poor Law Commissioners. Also a letter from **Mr. Coy**, Chairman of the Ballingarry Relief and Fever Hospital Committee wishing to be informed out of what funds the Medical Officer is to be paid." A reply was received from the Commissioners on 8th April, 1848 stating that "the Ballingarry Temporary Fever Hospital must be supported by the Board of Guardians out of the rates." Apparently the offer of Rev. George Gubbins to let his house was accepted because an expenses entry for 2nd May, 1848 reads "to the Rev. George G. Gubbins one year's rent of Temporary Fever Hospital, Ballingarry, £50."

A further entry in the Minutes gives the following information; "Doctor **Robert Odell** having proposed to let the Castle of Ballingarry with an adjoining field for exercise for the term of one year certain for the sum of forty five pounds, and for such further time as may be required; resolved that same be accepted and that the boys from Churchtown be removed thereto on the 5th of September and the Union School be in future continued there until new buildings are erected." *(Minutes of Board Meeting of Wednesday, 30th and Thursday, 31st August, 1848.)*

By September, 1848 some interesting changes had taken place. These are noted in the Board Minutes as follows: "The Vice Guardians report their having visited the Workhouse with it's several auxiliaries, Maiden Street, Square, Churchtown, Castletown and Ballingarry, and the usual order, cleanliness and regularity are observable in all. They recommend that Churchtown House (from whence the boys have been removed to Ballingarry Castle) be fitted up as dormitories for able-bodied men, to be taken there every evening to sleep under the charge of the Assistant Master ..". "Two clocks being much required for the use of the schools" and being informed that the National Board supply some at a reduced price, "it was resolved that application be made for same to the Commissioners of National Education..". "Castletown House and Ballingarry Castle, now occupied as auxiliary houses by the removal of the school girls and nine assistant women to the former and the schoolboys, four housemasters and two assistant women to the latter, and there being now accommodation for an increased number of Senior Inmates thereby to the following extent: Castletown - present accommodation (but capable by a small outlay to be made available for double the number) - 170; Ballingarry Castle - 130. Total 300. It is ordered that Ballingarry Castle be introduced into the upper column of minutes showing additional workhouses." Therefore, Ballingarry Castle was regarded as an Auxiliary workhouse in September, 1848.

The Grove Workhouse, 1850.

By 1850 it became obvious to Newcastle West Poor Law Union that a more local system was needed to administer the area lying between Ballingarry, Rathkeale, Croom and Granagh. Croom Poor Law Union was formed in March 1850 and a Workhouse was built in Croom in 1852. This building is still to be seen at the rear of the present Croom Orthopaedic Hospital. Croom Union was formed by taking part of Newcastle West Union, part of Rathkeale Union and part of Limerick City Union and forming them into a new Union. Mr. **Richard Costello** was appointed Clerk (pro tem) of Croom Union at a salary of £1-05-00 per week. The position of Master of the Workhouse was advertised as having a salary of £50 per annum. Initially Croom Board of Guardians experienced great difficulty in procuring Workhouse accommodation for the many poor people who sought food and shelter...." in consequence of the district containing no large village or town capable of affording much house accommodation for the paupers of the Union."

"We find that to act with economy, which the circumstances of the district requires, the most effective course to follow would be to maintain the Grove House at Ballingarry, which has been occupied by the girls of the Newcastle Workhouse, but it is situated in the Ballingarry Electoral Division part of the Union and capable of being made to contain from 1,000 to 1,300 persons. This is the largest establishment in our Union and suits well for the Electoral Division of Ballingarry - Castletown and that neighbourhood. For the other Electoral Divisions we propose to take a large establishment in the City of Limerick, capable of containing from two to three thousand paupers. All parts of Croom Union are within a moderate distance of the City of Limerick - from 4 to 8 miles, except those districts that can be accommodated at the Grove Workhouse. By that course we can concentrate on the two establishments all our paupers and have but two staffs. Most of our officers will find it far more convenient to attend to the conduct of the Officers in Limerick and Ballingarry than to scatter them in the several small houses which we can duly procure in this Union." *(Minutes of Board Meeting, 15th April, 1850)*

The Board of Guardians of Croom Union applied immediatly for a grant to enlarge Grove House. At a later Board Meeting the minutes have the following information. "Letter from the Poor Law Commissioners stating that they had under consideration a resolution of the Board of Guardians of Croom Union on the 22nd ult. requesting the Commissioners to grant funds to increase the accommodation at the Grove House, Ballingarry, and stating that the Commissioners will be prepared to apply to the Lord's of Her Majesty's Treasury for a grant for the purpose of enlarging the Ballingarry Workhouse on the understanding that such a tenure can be obtained as would justify an outlay of money on the premises ... Ordered that the Commissioners be informed that the Board have applied to **Mr. Maxwell** to know can a tenure of twenty one years be obtained at the Grove House and he expects to have the required information in the course of a week." By the end of May, 1850 Mr. Maxwell had required information for the Board of Guardians. "Mr. Maxwell having stated to the Board that his solicitor has informed him that all the interested parties have signed a consent to lease the Grove House and premises for 21 years and that it only requires the sanction of the Court to carry out the arrangement". Instructions to **Mr. Wilkinson**, Commissioner Architect were as follows regarding the extension to Grove House of covered sheds - "to be erected upon the boundary wall of the rear yard at the Grove House - such erection not to interfere with the permanent works proposed to be executed by the raising and roofing of the building surrounding the front yard, and that the Poor Law Commissioners be applied to for a grant of £200 for the purpose". *(Minutes of Board Meeting, 21st May, 1850)*

Work must have commenced immediatly to the raising of the coach house and stable roof on the outpremises of Grove House. An expenses item mentioned at a Board Meeting on 25th March, 1851 states :- "**James Mangan,** Carpenter's work at Grove House £3-13-08" A further communication from the Poor Law Commissioner reads "With reference to a resolution of the Board of the 14th ult. applying to the Commissioners for a grant of £200 for the erection of sheds at the Grove House, Ballingarry and stating that they will be prepared to remit the amount necessary, on the understanding that any deficiency which may be occasioned in the fund now available, for the enlargement of said Workhouse, shall be made good from the rates, and that the amount granted for extending the present Workhouse accommodation and for providing clothing, bedding etc. is £800. And it was resolved that the Guardians fully undertake to make good any sum that may be required to complete both the permanent works and the sheds at the Grove House".

The Minutes of the Board Meeting also record the following "Letter from Messrs. Geale & Dwyer, Solicitors, requesting to be furnished with a map of the Grove House and premises, in order to prepare a Lease; also requiring to be informed of the rent and the last Gale Day on which rent was paid and if the Guardians are in possession of the premises." Minutes of Board Meeting 6th July, 1850 record the following "Ordered that the Clerk give notice by handbills and by advertisement in the Limerick papers that the consideration of tenders for the several works at Ballingarry Grove House be postponed to next Board day - Tuesday, 16th July, 1850. At that Board meeting it was "Resolved that the Board, having proceeded to examine the tenders for completing the additional works at Ballingarry Grove Auxiliary Workhouse .... resolved unanimously that it was more desirable to appoint Mr. **John Foley**, Clerk of Works to get the additions completed, at a salary of 30/= per week and that the Commissioners be requested to sanction the Board's proceedings in this way, and place the funds granted for their execution in such a way as to enable them to meet the weekly payments, and proceed with the work with the least possible delay" ... "Resolved that Mr. **David Roche**, **Captain Green**, **Robert Maxwell**, **William Scanlan** and **Robert Cox**, esq. be appointed a Committee to see the additions at the Grove House carried out."

A further communication from the Poor Law Commissioners was received "sanctioning the appointment of Mr. **John Foley** as Clerk of Works to superintend the additions and alterations to be done at the Grove House and stating they had directed £100 to be sent to **Mr. Duncan** to provide for the weekly payments as suggested." Details of the Grove House contract were being considered at the Board Meeting of Tuesday, 22 October, 1850.

"The Board proceeded to the consideration of tenders for slating, glazing and painting of the Grove House, Ballingarry. The tender of **Thomas** and **James Mitchell** of Ballingarry for slating, rendering and tiling at the rate of 2/6 per square foot was accepted. Contractors to be found in all materials and labourers". At the Board Meeting of Friday, 19th November, 1850 we read from the Minutes "Resolved that the tender of **John Nolan** for painting and glazing at the Grove House be accepted at the sum of £17-08-09." Furnishing and bedding were considered at the Board Meeting of 24th Nov, 1850. "The Master reported to the Board that he required 100 pairs of blankets, 100 mugs, 500 yards of ticking, 500 yds. of sheeting, 300 yds. Cosy Wolsey and 200 yds. of Shambray, so as that he would be able to furnish the Grove House with the bedding etc. when finished.

Despite it's grandiose title, Grove House had the problems experienced in every household. "The Master reported to the Board that the kitchen flue of the Grove Auxiliary Workhouse took fire on Sunday morning. The fire was fortunately extinguished without loss of property." *(Minutes of Board Meeting 15th Oct. 1850)*

Inmates were moved according as more suitable premises became available. "Ordered that the boys from 5 to 9 years of age be removed from Castletown to the Castle Auxiliary at Ballingarry and that the women there be removed to the Grove."

Who were the people who saw to the day-to-day smooth running of the Auxiliary Workhouse in Ballingarry ? According to the Minutes of a Board meeting of 14th May,1850 we find the following officers recognised as officers of Croom Union:

Name of Officer	Office	Workhouse	Salary, Yearly
Johanne Curtin	Asst. Matron	Grove House	£15-00-00
Patrick Sullivan	Porter	Grove House	£08-00-00
Miss Clifford	Asst. Matron	Ballingarry Castle	£12-00-00
Mary Monahan	Nurse	Ballingarry (Fever) Hospital	£10-00-00

"It was also resolved that Doctor Odell who has heretofore been employed by the Newcastle Guardians as medical attendant of the Grove and Ballingarry houses at a salary £25 per annum, be continued for that duty as well as for the attendance at the Ballingarry Auxiliary and Temporary Fever Hospital at a salary of £60 per annum."

How many inmates were in the Workhouse at a particular time ? Croom Union gives the following data for the week ending 17th May, 1850 :

	Males	Females	Boys	Girls	Child 5-9 yrs	Child 2-5 yrs	Child U-2 yrs.
Remaining at last week	148	285	150	132	37	15	28
Admitted during week	77	115	44	44	23	8	22

Total Remaining, 795. Total Admitted, 333. Grand Total, 1,128.

How many were accommodated in Ballingarry Fever Hospital ? From the minutes of a Board Meeting in 1850 we read "The Board expects the Commissioners of Health will not require the Hospital to be operated under the Temporary Fever Act. This Board desires to represent that 24 out of the present number of patients in the Hospital (57) are from the Auxiliary Workhouses of the Croom Union and that by placing the Hospital under the Management of the Guardians in the way proposed a saving of £90 a year will be effected in salaries alone." Further details of expenditure are given in the Minutes of the Board Meeting of 31st December, 1850 :

Grove House	Pay Sheet	£ 26 - 12 - 07
Auxiliary Workhouses	Pay Sheet	£ 8 - 09 - 04
John Moloney	Glazing	£ 6 - 05 - 10
John Foley	Clerk of Works	£ 3 - 00 - 00
Auxiliary Workhouses	Balance of Pay Sheet	£ 5 - 14 - 10
Total		£ 50 - 03 - 02

Gradually all the legal obstacles to the acquisition of the Grove House were removed: "Letter from the Poor Law Commissioners stating for the information of the Board that they have received a communication from the Board's solicitor that the lease of the Grove House, Ballingarry is now duly executed". *(Minutes of Board Meeting 7th January, 1851)*. Therefore we can conclude that all the extensions were carried out during the year 1851.

The Grove House has long since disappeared. Only the foundations now remain. It was pillaged during the Famine times. It's stones were used in the building of the Parish Church and most likely in the building of the Convent also. The graceful portico and columns of the front door of the former Convent remind us of Grove House - because they once belonged to Grove House. But the ruins of the Grove Workhouse still remain. We can still view the raised sleeping platform of timber along a central wall. Using our imagination we can picture the inmates lying on their bed of straw along this raised platform. What thoughts crowd their minds as they waited for sleep to come ? Did they picture their own open hearth and flickering turf flame ? Or did they just blot out all such memories? After all, to stay by their own fire would have meant a slow death from starvation. In the Workhouse they were sure of having just enough food to survive.

PART VIII

The Encumbered Estates

The Encumbered Estates, 1850 - 1873.

Contrary to popular belief, not every landowner made it unscathed through the Famine. With the inability of their tenants to pay rents many estates became encumbered with debt. The British Government was anxious about this situation and to solve it established the Encumbered Estates Court by two Acts of Parliament in 1848 and 1849. This court was designed to facilitate the sale of insolvent landed estates whose owners had been bankrupted by the Great Famine, and thereby inject new capital, predicted by the Government to be British, into Irish agriculture. The court's three Commissioners were empowered, on a creditors' petition, to enforce the sale of any land or lease encumbered with debts worth more than half the annual rental. Creditors, including the petitioner, were entitled to bid for the land. The eventual purchaser could be awarded indefeasible title by the court. No compensation was offered to existing tenants for their improvements, and many new owners, used the opportunity to evict their tenants. In 1858 the Encumbered Estates Court was succeeded by the Landed Estates Court. In these records reference is made to strange terms like cab-beast, suit and service, heriot, messuages, etc. These are feudal terms and have little meaning nowadays. Also several people are listed as renting the one plot of ground. This practice arose when a group agreed to rent the land each being made liable for the rent in the event of the 'main' tenant not being able to pay. These would be families, relations or partners and might be a useful clue in assessing a genealogical connection. *The following are extracts from the Landed Estates Records in the National Archives.*

Townlands and their area in Acres, Roods and Perches.

Ballyelan	532-01-35	Ballygrennan	950-02-13
Ballyguileataggle	483-01-13	Ballyguilebeg	95-00-32
Ballykevan East	147-02-34	Ballykevan West	194-03-37
Ballyknockane	145-02-36	Ballynahaha	462-02-27
Ballynaroogabeg East	131-00-10	Ballynaroogabeg West	209-02-11
Ballynashig	149-01-13	Ballyneale	656-03-34
Ballynoe	661-01-22	Ballyroe East	169-00-37
Ballyroe West	99-02-35	Ballyvologe	282-00-07
Caherhenesy	235-03-13	Cloonregan	119-03-30
Cloontemple(a)	72-00-24	Common	653-03-26
Coolrus	1,030-00-09	Dollas	126-02-13
Doorlus	172-01-07	Downs	174-01-13
Durraclogh	443-03-34	Frankfort	518-02-09
Glenwilliam	552-00-01	Gorteen	82-00-28
Graigacurragh	609-00-01	Graigbeg	219-00-34
Grenagh	366-03-15	Kilbeg East	41-02-33
Kilbeg West	164-02-26	Killoughty	202-01-39
Kilmacanearla North	460-01-25	Kilmacanearla South	116-03-14
Kilmacow	1,078-01-35	Kilmihil	435-02-31
Kilmore	965- 03-06	Kilmore Demesne	112-00-10
Kilshane	28- 02-25	Kingsland	216-00-12
Knightstreet(a)	104-01-00	Lisduane	677-02-36
Lisduff	106-00-07	Liskennett East	235-01-20
Liskennett West	301-01-13	Lissamota	607-02-09
Lissavarra	152-02-39	Morenane	859-03-19
Rylanes(a)	88-01-23	Woodstock	27-01-16

Total Of Parish, 17,732 - 01 - 01.

In respect of the record of each estate there is a reference number, date of proposed auction, a declaration re ownership and location of the estate followed, in most cases, by a map and a detailed description of the estate. I have listed them in date of sale order. Measurements are in acres-roods-perches.

Auction, Friday July 19, 1850. Ref. V2, N26
In the matter of the Estate of William Cox, esq., owner. Ex parte Henry Irvine & others, petitioners. The lands of Ballinfrumpa in the Barony of Upper Connelloe in the County of Limerick.

Lot No. 1. Ballinfrumpa.
Thomas Neil, 17-02-00 Statute measure.   Thomas Cahull, 17-02-00 Statute measure.
Lots 2, 3 and 4 in the County Cork.

Auction; Friday 19 July, 1850. Ref. V2, N28.
In the matter of the Estate of John O Dell, Esq. Absolute order for sale dated 14 Feb, 1850. The lands of Bealdurogy, otherwise Ballydurogy, otherwise Lower Ballydurogy in the barony of Upper Connello and County of Limerick.

Patrick McDonnell - 16-01-22.   Mary Riordan / Connor Mangan - 29-03-35.
Denis & John Sheahan - 23-01-36.   Edmond Hallinan - 67-01-17.
Reps of the Rev John Graves - 57-00-14.   Patrick Grogan / Michael Grady - 04-02-32.
Bealdurogy Wood - 34-00-00.
Unoccupied, 80-02-30, 16-01-22, 09-01-20, 14-01-30, 03-00-00 and 23-03-37.

Auction; November 12,1850. Ref. V3, N39.
Rental of the Town and Lands of Ballinarogybeg, otherwise Ballinarogybeg Lynch with the commonage of the bog thereof. In the matter of the Estate of Thomas Henry O'Dell, owner. Held in Fee Simple. Part of the description reads as follows: 'there is a handsome cottage fit for the residence of a Gentleman, and flower garden attached.' No further details are given.

Auction, 24 June, 1851. Ref. V8, N30.
Rental of the lands of Ballynafranky and Gleneraha both now called Glenwilliam, Ballyguiletagill and Kilnamona. Held under leases for lives renewable for ever,and the lands of Gortroe, held in fee, all situate in Barony of Connolloe and Co. of Limerick.

Recapituation:(Acres - Roods - Perches.)
Ballynafranky/Gleneraha both now called Glenwilliam - 552-00-01
Kilnamona - 274-02-24. Ballyguiletagill - 483-01-13. Gortroe - 218-03-01.

Lot No. 1. Ballynafranky and Glenaraha, now called Glenwilliam. Plant. Measure.
Mrs. Mary Frances De Massy. The mansion house of Glenwilliam, with the garden, orchard and lawn thereto attached contains about 21-02-26. Gale days May 1, Nov. 1.
William O'Connell= 09-00-00.   William Reidy = 00-00-30.

Lot No 2. Kilnamona. Plantation Measure
Patrick Quaid, otherwise Patrick Quane = 169-02-10. Gale days 24 March, 24 June, 24 Sept. and 24 Dec. Lease executed to Denis Flaherty and John Flaherty, his son. Both are still living. Lessee is bound to furnish 10 horses to work one day in each year annually, or to pay an additional yearly rent of £5.

Lot No. 3. Ballyguiletagill. Plantation Measure.
James Nunan = 76-03-00. Tenant is bound to supply 10 horses, fully appointed, to draw turf or other matter yearly. Lease is made by George Massy, deceased ...and life of Edmond Nunan, son of Lessee, aged 9 years who is still living.

James Nunan = 02-02-00, Meadow Lot.   Robert Cox = 40-00-00.
Thomas Nunan = 62-03-23.   Edmond Curtin = 17-00-00
William Cullinan / Maurice Bennett = 07-02-00. Gale Days varied from the usual two to four in respect of above tenants.

Lot No. 4. Gortroe. Statute Measure. The Estate of George Thomas de Massy, Esqr.
Bog held by the following tenants.
John Ryan, jnr. = 06-02-00.   John Morrissey = 00-02-11.
Patrick / and late John Brusnihan = 00-02-11.   Peter Long = 00-03-15.
John Minahan = 01-00-13.   Mary Burns = 04-00-21.
John Browne = 02-01-00.   Mary Long = 01-01-10.
Daniel, Maurice and Patrick Donoghue = 17-02-13
Richard Morrissey / James Lee / John McAuliff / Margaret O'Brien = 04-00-10.
Frederick Massey = 01-01-36.

Part of Gortroe. Tenants names and holdings.
Patrick / late John Brusnihan = 05-00-35.   James Lee = 12-03-10.
John Ryan, jnr. = 11-00-20   James Daly = 02-03-02.
John Browne = 04-00-00   Thomas and Richard Hayes = 04-01-35.
Thomas Hayes = 02-02-30.   Margaret O'Brien = 11-01-20.
Richard Morrissey / John McAuliff / Maurice Launders = 21-02-02.
John Morrissey = 08-03-00.   Thomas Murphy = 06-02-25.
Mary Burns = 10-03-18.   John Ryan, snr. = 06-03-24.
Daniel, Maurice and Patrick Donoghue = 44-01-20.
Thomas Browne = 02-01-30.   Mary Long = 06-02-00.
John Minehan = 08-00-00.   Bog = 40-01-20.
John Ryan, jnr. (late Michael Shanahan) = 08-00-00.

Gortroe (contd.) Plantation Measure.
Daniel Donoghue = 09-01-21.
Patrick Donoghue = 09-00-21.
Maurice Donoghue = 09-00-21.

Note. *Proceedings by ejectment on notice to quit are pending against these three tenants.*

Mary Long = 04-00-02.
James Lee = 07-03-25.
John McAuliff = 04-01-28.
John Minehan = 04-03-30.
Thomas Hayes = 06-02-37.
Thomas and Richard Hayes = 02-03-01.
Thomas Hayes = 01-02-25.
John Ryan, jnr. = 06-03-09.
John Moracy = 05-01-23.
Frederick Massy = 00-03-26.

Note. These holdings were allocated a sequential number 1-24. Nine lots were shown as unoccupied on date of sale. The valuation describes the lands as partly of a superior quality, and part may be very much improved at a trifling cost. The subsoil, being porous, drains at very wide intervals will be sufficient. Lime is easily had, and there is a good supply of Turbary on the lands.

Auction on Friday, July 23. (No year given.) Ref. V2, N31.
In the matter of the estate of George Thomas de Massy, owner. Part of the lands of Gortroe situate in the barony of Upper Connello. Ordered to be sold in this matter.

Daniel, Maurice and Patrick Donoghue = 61-03-33.
Margaret Moracy / John McAuliff / Maurice Landers = 21-02-22.
John McAuliff, Margaret O'Brien and James Lee = 04-00-10.

Mary Long = 07-03-10.
James Lee = 12-03-10.
Mary Burns = 14-03-29.
James Daly = 02-03-02.
John Minehan = 09-00-13.
John Brown = 06-01-00.
Frederick Massy = 01-01-36.
Margaret O'Brien = 11-01-20.
Patrick (late John) Brusnehan = 05-03-06.
Thomas and Richard Hayes = 04-01-35.
Thomas Hayes = 02-02-30.
John Ryan, jnr. = 17-02-20.
Thomas Murphy = 06-02-25.
John Morasy = 09-01-11.
John Ryan, snr. = 06-03-24.
Peter Long = 00-03-15.
Thomas Browne = 02-01-30.
Unoccupied = 08-00-00.

Auction, 21st October, 1851. Ref. V11, N26.
In the matter of the Estate of George Thomas de Massy, a minor, owner. Ex parte Christopher Delmege, Esquire, petitioner. Rental of the lands of Ballynafranky and Gleneraha both now called Glenwilliam, Ballyguiletagill and Kilnamona held under leases for

lives renewable forever and the lands of Gortroe. Held in Fee.

Lot No 1. Ballynafranky and Gleneraha both now called Glenwilliam.
Mrs Mary Frances de Massy, Castle and Demesne lands = 34-03-21.
William O'Connell = 14-02-00.   William Reidy = 00-03-00.
In Receivers Hands = 552-00-01. This is let by the month purchaser can have vacant possession of the entire Estate save a house and 3 roods held by William Reidy who is a blacksmith. Glenwilliam is held under a lease for 3 lives, renewable forever, dated the 16th day of May, 1755 from Thomas Grady to Darby Grady at the yearly rent of 4s-7d per acre, plantation measure and a renewable fine of $9s-2^3/_4$ d on the fall of each life ..... The last renewable from De Courcy O'Grady to George Massy bears date 17 March, 1831, and one of the lives therein, namely. George Rollo Massy, is still living and now aged about 25 years.

Lot No. 2. Ballyguiletagill.
William Cullenan and Maurice Bennett = 35-01-34.
James Nunan, meadow lot = 04-01-13.   Robert Cox = 64-02-04.
Thomas Nunan = 101-03-21.   Edmond Curt n = 27-01-12.
James Nunan = 118-03-09*   In Receivers Hands = 131-00-00.
* son Edmond, aged 10, named as a life.
Ballyguiletagill is held under a lease dated 28 Sept 1742 from Thomas O'Dell to John Clanchy .... also yielding and paying immediatly on the death of every chief tenant of the premises, his Cab Beast for and in the name of a Herriott ..... the lessee was also bound to do suit and service to the Manor Court of said Thomas O'Dell.

Lot No. 3. Kilnamona. In the Receivers hands = 169-02-10.
Kilnamona is held under a lease dated 4 August, 1804 from John Pigott to George Massy. These lands were demised by George Massy, deceased, the grand-father of the present owner to Denis Flaherty, dated 1 Feb, 1827 and of Denis Flaherty, his son (both are still living) which lease has been evicted but the tenant has six months from 23 July, 1851, the date of the habere, to redeem his interest.

Lot No. 4. Gortroe.
Daniel, Maurice and Patrick Donoghue = 20-02-16. Proceedings by ejectment on a notice to quit pending against these three tenants.
Mary Long = 07-03-10.   Thomas and Richard Hayes = 04-01-35.
James Lee = 12-03-10.   Thomas Hayes = 02-02-30.
John McAuliff = 07-00-14.   John Ryan, jnr. = 17-01-31.
John Minehan = 09-00-13.   John Moracy = 09-01-11.
Thomas Hayes = 06-01-00.   Frederick Massy = 01-01-36.
Unoccupied = 78-02-03.

Auction, Tuesday 13th July, 1852. Ref. V17, N31.
In the matter of the Estate of George Thomas de Massy, owner. The rental of the lands of Ballyguiletagill held under a fee-farm grant situated in the barony of Upper Connello in the county of Limerick.
Ordered to be sold in this matter.

James Nunan = 118-03-09.
Robert Cox = 64-02-04.
Edmond Curtin = 27-01-12.
In Receiver's Hands = 131-00-00.
James Nunan, meadowlot = 04-01-13.
Thomas Nunan =101-03-21.
William Cullinan / Maurice Bennett = 35-01-34.

Auction, Friday 10th December, 1852. Ref. V19, N41.
In the matter of the estate of William Cox, Esq., owner. Ex parte: Henry Irvine & others. Rental of the estate and lands of Morenane situate in the barony of Kenry and of the lands of Lower Derryclogh and Upper Derryclogh situate in the barony of Upper Connelloe.

Lot No. 1. Part of the Lands of Morenane. Held in fee simple situate in the Barony of Kenry containing 477- 01- 26, Statute Measure.

Margaret McCarthy = 00-03-25.
Michael Murphy = 24-02-05.
Michael Maguire = 14-03-05.
Thomas Bourke = 00-01-10.
Mary Kennedy = 28-01-00.
John Kennedy = 21-03-00.
James Kelly = 16-03-35.
John Mann = 33-01-15.
Michael McDonnell = 10-02-30.
John and McDonnell = 27-02-17.
Thomas Kennedy = 00-00-29.
Water = 01-01-10.
Thomas Downes and Michael Neville = 26-02-03. There were four lots unoccupied.

Lot No. 2. Derryclogh Lower
Valentine Blake, Rep. of Michael Cagney = 13-03-00.
Valentine Blake, late Cornelius Regan and Cornelius Donohoe = 16-03-30.
John Kennedy = 26-01-00.
Edmond Kilbridge = 02-02-15 and 41-02-20.
Michael Donohoe = 12-03-00.
William Flannady = 24-02-20.
In owner's hands = 75-00-30.
Thomas O'Donnell = 21-00-30.
Bartholemew Hanly = 15-03-10.
Michael Quinn = 12-03-00.
William Sheahy = 13-00-00.
Myles Monckton = 65-02-20.
Reference is made to lease of Myles Monckton and Sarah Casey, otherwise Monckton.

Lot No. 3. Upper Derryclogh.
In owner's occupation = 101-03-19.

Auction, 10th December, 1852. In one lot. **Ref. V19, N45.**
In the matter of the Estate of John O'Dell, Esq., deceased continued in the name of William O'Dell, Esq. owner. Rental of the Estate & Lands of Bealdurogy Upper, Barony of Lower Connelloe, Woodstock, Caherhennessy, Ballyroe and Ballypierce in the Barony of Upper Connelloe and that part of Rylanes called Gortroe, or Drumroe situate in the Barony of Lower Connelloe; also the lands of Lower Rylanes, situate in the Barony of Lower Connelloe: all in the County of Limerick.

In the descriptive particulars to the sale, reference is made to the lands of Bealdurogy Upper; Woodstock; Caherhennessy; Ballyroe and Ballypierce: part of Rylanes called Gortroe or Drumroe are all held under lease of lives renewable forever bearing date the 7th Day of July, 1720 from John O'Dell to William O'Dell, subject to four shillings Irish for every acre plantation measure; therein demised as aforesaid; with a fat hog and a mutton at Christmas; or fifteen shillings in lieu of them at the discretion of the landlord; also a fat hen on 1st May and 1st Nov. every year, etc.

Bealdurogy Upper. Unoccupied: late the Reps.of the Rev. John Greaves = 102-01-18.

Rylanes Lower.
Patrick Grogan and Michael Grady = 20-00-20.
Connor Crummin = 01-01-11.

Rylanes Upper & Lower incl. Gortroe (Drumroe).
Unoccupied. Late the Reps. of the Rev.John Greaves = 42-01-20.
Denis Mangan = 30-00-00.   Unoccupied = 21-03-30.

Woodstock
Unoccupied. Late the Reps.of the Rev. John Greaves = 01-00-20.
John Fitzgerald = 14-03-10.   William Quinlivan = 00-01-06.
There is a mill upon this lot.

Ballyroe West including Ballypierce
Patrick Keating; late Hayes = 46-03-35.   Patrick Casey; late Gorman = 15-02-20.
Martin Daly = 00-00-30.   Thomas Moore = 04-01-36.
Patrick Hurley = 02-01-30.   Patrick Boyse = 14-01-10.

Caherhennessy
Darby Regan = 20-03-10.   Reps.of John Leo = 02-00-10.
John, Patrick and Callaghan Bowen in Co. = 17-01-13; 08-02-00 and 14-03-00
Denis Hogan and Matthew Kelly = 01-01-10.

Maurice Connell = 01-00-20.
Maurice Connell and Mary Egan = 12-01-20.
late Maurice Connell = 19-02-00.
Patrick Cagney and Michael Quinlivan = 03-02-20.
John Flemyng = 02-01-20.
Patrick Boyse, late John Hanrahan = 05-02-15 and 14-01-10.
Patrick Casey, late David Lee = 01-02-30, 00-02-20 and 00-03-20.
late James Burke = 00-03-30 and 00-03-25. late Dr. O'Dell = 10-02-25.
Bridget Grady = 13-02-20.
William O'Dell and Widow Frehan = 18-00-00 and 12-01-10.
Maurice Connell = 01-00-20.
Edmond Walsh = 09-01-30.
Patrick Keating; late Hayes = 04-02-00.
Patrick Boyse = 04-00-00.
Patrick Cane = 03-00-10.
William Quinlivan = 00-01-20.
Note. Here is a Fox Covert = 00-02-37.

Auction, Thursday 14 April,1853. Ref. V20, N70.
In the matter of the Estate of Garrett Russell Maume and Richard Russell Maume, minors. Rental of two Divisions of the Townland of Ballinoe. Held in Fee.

Ballinoe
Michael Shine, reps.of Richard Johnston = 09-00-11.
James Lyston = 119-00-08.
Terence Lyston = 140-03-27.
John Harnett = 97-00-37.
Patrick Lynch = 48-01-06.
Reference is made to the presence of a Tuck Mill.

Ballinoe: part of; called Garreeniska
James Lyston = 04-02-29.

Auction, Friday 28th October,1853. Ref. V24, N22
Incumbered Estate. Rental of the Fee-Simple Lands of Granagh containing 365-22-18 Statute measure in the Barony of Upper Connolloe. The Freehold Lands of Kilmacow called Ballyconneely containing 387-03-04 Statute measure in the Barony of Upper Connolloe (and other property in the Barony of Clanwilliam)

Lot No. 1. Granagh North Division
George Wellington Evans, Esq. = 213-00-10. Gale Days: May 1 & Nov. 1.
This lot was formerly let to James Mark Lynch, Esq. The Roman Catholic Chapel & yard containing 01-00-39 in above lot will not be included in sale.

Lot No. 2. Granagh South Division
Catherine Lyons, Reps. of Wm. Lyons and John Carroll = 121-03-23.
Catherine Lyons = 30-02-25.
Gale Days Mar. 25 and Sept. 29.

Lot No. 3. Kilmacow called Ballyconneely
William Power = 143-00-32 and 10-03-38. Gale Days are May 1 & Nov. 1.
David Martin Barry = 147-00-31. David Burns = 85-03-23.
The lands of Kilmacow otherwise called Ballyconneely are held under two leases bearing date respectively the 10th day of August 1804 from John Pigott, Esq., to James O'Shaughnessy, Esq., deceased, for three lives renewable forever on payment of a pepper-corn renewal fine, one portion of this lot containing 91-03-34 low land and 22-03-10 of Hill, Irish Plantation Measure, at the yearly rent of £1-3-0 late currency, being the £1-01-02$^{3}/_{4}$ present currency, for every acre late Irish Plantation Measure of the low lands and seven shillings late currency being 6s-5$^{1}/_{2}$d present currency for every acre, same measure of the hill adjoining thereto as above, together with a fat hog at Christmas, or in lieu thereof, one guinea of lawful money of Ireland.

Auction, 4 November, 1853. Ref. V24, N27.
In the matter of the estate of William Cox, Esq., owner. Rental of part of the lands of Upper and Lower Derryclogh situate in the Barony of Upper Connelloe and County of Limerick. Held in Fee in three lots. The rental of lot 2 will be considerably increased upon the expiration of the lease to Myles Monckton, tenant to the greater part thereof.

Lot No. 1. Derryclogh Lower
Valentine Blake, rep.of Michael Cagney = 13-03-00.
Valentine Blake, late Cornelius Egan = 14-01-20.
John Kennedy = 26-01-00. Thomas O'Donnell = 13-00-13.

Lot No 2. Derryclogh Lower
John Cox, jnr.= 02-02-09. Reps of Myles Monckton = 65-02-20.
William Shelley = 13-00-10. Gale days are Mar 25 & Sept 29.
Reference is made to lessee Myles Monckton and Sarah Casey, otherwise Monckton - both of whom are now living - in respect of the lease.

Lot No. 3. Derryclogh Upper
In owner's occupation = 101-03-19.

Auction Friday, 20 January, 1854. Ref. V26, N11.
In the matter of the Estate John Mason, Walker Jackson Mason and Myles Jackson Mason, owners. Valuable fee-simple and fee-farm Estates. The lands of Lisduane are with others held under a fee-farm grant bearing date June 22, 1592. The lands of Cappanihane are held in fee-simple being portion of the lands granted by patent of 36 Charles II, to Brook Bridges.

Lot No. 1 Lisduane
John Mason, Esq. = 53-00-30. David Bennett = 19-02-20.
No tenant = 31-03-20.

Lot No. 2. Lisduane, part of.
Edmond Cagney = 20-00-00. David Bennett = 58-00-30 and 20-01-30.

Lot No. 3. Lisduane = Untenanted.

Lot No. 4. Cappanahane, part of, otherwise Cooltus.
Myles Mason, Esqr. = 103-03-10. Patrick Clifford = 10-00-00.
Thomas Cagney = 06-00-30 and 01-00-25. Joan Malone (widow) = 00-00-25.
John Fitzgibbon = 07-02-15. Ellen Noonan = 00-01-10.
Denis Collins = 13-03-00. James Morrissy = 06-01-30.
Connor O'Brien = 04-03-05. Daniel Burns = 15-00-25.
Widow Hartigan = 00-00-18. William Lee = 02-01-60.
Connor Tuohill = 00-02-10. Richard Dundon = 20-00-35.
Patrick Clifford = 04-00-00. Jeremiah Clifford = 02-00-00.
Thomas Divane = 01-02-20. Patrick Condons = 49-01-00.
Patrick Drew = 26-03-20 and 09-01-00. Miss Mason = 124-02-20.
James Gorman = 05-01-35. Daniel Guerrin = 04-03-25.
John Cagney = 02-03-30. Patrick Lynch = 01-03-10.
Michael Lynch = 12-03-10 and 01-00-20. John O'Brien = 32-00-10 and 02-03-30.
Michael Tuohill = 06-03-00, 08-02-26 and 11-01-14.
Patrick McDonagh = 33-02-00 and 18-02-00.
John Gorman = 18-03-00, 01-01-10 and 04-03-20.
late John Ahern (now Thomas Maher) = 16-03-30.
Jeremiah Noonan = 06-03-10, 00-00-20 and 17-00-00.
Edmond Heffernan = 01-02-30 and 02-03-20.
Reference is made to the presence of a police Barracks

Auction Tuesday May 9th, 1854. Ref. V27, N50.
In the matter of the Estate of Christopher Hume Lawder, assignee of Daniel Dickson Power of Ashboro in the County of Limerick, Esquire, Owner. Ex parte, Mr William Irwin, petitioner. The lands of Ballynarogylynch, otherwise Ashboro, and Ballynarogybeg, otherwise Barry, situate in the Barony of Upper Connelloe in the County of Limerick held under a Fee-Farm Grant.
Lots 1 and 2 were lands in the Barony of Kenry, near Askeaton and Kildimo.

Lot No. 3. Ballynarogylynch, otherwise Ashboro
Daniel Dickson Power = 80-03-26.
Ballynarogybeg, otherwise Barry
Daniel Dickson Power= 131-00-10.

Auction 13 July, 1854. Ref. V30, N14.
In the matter of the Estate of John Tuthill and George Tuthill, Esqrs., owners. The lands of Kilmore, except the House Division there. The lands of Ballinleeny; and the lands of Doorlass, otherwise Thurlass situate in the barony of Connelloe and in the County of Limerick. Held in Fee Simple. Lots No 1-3 and No. 8 are not relevant to this area.

Lot No. 4. Kilmore, except the house division thereof.
Michael Holohan = 90-01-22.
This tenant has built a slated Grist mill on his holding.
Jeremiah Holohan = 89-01-21 and 03-03-05.
Mary Nunan = 10-01-20.   Margaret Martin = 00-00-37.

Lot No. 5. Ballinleeny, otherwise Kilmore, part of.
Patrick J. Hedderman = 179-01-03.   Mary Nunan = 15-00-09.
William McNamara = 07-00-09.   Edmond Fitzgibbon = 00-03-31.
Margaret Carroll = 04-02-05.   Margaret Sheehan = 51-00-18.
Jeremiah Holohan = 12-01-13.   Edmond Dooley = 01-02-02.
David Walsh = 03-02-04.   Michael Holohan = 00-00-30.
Thomas Mahony = 01-02-32.

Lot No. 6. Ballinleeny, otherwise Kilmore, part of.
Michael Callaghan = 12-02-14.   Lieut. Col. Wm. Jones = 09-00-10.
James Sheehy = 177-01-01.   Denis Nunan = 42-01-07.
Thomas Callaghan = 85-03-16.   Timothy Collopy = 48-02-15.

Lot No. 7. The lands Doorlass, otherwise Thurlass, otherwise Kilmore, part of.
Thomas Graddy and Patrick Graddy = 117-00-13.

Auction 19 May, 1857. Ref. V45, N23.
Rental of part of the lands of Rylanes and part of the lands of Cloontemple situate in the Barony of Upper Connelloe in the County of Limerick. Held in Fee. In the matter of the Estate of

George Thomas De Massy, Esqr. and William Hamo De Massy, Esqr. owners. Ex-parte petitioner, Mrs. Mary Frances De Massy.
Lot No. 1. Rylanes, part thereof called the Brickfield and part thereof called the Sweepsfield.
Edmond Hallinan = 11-00-02.   William Fitzgerald = 08-02-22.
Poor Law Commissioners = 04-00-00.
The premises demised are described as The Grove House, offices, yard and gardens.
Cloontemple, part of.
Unlet. Late James Mulcair = 137-03-07.
Rylanes
Unlet. Late Denis Crotty = 01-01-00.
No. 2. Rylanes, part of.
Paul Broderick = 00-02-31.
The premises comprised in this proposal are described as the house in the Town of Ballingarry in possession of said Michael Cavanagh, together with the back yard and garden to the rere thereof. Said Catherine Cavanagh, widow of Michael, is now the wife of John Hogan and they emigrated to America in 1853 where they are now residing.
Philip Hurley = 00-00-28.   John Riordan = 00-00-27.
Patrick Broderick = 00-00-32.
Lease to John Scanlan, deceased, and John Scanlan.
David Fitzgerald = 00-00-13.
Cloontemple, part of.
Revd.G.G. Gibbings = 02-00-30.   William Scanlan = 02-00-22.
References are made to Wm. Scanlan, Hugh W. Scanlan and Matthew Scanlan, deceased.
Patrick Donoghue = 00-00-22.   Thomas Sullivan = 00-00-23.
Roger Dillane = 00-00-13.   Joseph Granville = 01-02-17.
The rent payable by Joseph Granville is one pepper-corn. This premises was previously occupied by Robert Carey.
William O'Dell,Esq.= 02-01-38.   James Donnelly = 00-00-26.
Frederick Massy = 03-01-20.   John Murphy = 00-00-08.
James Hoare = 00-00-15.   Patrick O'Donnell = 00-02-20.
John Cox = 00-00-15.   William Lenihan = 00-00-09.
William Hartigan = 00-00-13.   William Ahern = 01-01-03.
Denis Crotty = 00-03-06.   Michael Hannon = 00-01-09.
Edmond Bowen = 00-03-06.   Patrick Boyce = 02-00-39.
John Bowen = 01-01-06.

Michael Connell, reps. of Patrick McMahon = 00-00-30.
William Lenihan, reps. of Michael Walsh = 00-00-11.
The premises are the house & premises in Pound Lane as was held by William O'Brien and his under-tenants, together with half the lot of ground in Lyon's Field,...and situate above John Condon's holdings ...

Patrick Dunne = 00-00-31.
Robert Maxwell = 00-00-10.
John Keating = 00-03-14.
John O'Grady = 00-02-15.
Roger Sweeney = 00-00-22.
Daniel D. Power = 01-03-27.

Michael Regan = 00-02-09.
James Donnelly = 00-01-33.
Edmond Tracy = 00-00-25.
Patrick Fenaughty = 00-00-22.
Michael Molony = 00-00-32.
Jeremiah Browne = 01-00-29.

Reference is here made to a Paddock-Garden.
Thomas Keeffe and Patrick Casey = 01-02-09.
Michael Guiry = 00-01-30.
Margaret Hogan = 06-03-23.
Owen Dunn = 01-04-14.

John Connell = 01-00-10.
Patt Hurley = 00-02-33 and 00-01-39.

Auction, Thursday 23rd February, 1860. Ref. V57, N39. In 3 Lots.
In the matter of the Estate of John Baker Graves, Henry Meggs Graves, Sybella Baker, otherwise Graves, and the Rev. Hugh Baker, her husband, Frances Baker, Margaret Drought otherwise Graves, and Philip Drought her husband, Daniel Dickson Power and Henry Maunsell. Owners. Ex parte William Henry Linnaeus Walcott and Susanna Sarah Walcott. Petitioners. Rental and Particulars of the Impropriate Tithe Rent - Charge of the Parish of Ballingarry. Premises in the town of Ballingarry or Knight Street with the tolls of Whitsun Monday's Fair of Ballingarry and Knight Street Mill, Cottage and Garden, situated in the barony of Upper Connelloe in the County of Limerick. Held under lease dated 14th March 1727 for lives renewable forever. And the mill and part of the lands of Woodstock situate in the same barony and county. Held under lease dated 7th November, 1800 for lives renewable forever.

Lot No 1. The Impropriate Tithe Rent-Charge in lieu of composition for Tithes of the Parish of Ballingarry in the County of Limerick, being £451-00-06 sterling yearly as per the Applotment book of the said parish, and held under lease dated 14 March, 1727 from the Earl of Orrery to Francis Cornwall, for three lives renewable forever.

No.	Denominations	Qty. of Land	Net amount rent-charge less 25% Stg.
1	Coolrush	1,011-00-18	31-18-03
2	Kingsland	212-00-06	06-15-05
3	Ballinlyny	662-02-26	20-09-10$^1/_2$
4	Kilmore	402-03-24	13-01-01$^1/_2$
5	Granagh	374-02-07	11-19-00$^1/_2$
6	Doorlasbeg	170-00-13	04-04-07
7	Liskinnit	537-00-09	15-12-01
8	Grangueacurra	604-02-10	17-14-10
9	Lisduane	674-00-07	18-18-03
10	Grangebeg	340-00-01	09-00-10$^1/_2$
11	Everground	21-00-09	00-14-04$^3/_4$
12	Lisduff	106-03-27	03-03-07
13	Kilmacneerla	575-03-03	14-00-11
14	Bantabee	298-02-13	10-10-07
15	Kilmacow	774-00-13	26-14-00
16	Ballinaha & Commons	472-03-36	12-14-00
17	Ballynockane	145-03-05	05-16-04
18	Kilbeg	203-01-06	05-10-06
19	Lisavarra	150-02-34	03-16-10
20	Caherhennissy & Commons	231-02-07	06-09-04
21	Ballyrow Nash	176-03-17	03-19-11$^1/_2$
22	Ballyroe, O'Dell & Commons	126-02-07	03-01-00$^1/_4$
23	Woodstock	24-01-07	00-17-01
24	Lisamota	605-02-10	14-13-10
25	Kilshanabbey	31-00-29	01-07-00
26	Rylans	98-03-09	04-04-04
27	Night-St. or Knightstreet	84-03-18	03-16-07$^1/_2$
28	Cloentemple	35-00-07	02-00-05
29	Killoughta	225-01-38	05-15-02$^1/_2$
30	Ballyvalogue	247-03-32	06-03-04$^1/_2$
31	Ballyguile Jagil	473-03-09	12-12-10
32	Downs	174-03-30	06-08-07$^1/_2$
33	Ballinarogy	331-01-36	10-09-06$^1/_2$
34	Ballycavin	342-02-15	07-15-11$^1/_2$
35	Frankford	511-03-31	10-11-02
36	Hoaresfield	04-00-07	00-33-10$^1/_4$
37	Clounregan	113-00-26	04-15-11$^3/_4$

No.	Denominations	Qty. of Land	Net amount rent-charge less 25% Stg.
38	Gurteen	78-02-31	02-11-03
39	Ballygrinnan & Commons	1,006-00-34	25-18-04
40	Ballynashig	149-01-02	03-07-02$^{1}/_{2}$
41	Ballyguilobeg	117-02-38	02-14-10
42	Ballyelane & Commons	607-03-20	15-02-05æ
43	Ballyneale	649-00-00	14-03-02æ
44	Kilmihill	158-00-04	03-10-10
45	Kilmichael & Commoms	294-03-31	07-01-09
46	Glenwilliam	539-01-34	11-08-04
47	Doroclogh	437-03-01	09-12-03
48	Ballinoe	601-00-34	17-04-04
Totals		16,218-01-36	£451-00-06

Lot No. 2. This is the town section of Ballingarry. There is a map for this section which I felt would not be worth reproducing as it is small and very detailed. For ease of reference I have kept the map references. They are reproduced here in the sequence as listed in the records.

Map ref. 1-2. Town and lands of Knockard and the Long Castle.
Tenant Thomas Fitzgerald = 42-00-09 statute measure. Lease from Alexander Cornwall to David Fitzgerald, dated April 10th, 1777 of the town and lands of Knockard, with the Long Castle, situate in the town of Ballingarry, for three lives, with covenant for perpetual renewal. The lives are all dead and no renewal has ever been made. Lease contains a covenant on part of the Tenant, his heirs and assigns to grind his and their corn at Knight-Street mill, Ballingarry under pain of 5/= for every neglect or refusal to do so. There is a public right of way through this holding by the passage E to F on map.

Map ref. 3-4. The Castle, Field, Houses and Garden, Knight St.
Tenant Thomas Fitzgerald = 11-02-28 statute measure. Lease from Alexander Cornwall to David Fitzgerald dated January 13th, 1779 of the Castle Field and houses in the Town of Ballingarry with the Kercher Field and a quarter of an acre of the field adjoining thereto, for three lives renewable etc. On this holding are two houses with shops, yards and offices. There is a right of way through the passage marked B,C & D on the map from Castle Lane to holding No 3 on map.

Map ref. 5. Ground and Dwelling House.
Tenant Michael Quilinan = 00-01-24 statute measure. Lease from Catherine Ann Graves to Cornelius Scanlan, dated August 1st, 1828 for lives of lessee, John & Joseph Scanlan of whom John is living. There are ten houses on this holding one of which is slated, two stories high with shop fronting the main street.

Map ref. 6-7. Dwelling House and premises.
Tenant John Sheehy = 00-00-19, statute measure. This holding consists of a slated house, shop, yard and garden.

Map ref. 8. Dwelling House, back yard & premises.
Tenant William Hurley = 00-00-10 statute measure. Lease dated September 27th, 1825 from Catherine Ann Graves, widow, to Denis Hurley and Philip and William Hurley, his sons, the last two of whom only are living. This is a house, shop and small garden.

Map ref. 9-10. Knight Street. House & haggard, with the Tolls of Whitsun-Monday's Fair of Ballingarry.
Tenant Michael Hallinan = 00-00-19 statute measure

Map ref. 13. Knight Street, House and yard.
Tenant Rev. George Gough Gubbins = 00-00-08 statute measure. Tenant is in possession as assignee of James Falkner by lease dated April, 1820 from the Rev. John Graves for lives of William Hurley, James Falkner and Edward Fitzgerald, all of whom are living.

Map ref. 11-12. Houses in Ballingarry.
Tenant Patrick Meade = 00-01-37. On this holding are seven houses, yards, offices & gardens, two being slated.

Map ref. 14-15 and 16-17. Houses and gardens in Castle Lane.
Tenant Robert O'Dell, assignee of Rev. Thomas Gibbings = 01-02-05. The description in this lease is 'Garden formerly held by Connor and Alicia Farrel, also Mangan's house in Castle Lane, also Hogan's house in Castle Lane and 1/4 acre of ground in the Castle field or garden.' The houses are slated and in good repair.

Map ref. 18. Houses in Castle Lane.
Tenant Reps. of James Russell = 00-03-02, statute measure. There are three houses in this holding.

Map ref. 21. Maras two fields, part of Knight Street.
Tenant Robert O'Dell, assignee of Edmund Fitzgerald = 04-03-12. Lease dated March 24th, 1821 from Catherine Ann Graves to Edward Fitzgerald

two fields to the west of Ballingarry being part of Knight Street, called Maras Fields.

Map ref. 19-20. House and land.
Tenant Robert O'Dell, M. D. = 01-01-38, statute measure. Tenant at will. Slated house in excellent repair.

Map ref. 24-25. Knight St. House in Castle Lane, with ground attached thereto. Tenant Garrett Russell = 00-02-05, statute measure. Lease dated June 11, 1822 for lives of Garrett Russell, the lessee, John Russell and Thomas Russell, all living.

Map ref. 26. Knight Street. Two houses, back houses, yards and gardens.
Tenant Patrick Meade = 00-02-16, statute measure. Lease dated October 14, 1790 from Crosbie Morgell to James Meade for ninty nine years. Contains covenant to grind corn and malt at Knight Street mill etc. as 1-2 above.

Map ref. 27. Knight Street. Houses and lands.
Tenant: Patrick Meade == 00-00-25 statute measure.

Map ref. 30. Houses and lands.
Tenant John Connell. No details.

Map ref. 36-37. Houses and lands.
Tenant Roger Grady, (late David Costello) = 01-01-13, statute measure.

Map ref. 29. Lands..
Tenant John O'Connell, (late John Cavanagh) = 01-02-04, statute measure.

Map ref. 34-35. Knight Street. House, garden and land, the Castle field.
Tenant Garrett Carmody = 00-02-21, statute measure. Lease dated April 10, 1792 from Crosbie Morgell to Catherine Shanahan and James Scanlan for ninty nine years. The lease describes the premises as part of Shanahan and Falvey's tenement at Knight St. in Ballingarry. Contains covenant re grinding corn at Knight St. mill.

Map ref. 38. House and garden.
Tenant Thomas Tracey = 00-03-09. Lease dated September 9, 1794 from Crosbie Morgell to John Shelton for three lives etc. Renewed 1839 to Catherine Shelton, spinster, Limerick City for lives of Ellen Sharkell, otherwise Shelton, daughter of lessee, c'estui qui vie, in original lease, and William Hamo Massy and George Rollo Massy, then aged respectively 18 and 12 years.

Map ref. 39. Three houses.
Tenant Nicholas Madigan = 00-03-06, statute measure.
Map ref. 40-41. Houses and Lands.
Tenant Daniel Dickson Power = 01-00-17, statute measure.
Map ref. 42-43. Downs Road. Two houses, yard and premises and building ground.
Tenant Frederick Massy = 00-00-16, statute measure. Lease dated May 4, 1844 whereby Richard Dundas Graves demised to Frederick Massy two houses at the corner of the Downs Road, Knight St., tenanted by Darby Twomey and Mary Curtin for lives of Jeremiah Dineen, John Dineen and David Herlihy.
Map ref. 44. Police Barracks.
Tenant John Bowen = 00-00-07, statute measure. Lease dated December 29, 1836 whereby Richard Dundas Graves demised to John Bowen the ground whereon the Police Barracks is partly built for lives of Jeremiah & John Dineen and David Herlihy.
Map ref. 46-47. House, four Tontine buildings, backyard and a lot of ground belonging thereunto. Also one acre of land, Plantation measure, adjoining Kelt's Forge.
Tenant Jeremiah Dineen = 02-01-05, statute measure. Lease dated September 29th, 1825 for the lives of William James Graves, John Dineen and Edmund Blake of whom Edmund Blake, son of Michael Blake of Gurteen, Co. Limerick, farmer, is the survivor
Map ref. 48. Ground in Knight Street.
Tenant Jeremiah Dineen = 06-02-35 statute measure. Lease dated September 29th, 1825 for three lives, Charles Conyers, son of Rev. Edward Conyers, Jeremiah Dineen and Mary Dineen, second son and daughter of lessee.
Map ref. 28. Premises formerly in possession of Edmond Connell with two Houses and Haggard.
Tenant John O'Connell = 00-01-11 statute measure.
Map ref. 31. Five houses and garden.
Tenant John O'Connell = 01-03-20 statute measure.
Map ref. 49-50. House and land.
Tenant Nancy Madigan, widow = 05-01-27 statute measure. Lease dated September 13th, 1852 to Eugene Madigan, etc.
Map ref. 53. Ground, part of the Knight Street, being part of the Fair

Field.
Tenant Thomas McCarthy, M.D. = 00-00-18 statute measure. Lease dated July 9th, 1825 to Thomas Gleeson and for lives lessee, Thomas Gleeson, his son and Edward O'Dell, 5th son of Robert Dean O'Dell and the survivor of whom Thomas Gleeson the son only is living.

Map ref. 54. Ground part of Knight Street being part of the Fair Field.
Tenant Thomas McCarthy, M.D. = 00-01-00 statute measure. Lease dated July 9th, 1825 to Robert Dean O'Dell for lives of Robert O'Dell, Thomas O'Dell and Edward O'Dell, 2nd, 4th and 5th sons of lessee, the two first of whom only are living.

Map Ref. 55. The Fair Field to the rere of O'Dell's and Gleeson's premises.
Tenant Thomas McCarthy, M.D. = 03-01-18 statute measure. This comprises the plot of ground known as the Fair Field and strip at rere of holding no. 30.

Map Ref. 51-52. House at the Tontine next the Custom Gap.
Tenant Deborah Burk = 02-03-14 statute measure. Accepted proposal dated March 12, 1818 for three lives of whom one of the lives, namely, Mary Anne Egan only is living. The proposal describes the house next the Custom Gap at the Tontine, Ballingarry with the back ground adjoining the stone wall which runs between the same and the Fair Field and which ground extends to the rivulet or watercourse at the east side thereof. Consists of land and five thatched houses.

Map ref. 32-33. House, yard and garden in Knight St. being about half the tenement called Falvey's and Shanahan's tenement.
Mary Jane Cavanagh, widow, repesentative of Honora Falvey and Edmund Baggott = 00-00-36, statute measure. There was an obligation to grind corn and malt in Ballingarry mill etc.

Map ref. 22-23. House and garden in and near Knight Street.
Tenant Margaret Egan = 00-01-39 statute measure. Proposal by Thomas Egan and accepted by Crosbie Morgell dated May 17, 1777 for three lives of whom Mary Anne Egan is still living.

Totals
Valuation = £413-00-00. Area = 95-00-13 statute measure. Yearly Rent = £200-02-06.

Lot. No. 2. A list of the Tolls payable at the Whitsun - Monday Fair of Ballingarry.

For Each Cow, Bull, Bullock or Heifer sold	6d
For Each Two-Years old sold	4d
For Each One Year Old sold	3d
For Each Horse, Mule or Gelding	1/=
For Each Pig sold	3d
For Each Car with Pigs or Slips	1/=
For Each Car with Plants or Cabbages	6d
For Each Load of Spades, Trees or Tents	4d
For Each Load of Apples	6d
For Each Hardware Stand	4d
For Each Tent, Licensed to sell Liquor	3/=
For Each Coffee Tent	1/6d
For Each Load of Cans, Gallons or Cooper's work	6d
For Each Load of Smith's Work	6d
For Each Soft Goods stand	4d
For Each Bread Car or Standing	4d

Lot No. 3. Knight-Street Mill, Ballingarry, held under lease dated 14th March, 1727 for three lives renewable forever and Woodstock Flour Mill, held under lease dated 7th November, 1800 for three lives renewable forever at the yearly rent of £02-01-06$^1/_2$ sterling, and a renewable fine of £01-00-09$^1/_4$.
Map ref. 57.
Knight-Street Mill commonly called Kennedy's Mill and land and Mill House within one quarter (1/4) of a mile of Ballingarry.
Prudence Brownrigg = 00-03-30
Map ref. 58. Woodstock Mill & Cottage. 01-00-30 statute measure.
Totals
Valuation = £56-00-00. Area = 02-00-20 statute measure. Yearly rent = £58-00-00.

Auction July 6, 1865. Ref. V78, N19.
In the matter of the Estate of Richard Harte, Esq. owner and petitioner, in one lot. The town and lands of both the Courrusses, otherwise Coolruses, known by the name of Coolruss. Held in Fee-Farm. Agent of the Estate, Michael Kerin, Esq.

Coolruss

Martin Carroll, jnr. = 176-02-19.
Patrick Lyons = 125-00-00.
William O'Donnell = 24-07-10.
John O'Brien = 48-00-00.
Thomas O'Brien = 85-00-00.
Thomas Sheils = 04-15-00.
Cornelius O'Brien = 10-10-03.
James Dundon = 05-00-00.
Honoria Sheehan (widow) = 01-03-21.
William Maher = 23-01-02.
James M. Lynch,Esq., = 196-03-29.
Anstance Ryan (widow) = 16-00-33.
Thomas Dillon = 01-03-34.
David McCarthy = 00-01-20.

Michael Murphy = 80-00-00.
Denis O'Donnell = 32-00-00.
Martin Carroll, snr. = 60-00-00.
James Bourke = 11-00-00.
Thomas Burns = 63-07-00.
Jeremiah Noonan = 40-00-00.
William Mahony = 06-00-00.
Patrick Burns = 03-00-00.
Edmond Barry = 05-00-09.
John Leahy = 03-01-00
William Cuthbert = 49-02-30.
Michael Burns = 14-02-35.
Edmond Noonan = 11-00-20.

Auction 11 February, 1873. Ref. V109, N19.
The lands of Kilmacanierla North. Held in Fee. In the matter of the estate of Denham William Jephson Norreys and Thomas John Franks, Trustees. For sale under the Trusts of Will of William Hume Franks, deceased, owners and petitioners

Kilmacanierla North

Patrick Cagney = 81-00-27.
Thomas Ahern = 88-00-01.
Patrick and James O'Shea = 108-00-35.

Thomas Connor = 27-01-01.
Daniel Byrne = 72-01-14.

Reference is made as a condition of lease 'not to sell or dispose of any hay, straw or unthreshed corn off the lands, but to spend the dung and manure to be made upon the premises in a proper and husbandlike manner.' There are no further details of this sale.

PART IX

History of the National Schools, 1841 - 1900.

Ballingarry.

Prior to 1800 there was no education system worthy of the name. However, after the Act of Union, Jan 1, 1801 and in tandem with developments in Britain, the system was changed. In 1831, **Lord Stanley** introduced the National Education Board. This in turn set up a Board of Commissioners to control primary education and the state was to provide non-denominational primary schools. These were the National Schools. Part of the function of the Board was to grant aid the setting up of the national schools. These were voluntary parochial, with a clergyman as manager. *Records of the national schools are kept in the National Archives in which this article was researched.* **It should be noted that by 1870 only 34% of the teachers nationwide had formal training.**

On Jan 12, 1841 **Archdeacon Michael Fitzgerald,** parish priest of Ballingarry made application to the Board of National Education on the application form and wrote as follows :

Gentlemen,

The site of the proposed National school of Ballingarry is in the centre of the town, on ground rather elevated, and within about eighty feet of the river. It has a front of 44 feet towards the street by fifty feet of rear or back ground. It will be leased to the Board or to such Trustees as the Board shall approve at a rent of 40 shillings a year for the term of three lives of the respective ages of twenty seven, nine and four years; an additional term of thirty one years to commence from the extinction of the last survivor of the lives. I myself am the person to make the lease and I hold the premises under a lease from **William Scanlan**, Esq. of Ballyknockane who himself holds under a lease of lives renewable forever from **Thomas Odell,** Esq. of the Grove, the owner in fee. The fee is likely to be sold 'ere long but Mr.Scanlan's lease is over sixty years -- consequently antecedent to all claims and incumberances affecting Major Odell's property.

I am not at present prepared to name the trustees as I do not clearly understand what the power of those trustees over the proposed school is to be - but the Board shall be satisfied as possible. As to the numbers likely to attend I beg to repeat that the population of this town was at the last census (1831) over two thousand and as there is a considerable population at least one thousand more located within a circuit of one mile from the town the attendance may be estimated at two hundred boys and one hundred girls at the least.

Two school rooms would be required and I propose to build a house of two stories containing two apartments-one overhead for the girls and one below for the boys. The upper room to be forty feet by twenty which is what the ground in front will admit of and the lower room to be enlarged by means of a return of one storey of twenty feet by twenty opening from the centre of the outward apartment. The girls schoolroom to be accessible by an external flight of steps.

I forgot to state the proposed site is quite unconnected with any House of Worship and I have only to add that as many feet to rear as the Superintendent shall deem necessary shall be given without any addition to the yearly rent of forty shillings. Humbly submitting the premises to the kind consideration of the Board of National Education.

Signed**, Michael Fitzgerald,** R.C. Archdeacon & P. P. of Ballingarry.

P.S.....My own tithe to the proposed site is founded on the assignment of a lease under William Scanlan, Esq. for the term mentioned above three young lives and thirty one years after - the tithe being in all respects quite unexceptionable

The Superintendent investigated the application and filled in his report sheet which entailed answering a series of standard questions concerning the application. Among his replies he submitted as follows :

Townland = Knightstown, in the centre of the town.
Size of school = Forty four feet by sixty feet.
Proposed number to school : Males = 360. Females = 140.
The population of the parish is over 7,000 of whom 4,500 would feel such a school an acquisition. In the town are two mixed schools and one for females exclusively, not capable of accommodating 50 pupils each and usually thronged, one at Fortwilliam, same district; one at Lisamota, same district; one at Kilmicheal, same district and one at Knockfierna, No. 3 District, each attended by from eighty to one hundred pupils but not capable of accommodating half the number. The **Rev. Mr. Gubbins** objects on two principles: general unsoundness in the system and that this school being built would preclude the chance of having one upon a more sound system. I find the entire town of Ballingarry with a population of nearly three thousand extremely dependent upon two or three schools of a very inferior class without any accommodation. The population, including a circuit of two and a half miles, cannot be less than four thousand. Upon those grounds would recommend that it be entertained favorably. He further states 'while stopping at the Hotel with a view to the inspection of Baleanlanan and Castletown schools, **Mary Parsons** asked me about this application, expressing the greatest interest in it. Date of visit 25 Feb. 1841. **Michael McSheehy,** Superintendent of National Schools.
A decision to grant aid the building of the school was given on 31 March, 1841 but subject to a qualification viz. 'that as the --- and Grantor is only a tenant under a lease and therefore liable to eviction it will be necessary for the Trustees to covenant to indemnify the Board to the full extent of the Grant.'

The school was formally opened on 8 November, 1841 under the 'superintendance' of **Michael Shanahan,** aged 23, the first teacher. In 1842 an application was made for the salary of Michael Shanahan. In the application it stated that Mr. Shanahan had been inspected by the school Superintendent Mr. McSheehy, there were local funds of £10 to meet the teachers pay 'as nearly as I can judge', and the scholars pay 'from 3/= per quarter to 6d per quarter.' Mr. Shanahan had one school room and 75 pupils (male). The application was successful and Mr. Shanahan was awarded a salary of £8 from 1 Nov.

In 1841 the school was grant aided by £134 for building, £15 for fitting up and £2-8-6 for requisitions. Local contributions were £106.oo

In 1842 an application was made for the salary of **Mary Ryan,** (24), the first female teacher. In the application it was stated that 'she was recommended to the priest by some very respectable persons in the City of Limerick of which city she was then a resident.' There were 55 scholars, all females. They paid from 5/= to 2/= per quarter. It also stated that there was an assistant (female) employed. The application was successful and Mary Ryan was awarded a salary of £8 from Nov.1, 1841. An idea of the running costs of the school is given by the following list of requisites costs:

1842 = £01-07-11	1843 = £01-07-11	1844 = £00-12-11
1845 = £00-10-00	1847 = £00-14-10	1849 = £03-06-09

As well as Michael Shanahan, the following were identified as teaching in Ballingarry National School: 1843, **James Quinlan** 1845, **Pat Shanahan,** and 1849 **James Moore.** As well as those female teachers already mentioned **Margaret O'Dwyer** is shown as a teacher in 1853. On 26 July, 1864 an application for salary for an assistant teacher, male, was made in respect of **Edmund Leahy**, aged 18. It was stated he was a former pupil of the school. In the course of recommending this application the Inspector wrote: 'The Ballingarry schools are rising very much in public estimation; the manager gives a good deal of attention to them in which he is ably assisted by his two curates, and the teachers are very painstaking. In consequence of their ----? the attendance has increased very much so that I would strongly recommend the application to be granted. Dated 29 Aug. 1864**.** The Inspector adds a note - 'the school had just been re-opened on the day after Midsummer Vacation'. In the correspondence dealing with this application for salary in 1864, the following teachers were identified by name: **Patrick Coghlan** and **Patrick Bouhan**. They were teaching 143 boys, and the average attendance for the previous six months were 90.4 days. **Edmund Leahy** was assistant teacher. The female teachers were: **Ellen Coghlan, Mary Tuohill** and **Mary McInerney**. In 1882 the following teachers were identified as teaching in Ballingarry: Principal **Timothy O'Regan**, Asst. **Timothy Condon**, Asst. **John O'Regan**. The monitors were **Thomas Kerriss** and **Denis O'Regan.** In 1886 an application for a salary for an Assistant Teacher was made in respect of **Margaret Blake.** She was baptised 21-01-1865. She initially taught as a monitor and continued her services thereafter.

The Convent School.

Late in 1887 or early in 1888 a decision was taken to split the National school by taking the girls out of it and having them taught by the Sisters of Mercy in a separate school. There were on average 127.2 pupils for the quarter ended Sept. 1887. On the return for that quarter it states that there was no school on 5th July as 'Races Convenient.' The teachers in the old school on 30 Sept. 1887 were: Principal, **Mary McNamara.** The two Assistant teachers were **Mary O'Connell** and **Margaret Blake.** The monitor was **Hannah Cullom,** aged 14. On the 25th May, 1888 the OPW approved a loan of £1,000 to be applied as follows: £500 to recoup the amount already expended on the school house which is partly built and £500 to complete the undertaking. The file for quarter ended Sept. 1888 records that the teachers in the school at dissolution were retired and **Hannah Cullom** was transferred to the new school.

The following information was supplied to me by Sr. Delia Curtin, Convent of Mercy, Abbeyfeale.
It is reproduced here with her kind permission.

At the request of the Parish Priest, Ballingarry, the following Sisters went to Ballingarry -

1. **Rev. Mother** (at that time) **de Sales Cotter,** (1st May, 1830 - 23rd Feb, 1902)
2. **Sr. M. Gonzaga Curtin,** (15th Feb. 1857 - 26th March, 1929)
3. **Sr. M. Baptist McSweeney,** (11th Nov. 1860 - 28th Jan. 1945) and
4. **Sr. M. Agnes Curtin**, (1st Sept. 1864 - 25th Dec. 1940)

The circumstances of the foundation were as follows. The Turrett House was offered to the parish priest - **Rev. Timothy Ryan Shanahan**. He had just built a new parochial residence. The cost of the original building (the convent) was £3,000. Money was raised in the USA. It was built on a site formerly occupied by Echo Lodge - a long thatched dwelling. He had therefore two residences at his disposal. Through Most Rev. **Dr. Dwyer**, Bishop of Limerick and at his request, the Sisters set out from Abbeyfeale. They travelled by train to Rathkeale, accompanied by **Rev. Timothy Curtin,** later Parish Priest of Croom and **Rev. Casey,** P.P. of Abbeyfeale.

At Rathkeale they were met by **Rev. T. R. Shanahan**, P.P. Ballingarry and **Rev. T. Liston,** C.C. Rathkeale. They travelled by horse-drawn carriage to Ballingarry where they were met by a big crowd from Ballingarry, Granagh and the surrounding parishes. The Redemptorist Fathers were giving a mission in the parish at the time and they had organised the children in procession to the then parochial house and now to become a Convent. The local band from Rathkeale played. When the carriage reached the entrance door **Father Shanahan** made a formal speech of welcome, on his own behalf and on behalf of the parishioners. Benediction of the Blessed Sacrament was given in the front hall. Crowds who could not get in knelt outside in the lawn. It was the 15th. August, 1888. The new school was in process of being built but was not yet ready, so the summer vacation was prolonged until 24th Sept., 1888. The attendance at the school rose from about 90 to 280. Classes were also held in the Convent itself. It is not clear, from the account given, if the Sisters actually taught for some time in the old school (in Turrett Street). The rise in attendance would seem to point to this. *(My thanks to Sr. Curtin for above.)*

Rathkeale. Nov 2nd. 1888.

Gentlemen,

In answer to letter (L15440) of 30th October I beg to submit the following report with regard to the changes in the working and arrangements of the above school. The old school (Ballingarry Female) closed for vacation on the 14th August, 1888 and when it was re-opened after vacation on the 25th September, 1888 it was placed in the charge of the Sisters of Mercy, the services of the old staff, save one paid monitor thus disposed with. The new teaching staff consists of six members of the Community, 1 monitor paid by the Commissioners and eight monitors paid by the Community. New schoolrooms, adjoining the Convent and capable of containing about 300 pupils, have been in use since 25th September. Two of these school rooms will be devoted to the use of a thoroughly organized Infants Department, including both boys and girls, and three for the use of the remaining classes. The schoolrooms are now complete, with the exception of maps, desks and forms. At present the old desks and forms of the Ballingarry Female school are being used but new ones have been ordered to replace these. The average attendance for the month of October, 1888 was as follows: Boys, 39. Girls, 209.

I am, Your Obedient Servant, **John McNeill**.

The Secretaries, Education Board.

An application form was submitted on Nov 12,1888 applying for salaries and aid towards books. The following points were made.

1. The school was established on 25 September, 1888.
2. Situated in town of Ballingarry. Population about 400.
3. Manager's name: Revd. **Timothy Ryan Shanahan**, P.P.
4. The teachers are Sisters of Mercy.
5. They left Abbeyfeale Convent to take charge of present school.
6. The school was erected on a loan from Board of Works; is single storied and has five apartments.
7. Local funds available = £50.
8. Local fund is raised through proceeds of annual sermon and various similar sources.
9. School fees are charged as follows:10/= a quarter for instrumental music and 5/= a quarter for French.
10. Average attendances: September 1888 = 184.5, Male and Female.
    October 1888 = Male, 39.8. Female, 209.8
11. Patron: the Bishop of Limerick. R.C.

The new school had teething problems as the following unsigned letter reveals.

Ballingarry Convent National School.
17 November, 1888.
The teachers of the above school will thank the Secretaries if they kindly send free stock as soon as possible. The school is furnished and the attendance increasing daily. It is very difficult to manage an Infant class room of about 150 pupils without tablets or black boards. The supply of slates is scanty, no maps or other things that are indispensibly necessary.

This undated letter was sent to the Board of Education.

Dear Sir,
I reply to your communication 12th inst. (which remained unanswered by me owing to a sharp attack of bronchitis.) The new schools are built on my own lands, but at the instance of the Board of Works, I have made a sub-lease of them and of a large plot of ground adjoining for the purpose of a playground, to myself and to another, at the nominal rent of one shilling a year in view of my obtaining the desired loan from the Board. The schools are, I am happy to say, a grand success. On last week the average attendance was over 280, almost treble the highest attendance ever attained. This is most satisfactory considering that it was only on the 25th September last the Sisters took charge of them and I am

confident the attendance will reach a much higher figure. The Patron is the Bishop, the most Rev. **Dr. O'Dwyer,** the Palace, Limerick or his successor for the time being. I am myself the manager. **James Mangan** and **D. Hallinan**, two of the persons named in the deed of 1841 are dead, the third, **Michael Hallinan** is living. The schools were hitherto used distinctly as male & female schools - the male school on the ground floor, the female school overhead. I shall as soon as possible throw in the female school, now vacant, into the male school and thus provide for it additional accommodation for a long time much needed.
I Remain Dear Sir, Yours Very Truly, **T. R. Shanahan.** By reference to the Sisters above this letter would be dated 1889. The Board queried the accuracy of the fate of **D. Hallinan** and Fr. Shanahan had to ruefully admit that in fact **D. Hallinan** was still living but Michael had died.

Granagh National School.

On 4 March, 1856 a Request for Aid for Teachers Salaries and Books Supply was made to the Board. The following are extracts from the application:

Description: Ballingarry is in a westerly direction. House (School) is divided into two apartments, newly thatched and well lighted. There are two school rooms. One is 27ft. long; 16ft. breadth and 10ft. high. The other is 17ft. long, 16ft. breadth and 10ft. high. There are five desks and seven forms in one room and three desks and five forms in the other. *(note: the word 'forum' was used in the report but was amended to read 'form' in each case).* All are in good condition. Names of the teachers were **Michael Monckton**, age 48 and **Margaret Monckton**, age 19. The average attendance at present is 88 males and 80 females. The school hours are 10.00am to 3.30pm, Monday to Friday. An hour each day is set aside for Religious Instruction. Books used in the school are those published by the Board, namely, 1st, 2nd, 3rd, 4th and 5th Books. Visitors are admitted during school hours. The manager was **Rev. James H. Roche**, Ballingarry.

The report on this application is dated 10 March, 1856. It states: The school opened on 28 January, 1856. There are 100 dwellings within one half mile of the school. There is a school at the village of Knockfierna under CH. Ed. Soc. of which the Rector is Patron. It was stated that the previous school had been taken off the Commissioners Rolls on 31 December, 1855 as the teacher was ineffective, the house was unsuitable and the school was unsuccessful. *A note indentifies this school as Ballinleena.* The school is built of stone and lime. It is thatched. It was a private house adapted to the present purpose. The rent is £2 per annum payable to **James Lyons,** Granagh. The floor is of earth and rooms are plastered but not ceiled. There is no blackboard but they have a clock. Teachers annual income of school is about £8. The pupils attending are stated to be children of farmers labourers and poorer class generally.

On 1 March, 1856 it was decided to aid the school: £17.00 each to **Michael Monckton** and **Mary Monckton**. In August a book press and teachers desk was supplied.

On August 7th, 1858 the Board wrote to the manager and complained as follows: "It is forbidden by the Rules of the Board for a teacher in it's service to be connected with a public house. That therefore, this teacher (not named) must give up all connection with the public house herein referred to (not identified) or be prepared for the withdawal of his salary.' On 13 October, 1856 a letter requesting aid towards the salary of an Assistant teacher in Granagh National School was made. It stated that there were two teachers: **Michael Monckton**, £17 and **Margaret Monckton**, £14. There were two Assistant teachers: **Patrick Condon**, age 20 and **Mary Monckton,** age 23. Prior to this it was stated that **Patrick Condon** had conducted Ardagh school for three months. He left on 1 April, 1855. **Mary Monckton** had previously conducted Ballinlena School for two years. She left on 2 Nov, 1855. They were appointed to Granagh School on 18 Aug, 1856. The school was described as having two apartments divided into male and female. On the rolls there were 123 males and 112 females. Average attendances were 83 males and 77 females. It was signed by (Rev) James H. Roche, Manager. This application was approved to the amount of £14 per assistant teacher.

In a file dated 25 Feb., 1861 there is a curious note with reference to **Mr. Enright's** letters.

If **Mr. Robinson** discharges his duties properly there will be no problem with the Board. No further details are given. On March 16, 1861 **Mrs. Long** becomes a teacher in what is now a mixed school. On 11 November, 1861 an evening school was established in Granagh. On 28 Nov, 1861 an application was made to the Board requesting aid for this evening school. The application was in question and answer format. The following points were made in the application: teachers were **John Long**,

Principal in Day School and **Michael Monckton**, Assistant in Day School. Classes were from 6.00 pm to 9.00 pm, Monday to Friday. On average there are 50 attending classes. They were all local workers. They paid one penny each per week but 'more than half are taught gratuitously.' The curriculum is the three 'R's - reading, writing and arithmetic. This application was signed by **Rev. James Enright**, Manager.

In dealing with this application the following information was given :

Date of Visit	16 Dec., 1861	
On Inspection	49 Males	11 Females
Average Attendance	40 ,,	8 ,,
Number on Books	42 ,,	9 ,,
Attendance at Day School	7 ,,	3 ,,
Average Age	14 ,,	12 ,,
Number of Adults	25 ,,	5 ,,
Average age Adults	20 ,,	18 ,,

It was stated in the report that the students (adults) were mostly employed locally as farm servants. The ages of the teachers were also given. **John Long**, Principal, age 22, **Michael Monckton**, Assistant, 61 and **Mary Long,** Assistant, 26. They were deemed to be competent and of good character. Recommended: 'Such a school as this will do great service to this neighbourhood. It is likely to be well attended. Aid is recommended.' Early in 1862 the sum of £5 was granted. This particular initiative lasted until 31 Oct, 1865 when an Inspector recommended that he was of the opinion that it is undesirable to continue grants to it.

   On August 5, 1867 the **Rev. C. McCarthy** became manager as **Rev. J. Enright** emigrated. **Michael Cahill** was an Assistant and **Thomas O'Sullivan** a Monitor. In 1869 teachers identified in Granagh were **Mary Twohill**, Principal and **Mary Long**. On 31 July, 1878 an application was made for salary of an Assistant teacher. This assistant was **Margaret Long**, age 19. On 3 Aug, 1878 the following information was supplied to the Board. **Ellen Joyce**, Principal. Average attendances in the female School:

Quarter Ended December, 1877	48.4
Quarter Ended March, 1878	58.2
Quarter Ended June, 1878	64.7
Quarter Ended September, 1878	59.3

The manager was the **Rev. T. R. Shanahan**. The result of this application was not noted.

In 1878 **Margaret Long**, now **Walshe**, was a teacher. On June 4, 1879 the Principal was reprimanded to keep the correct time as the school clock was forty minutes fast. On September 1, 1880 **Ellen Leeny** was Principal. In 1883 Miss **Margaret O'Brien,** now **FitzGerald,** is a teacher. In 1886 **David Cahill** was a Monitor. In May 11, 1891 **Margaret McEniry** was a teacher in Granagh. In 1896 **John Long** died. A request to the Board of Education for financial assistance for his widow and children was turned down on the basis that the Board had no power to dispense funds in this way. In 1899 the **Rev. W. Downes**, P.P., is the Manager.

PART X

Late 19th Century Records.

As the century draws to a close the need for genealogical records is not as acute due to the registration of births, deaths and marriages, greater use of newspapers for recording these events and the 1901 census. However, it is right to place as many people as possible in their place and in their time. These records help in this respect.

1864 July 22. Registry of Sheets and Notices. Posted by Patrick Boyse on the Court House of Ballingary and retained a copy in his own house.

1874 - 1879. Grand Jury Records. *(Nat. Lib. ref IR 94144 L3)*

1874. Contracts commencing Summer. Michael Cronin, work at Glenwilliam and the upper cross at Ballingarry, including footpaths and pavements. Thomas Ahern, between Granagh chapel and Fort Edmond. Patrick Gilborne, between Kilnamona and Kilcroig Cross. William Purcell, between Dollas and Ballyknockane. Michael Lee, between Sunday's Well, 3 roads at Clounregan and the barony bounds at Doonbeirne.

1875. Contracts commencing Spring. James Hickey, the Commons and Kilmacow. William Anderson, between Castletown and Coolruss.

1875. Contracts commencing Summer. Henry Preston, between new line at Shanavoho and the ford near Granagh lime-kiln. Robert Morrison, between Quin's cross at Gortroe and bounds Gurteen / Kilmurry.

1876. Contracts commencing Spring. William Anderson between Patrick Daly's in Doroclogh and Quin's house at Gortroe. Daniel Byrne, between Andew Moylan's house and the bounds of the County Cork.

Other contractors mentioned in this decade around the Ballingarry area were: Joseph H. Bouchier, Edmund Burns, John Corkery, Michael Danaher, Richard Fennell, David Hickey, Cornelius O'Brien, William O'Connell and John Reidy.

1878. Summer Assize. At these Assizes it was also resolved that the Special Road Session previous to Summer Assizes for the Barony of Upper Connelloe would be held on Friday, 9th May, 1879 in Ballingarry.

The following is an example of what was required of the 1879 contracts:

William Power. Between 3 roads at Lisamota and cross roads at Commons. To have a carriageway 20 feet wide. Annual supply 200 cubic yards of broken stone, or 200 of gravel, to be applied during the Winter and Spring months. Footpaths, channels, parapets etc. to be kept in repair.

Cornelius O'Brien, to close a dike and widen the road at Shanavough Church, near Thomas Bourke's house.

The sum of £1,200-17-09 was levied on the barony at these assizes.

1879. Cess Payers selected by the Grand Jury at Spring Assizes,
Robert Cox, Ballinamona. Patrick Hederman, Kilmore. Thomas Lloyd, Heathfield. Henry Sheehy, Fortwilliam.

Rathkeale Parish. To Henry Sheehy. Compensation for 11 winds of hay maliciously burned on the lands of Ballinamuckee on night of 6 August, 1878 - £25.

1886. Francis Guy's Postal Directory of Munster.
Ballingarry.

Post town and parish. Population of town, 795. Population of parish, 3,143. The town is situated in the pleasing and sheltered valley on the road from Rathkeale to Charleville. Several religious houses were founded here at a very early period, and within the limits of the parish are traces of ancient buildings of various kinds. The adjoining parish of **Cloncagh,** population 624, served from this post office.

Postal address - Ballingarry, Limerick. Money order & telegraph office. Postmaster & stamp distributor John **Sheehy**. Conveyances - Adare (Limerick, Foynes and Newcastle ry.) nearest station. A public mail car in conjunction with trains from Adare. Poor Law Union of Croom. Dispensary and registration district of Castletown, population 5,279, including electoral divisions of Ballingarry, Ballyagran, Ballygrennan,

Ballynoe, Castletown and Coolrus. Medical Officer & Registrar is Dr. H. G. **Moloney**. The Relieving Officer is Richard **Liston.** Rate Collector is John **Costelloe** and Edward **Vaughan** is the Clerk of Petty Sessions. Petty sessions are held every second Wednesday. The population of the district is 7,390. It is the Quarter Sessions District of Rathkeale and the constabulary district of Adare. Sergeant P. **McCormack** is in charge of Ballingarry Station.

Gentry and Clergy.
Thomas R. D. Atkinson, J.P., Glenwilliam Castle.
Robert Cox, Ballinamona.　　　　　　Robert Cox, Ballynoe.
Rev. Timothy Curtin, C.C.　　　　　　Rev. William Fitzgerald, C.C.
Grady Conyers, Ashborough.　　　　　Rev. John Johnson. A.B., Rector.
Henry Moloney, MD; MCH; QUI; LM.　Edmund Moroney, J.P., O Dellville.
Michael Scanlan, Ballyknockane.　　　Michael Scanlan, Kilbeg East.
Rev. Timothy Shanahan, P.P.　　　　　Charles Townley, Turrett House.
Thos. William Wilkinson, J.P., St. Oswalds.

National School Head teachers. Male, Timothy O'Regan. Female, Julia Guinea.
Hotel, Michael O'Connell.
Car owners were John Dunworth, John Griffin, Thomas Fitzpatrick and Andrew Nolan.
Cattle Dealers were Patrick Columb, Thomas, Daniel and Michael O'Connell, James Shanahan and John Supple.
Drapers were Henry O'Brien, Patrick Maher and Edward Hartnett.
Emigration Agents were Andrew Nolan and Maurice O'Regan.
Grocer: Andrew Nolan.
Shopkeepers were Stephen McCormack, Michael Maher, Henry O'Brien, Michael O'Connell and John Sheehy.
Tradesmen. Jeremiah Dineen and James McCormack were carpenters. Thomas Fennell, Daniel O'Shea and James Taylor were Smiths & Farriers. Daniel O'Mara was a bootmaker.
Vintners. Thomas Bourke, John Butler, Anne Bowen, Edward Hartnett, Michael Quaid and Daniel Tierney.

Principal Farmers, Ballingarry Parish.
John Bennett, Ballynahaha.　　　　　Michael Croake, Frankfort.
James Irwin, Frankfort　　　　　　　John E. Irwin, Ballykevan East
Charles McCarthy, Ballykevan West　Thomas McDonnell, Fortwilliam.
Ellen Mangan, Frankfort

Principal Farmers, Cloncagh Parish.

Condon, David. Ballinaroogamore South
Curtin, Michael. Gorteen East

Hannigan, Edward. Gortnacreha Lower

Keating, Mary. Ballybeggane
Lyons, Patrick. Ballynarooga
Quaid, George. Ballykennedy South
Wall, Patrick. Teernahilla

Condon, Margaret. Ballyhahil
Gilburne, Patrick. Ballynaroogamore
Howard, Bartholemew. Teerveena
Liston, James. Gortnacreha
McCarthy, Mary. Ballyhahil
Wall, Patrick. Gorteen west
Walsh, Eliza. Ballykennedy

1891 - 1895. Grand Jury Records.
1891. Names of people and townslands in the Ballingarry region.

Begley, Daniel	Clouncagh.	Bourke, Edmond	Ballyagran.
Carmody, Jeremiah	Kilfinny.	Casey, Patrick	Ballinamuckee.
Hickey, James	Clouncagh.	Hogan, Patrick	Lisamota.
Houlihan, James	Fortwilliam.	O'Brien, Daniel	Ballinaha.
O'Kelly, Thomas	Lisamota.	Tierney, Daniel	Ballingarry.
Tierney, Michael	Fortwilliam.		

1892.

Hickey, Timothy	Clouncagh.	O'Donnell, Thomas	Derryclough.
O'Donoghue, T.	Derryclough.	Kennedy, John	Derryclough.

1893.

Ahern, Denis	Ballynoe.	Ahern, Michael	Derraclogh.
Ambrose, Patrick	Ballyhahill.	Anderson, William	Ballynoe.
Blake, David	Derryclough.	Bresnihan, Cornelius	Gortroe.
Broderick, Thomas	Knockfierna.	Byrnes, Daniel	Knockfierna.
Cagney, Daniel	Ballinaha.	Cagney, John	Ballinaha.
Casey, James	Ballyguile.	Casey, Michael	Ballyea.
Clifford, John	Kilmihill.	Clifford, William	Kilmihill.
Curtin, Cornelius	Knockfierna.	Donohue, Daniel	Kilmihill.
Dore, James	Kilatal.	Fitzgibbon, John	Gortroe.
Fitzgibbon, Michael	Derryclough.	Hannan, Michael	Ballyea.
Hannon, John	Downes.	Hanrahan, Daniel	Morenane.
Harnett, William	Kilmore.	Hennessy, John	Ballyhahill.
Hickey, James	Kilmacow.	Hickey, James	Lisduff.
Howard, Bartholemew	Tiervena.	Howard, James	Ballingarry.

Keating, John	Ballyroe.	Kilbridge, John	Kilmacow.
Lee, James	Ballynoe.	Mahony, William	Coolruss.
McCann, John	Caherhennessy.	McDonagh, Pat	Cappanihane.
Morrissey, Edmond	Lisduane.	Morrison, Robert	Derryclough.
Murphy, Michael	Gurteen.	Murphy, Patrick	Derryclough.
Noonan, Edmund	Kilmihill.	O'Brien, David	Ballingarry.
O'Brien, Thomas	Ballinaha.	O'Brien, William	Doorlusbeg.
O'Connor, John	Glenwilliam.	O'Grady, Michael	Woodstock.
O'Shea, Thomas	Coolruss.	Roche, Maurice	Kilnamona.
Quaid, John	Gortroe.	Shea, Daniel	Ballingarry
White, John	Knockfierna.		

1894.

Begley, Daniel	Clouncagh	Bridgeman, John	Knockfierna
Corkery, John	Heathfield	Fitzgibbon, George	Ballygrennan
Hanly, Bartholemew	Clouncagh	Hartnett, Timothy	Ballyroe
O'Grady, Michael	Woodstock		

1895. Cess Tax payers selected by the Grand Jury at Spring Assizes, Conneloe Upper.

William Irwin, Lisheensheela, Kilmeedy. Grady Conyers, Ashboro, Ballingarry.
James Gorman, Kilmacow, Ballingarry. John O'Keeffe, Clonregan, Ballingarry.

1895. Lower Connelloe. Henry Sheehy, Springmount, Ballingarry.

1894. Slaters Commercial Directory.
County Limerick.

His description of the county is similar to previous directories but he makes the following interesting observations. Pasturage is now more attended to than tillage; large quantities of agricultural produce are exported from the county, the butter being a great commodity. The manufactures are coarse woollens, paper, flour and meal. The entire face of the country, notwithstanding it's great natural fertility, presents a denuded appearance from the paucity of woodlands and hedgerows, those great embellishments of scenery.

General Statistics.
Asses = 10,815.
Milch Cows = 101,652.
Sheep, over 1 year = 49,498.
Pigs = 53,924.
Poultry = 446,074.
Tillage Including Meadow = 161,253 acres
Turf Bog = 11,643 acres
Barren Mountain = 24,925 acres

Horses = 17,778.
Cattle,other = 140,259.
under 1 year = 30,102.
Goats = 14,356.
Plantation = 8,431 acres
Pasture = 425,256 acres
Marsh = 4,592 acres
Roads,Fences,etc = 26,268 acres
Total = 662,368 acres

BALLINGARRY.
Post, Money Order & Telegraph Office & Savings Bank. Edmond **Sheehy**, postmaster. Letters from Limerick arrive at 6.40a.m. & 7.30p.m. Dispatched at 8.00 & 8.25 p.m. The petty sessional district comprises 36,849 acres; containing 108 townlands; Edward **Vaughan**, clerk.

Clergymen. Church Of Ireland, Rev.George Dart. Catholic, Rev.Timothy Shanahan, P.P., Rev. Mortimer McCoy, C.C. and Rev. Stephen Culhane, C.C.

Private Residents.
Atkinson, Thomas Durbin, J.P., Glenwilliam Castle.
Conyers, George F., Liskennett   Cox, Thomas, J.P.
Hedderman, Daniel, J.P., Ballyneale   McDonnell, Thomas. Fortwilliam
Moloney, Henry G., M.D., Odell Ville
Moroney, Edmund, J.P., Odell Ville
Wilkinson, Thos. Wm., J.P., St.Oswald's

Shopkeepers.
Thomas Burke, John Butler, Julia Guinea, Edward Hartnett, Andrew Nolan, Michael O'Connell, Michael Quaid and Edmond Sheehy.

Medical Doctor.
Moloney, Henry G.; M.D., Odell Ville. Physician & Surgeon. Medical Officer,Castletown dispensary district.

Farmers.
John Bennet, Ballinaha. Michael Croke, Frankfort. William Hedderman, Ballygrennan. James Irwin, Frankfort and Thomas McDonnell, Fortwilliam.

PART XI

C. of I. Births, Deaths and Marriages

The final section of this book is the traditional one of births, marriages and deaths. While researching these records I was able to identify families and at the end I have listed these.

Births / Baptisms in Ballingarry, 1800 - 1869.

The following are extracts from the Church of Ireland parish records of Ballingarry held on microfilm in the National Archives. Ref. No MFCI - Reel 16. In some cases it is very hard to make out the correct spelling. In any cases of doubt these microfilm records should be consulted. I have used abbreviations where I thought appropiate. In the absence of a townland I have used the townland column for explanatory comments like father's profession.

Year	Date	Name	Parent(s)	Townland
1800	Jan, 19	**Massy**, Wm. Godfrey	George	Glenwilliam
	Apr, 11	**Cox,** Mary	William	Ballynoe
	May, 04	**Mason**, Clifford	John	Lisdwane
1801	Jan, 11	**Scanlan,** John	Michael, jnr	The Grove.
	Mar, 22	**Cox** , Constance	William	Ballinoe.
	May, 25	**Fetherston,** Robert	Robert, M.D.	- - - - - - -
	Nov, 20	**Graves**, Sidney Sybella	Revd. John	Ballingarry.
	Dec, 01	**Massy,** John	George	Glenwilliam.
1802	Jan, 24	**Browne,** John (At the Grove)	John	Danesfort
	Mar, 07	**Mahony,** Margaret	Thomas	Ballinaruga.
	Aug, 02	**Cox,** Aphra Augusta	William	Ballinoe.

Year	Date	Name	Parent(s)	Townland
1803	--- --	**Tuthill,** Deborah Frances	Mrs. Tuthill	Ballyscanlan.
	Mar, 14	**Lee,** Patrick Peppard	Patt	Ballyscanlan.
		(Patt from Cappagh, Rathkeale Parish.)		
	Mar 14	**Field,** Deborah Frances	----	Ballyscanlon
	Mar 16	**Odell,** Thomas Alexander	John	Odellville.
		(John, Late a Lieutenant in the Navy.)		
	Jun 08	**Graves,** Harry	Rev. John	Ballingarry
	Sep 08	**Massy,** Rosina	George	Glenwilliam.
	Sep 19	**Cliffs,** Anthony	John	Kilfinny.
		(Father a Freeholder of Kilfinny Parish: brought to Ballingarry.)		
1804	Jun 02	**Odell,** Anna Maria	John	Ballingarry
	Nov 05	**Brown,** William	Captain John	The Grove.
	Dec 16	**Massy,** William	George	Glenwilliam.
1805	--- --	**Airey,** George	John	Glanaraha.
	Aug 06	**Odell,** Sarah	John	Turrett St.
	Sep 17	**Graves,** Catherine Anne	Rev. John	Fortwilliam.
	Nov 29	**Odell,** John	Thomas	Odelville.
1806	Apr 13	**Brown,** Sarah	Captain John	Danesfort.
	Oct 15	**Cox,** Elizabeth Vowel	William	Ballinoe.
	Nov 23	**Odell,** Henry	T. A.	Odelville.
1807	Jan 4	**Massy,** William	George	Glenwilliam.
	Feb 1	**Fitzgibbon,** Sarah Eliza	Thomas ?	The Turrett.
		(Grand-daughter of Thomas Odell.)		
	May 25	**Brown,** Henry	John	Danesfort.
	Jul 20	**Scanlan,** Hugh Wheeler	Michael	Ballyknockane.
	Jul 28	**Monkton,** Mary Anne	George	Ashborough.
	Sep 08	**Graves,** Sybilla	Rev. W.	Fortwilliam.
	Dec 03	**Odell,** Thomas Henry	T. A.	Odelville.
1808	Jan 08	**Massy,** Godfrey	George	Glenwilliam.
	Mar 03	**Odell,** Robert	Robert	The Grove.
	Mar 05	**Gubbings,** Robert	Robert	The Grove.
	May 18	**Raymond,** Samuel	James	The Grove.
1809	Feb 08	**Tavern,** Joseph	Private E. D.	7th Drag. Grds.
	Mar 05	**Navenham,** Noble H.	Noble H.	--------
	Apr 09	**Elliott,** William John	Sergeant.	7th Drag. Grds.
	Jul 30	**Graves,** Rachel Dundas	Rev. J.	Fortwilliam.
1809	Jul 30	**Monkton,** Margaret	George	Ballingarry
	--- --	**Brown,** Thos. Anty. Southwell	John	Danesfort.
	--- --	**Raymond,** Aphra	James	--------

Year	Date	Name	Parent(s)	Townland
1810	May 28	**Magree,** George Henry	- - - - -	Glenwilliam.
		(Son of the Widow Magree, late of Limerick.)		
	Nov 03	**Monkton,** John Cornwall	George }	
		Monkton, Miles	George } Twins	Ballingarry
	Nov 4	**Odell,** Sarah Pierce	Thomas A.	Odellville.
	Dec 10	**Scanlan,** Matthew	Michael	Ballyknockane.
	Dec 23	**Casey,** Henry	Dobbyn	Ashborough.
1811	Mar 15	**Graves,** Margt. Cath.	Rev. John	Fortwilliam.
	Jun 9	**Brown,** Frances	John	Ballyknockane
		(John a Captain in the Co. Limerick Militia.)		
	Sep 13	**Massy,** Hugh	George	Glenwilliam.
	Oct 23	**Abbott,** Sarah Eliza	John	Turrett St.
	Oct 27	**Chadwicke;** Thomas Alexander		
		(Father in the Tipperary Militia, at Odellville.)		
1812	Jan 15	**Brazil,** Petty Lucinda	Mr. Brazil	Glenwilliam.
	Apr 19	**Odell,** Samuel	T. A.	Odellville.
	May 14	**Graves,** William James	Rev. John	Ballingarry
1813	Jan 31	**Woods,** Mary Ann	Joseph	1st Drag. Grds.
	Feb 7	**Ram,** Elizabeth	William,	1st Drag. Grds.
	Apr 16	**Odell,** Mildred	Councelor	The Grove.
	Jun 19	**Monkton,** Sarah Elizabeth	George	Ballingarry
	Sep 8	**Butcher,** Mary	Richard	1st Drag. Grds.
1814	Mar 16	**Raymond,** Catherine	James	Ballyknockane.
		(of Hollywood)		
	Apr 5	**Graves,** Margaret Elizabeth	Rev. John	Ballingarry.
	Jun 26	**Odell,** Catherine	T. A.	Odellville.
1816	Jan 22	**Raymond,** Frances	James	The Grove.
	Feb 20	**Graves,** Elizabeth Jane	Rev. John	Ballingarry.
1817	Jan 26	**Casey,** George Monkton	Dobbyn	Ballingarry.
	Jun --	**Brown,** Phoebe	John	Coolruss.
1818	May 15	**Scanlan,** Constance	Michael	Ballyknockane.
1819	Jan xx	**Odell,** Maria	Major	Ashborough.
	Apr 3	**Raymond,** John Crone	James	The Grove.
1819	Jul 11	------, Mary	A foundling	Ballingarry.
	Aug 25	**Odell,** Edward	Robert	Ballyroe.
1820	Feb 20	**Massy,** William Hamo	George, Eliza	Glenwilliam.
	Feb xx	**Odell,** Henry	Thomas/	
			Amelia	Odellville.
	Feb xx	- - -, - - - -	A foundling	Ballingarry.

Year	Date	Name	Parent(s)	Townland
1820	--- --	**Cox**, Eliza	John / Catherine	Ballinamona
	--- --	**Ryan**, Margaret Lucy Odell	-------	Ballyhahill
1821	Aug 20	**Massy**, Aphra	George	Glenwilliam.
1822	Jan 27	**Odell**, Henry	Major / Jane	--------
	May 12	**Dent**, Hobart	Benjamin / Catherine	42nd Regiment.
	May 19	**Skinner**, Robert	Robert	42nd Regiment.
	Jul 15	**Massy**, Eliza Maria	George	Glenwilliam
	Sep 29	**Dixon**, Priscilla	John / Anne	1st Rifle Brig.
1823	Mar 5	**Odell**, Frances Sophia	Robert Deane	--------
	May 3	**Hayes**, Maria	Benjamin / Mary	1st Rifle Brig.
	Jul 28	**Odell**, Alexander John	T. A./ Emilia	Odellville.
	Aug 3	**Balls**, Mary Anne	Thomas / Elizabeth	1st Rifle Brig.
	Oct 23	**Nash**, Frances Jackson	Capt. Edmond	--------
	Nov 25	**Wood**, William	Humphrey / Anne	39th Reg. Foot.
	Dec 24	**Davis**, Mary	Richard / Margaret	39th Reg. Foot.
1824	Feb 22	**Moore**, Mary	William / Martha	A constable
	Mar 14	**Gibbings**, Arthur	Rev.Thomas / Agnes	Charleville.
		(Rev. Thomas, Vicar. Child born in Charleville)		
	Apr 23	**Odell**, Anne	Major / Jane	Ashborough.
	May 20	**Hoseland**, James	Charles / Maria.	Corp. 39th Foot
	Jun 6	**Gasore**, Mary Anne	John	A constable.
1824	Jul 24	**Healy**, Christopher	John / Mary	Ballingarry
	Sep 3	**Ryan**, Southwell William	Southwell	--------
	Dec 12	**Leysant**, Mary Anne	John A./ Maryanne	6th Rgt. Foot
1825	Mar 5	**Daxon**, Richard Power	William	Ballinakill
		(William from Kilmorane, Co. Clare.)		
	May 7	**------**, Kitty	A foundling.	Died July 19.
	Jul 17	**Odell**, Henry Crone	Robert Deane	
	Oct 30	**Graham**, Henry	Henry / Catherine	1st Rifle Brig.
	Nov 23	**Stavally**, James	Robert J.	Newcastle W.
1825	Dec 4	**Lewes**, Barbara	Peter / Anne	A constable
	Dec 5	**Perkins**, Eliza	Sylvan	--------
	Dec 19	**Langton**, Donas?	James / Barbara	Coolruss.
		(Baptised in Coolruss by Rev. Robert Fitzgerald.)		

Year	Date	Name	Parent(s)	Townland
1826	Jan 8	**Healy**, Richard	John / Mary	- - - - - - -
	Feb 19	**Smith**, Sarah	Robert / Margaret	Limerick.
	Feb 23	**Odell**, Edmund Westropp	Major Thomas/ J. Caroline	Ashborough.
	Feb 27	**Power**, William Daxon	Samuel D.	Ballinahaha.
	Jul 25	**Daxon**, Francis	Richard / Aphra	Ballyknockane
	Aug 17	**Massy**, George Rollo	George	Glenwilliam.
	Aug 24	**Moore**, Martha	William	The Grove.
	Aug 29	**Barlow**, Maria	John	25th Rgt. Ft.
	Oct 31	**Tarff ?**, Eliza	Joseph / Eliza	Coolruss.
	Dec 31	**Davis**, ------	John / Elizabeth	26th Rgt.Ft.
1827	Mar 31	**Gibbings**, William Robert	Revd.	Glebe House
	Apr 23	**Nash**, William	Capt. Edmund	Fort Edmond.
	May 28	**Mason**, Henry Robert	Southwell	
1827	May 28	**Hodgins**, Eliza	Edmond / Jane	A constable.
	Jun 28	**Ryan**, Henry Robert	Southwell / Anne	Clerk/Sexton
	Aug 28	**Standish**, John Langford	Richard / Elizabeth	Frankfort.
	Sep 25	**Healy**, John	John / Mary	Ballingarry.
	Sep 28	**Harte**, Helena Alicia	Sam. Dickson / Anne	Ballingarry.
	Oct 20	**Fisher**, Mary Rebecca	James / Aphra	Limerick.
	Nov 3	**Crowley**, Jane	Thomas,	Scrip.Reader
1828	Feb 1	**Moore**, Martha	William.	- - - - - - -
	Feb 7	**Daxon**, Mary	Richard	Ballinahaha.
	Feb 17	**Moore**, Jane	William	37th Rgt. Ft.
	Mar 22	**Donnelly**, Mary Anne		A constable
	Mar 31	**Massy**, Hugh Ingoldsby	George	Glenwilliam.
	May xx	**Alexander**, John	James / Elizabeth	A constable.
	Sep 27	**Lorzet?**, Rebecca	Peter / Anne	A constable.
	Nov 29	**Holmes**, Edmund	John / Bridget	Ballingarry.
	Dec 3	**Standish**, William Henry	Richard	Frankfort.
	Dec 21	**Browning**, William Thomas		A constable
1829	Mar 1	-----, Jane	A foundling	Ballingarry.
	Mar 22	**Healy**, George	John / Mary	Ballingarry.

Year	Date	Name	Parent(s)	Townland
1829	Mar 22	**Fisher,** Aphra Jas. Constance	James / Aphra	Limerick.
	Mar 25	**Odell,** Henry Edmund	Major T./ Jane	Ashborough.
	Apr 26	**Cox,** Rosetta	William/ Elizabeth	Ballyneale.
1829	May 10	**Partridge,** Anne	Richard / Ellen	36th Regt. Foot
	May 11	**Marks,** S.	John	Fort Edmund.
	May 17	**Richardson,** Samuel	Colour Sgt./ Ellen	36th Rgt. Ft.
	Jun 11	**Graves,** Hugh Baker	Captain / Anne	Coolruss.
	Jun 12	**Odell,** William Fitzwilliam	Wm. Robt./ Catherine	Ballingarry.
	Aug 8	-----, Jane	A foundling	Ballingarry.
	Aug 10	**Massy,** Godfrey	George	Glenwilliam.
	Aug 16	**Daxon,** Aphra	R. Dickson / Aphra	Ballingarry.
	Oct 18	**Hodgins,** John	Edmund	A police sub-constable.
	Nov 22	**Odell,** Wycherly	Capt. Robt D.	Fortwilliam.
	Dec 25	**Standish,** Thomas	Richard	Frankfort.
1830	Jan 3	-----, Anne	A foundling	Ballingarry.
	Jan 3	**Alexander,** Thomas	James / Elizabeth	A constable.
	Feb 5	**Power,** Samuel Dickson	Samuel D.	Ballinakill.
	Sep 5	**Switzer,** Eliza	John/ Margaret	Ballingarry.
	Oct 30	**Hunter,** Milly Emily	Henry / Sarah	Rossmore.
	Nov 9	**Cox,** Mary	William	Ballinoe.
	Dec 9	**Massy,** Frances Scanlan	George	Glenwilliam.
1831	Jan 5	**Daxon,** Alice Anne	Richard D.	Ballyknockane
	Feb 6	**Loze,** Anne	Peter / Anne	A constable.
	Feb 7	**Hickie,** Alicia	Michael / Mary Anne	Ballingarry.
	Mar 17	**Healey,** James	John / Mary	Ballingarry.
	May 7	**Cox,** Constance	John / Barbara	Ballineale.
	May 8	**Alexander,** Elizabeth	James / Elizabeth	Ballingarry
	Jun 12	**Nash,** Frederick Singleton	----- / Maria,	Finchley. Croagh
	Jul 12	**Hanrahan,** Catherine	Laurence / Margaret	Caherhennessy
1831	Oct --	**Power,** -----	Samuel D.	Ballinakill.
	Oct 18	**Standish,** Milicent Anne	Richard	Frankfort.
	Nov 25	**Odell,** Selina Sarah	Wm. Rob./ Catherine	Ballingarry.

Year	Date	Name	Parent(s)	Townland
1831	Dec 31	**Lebert**, Anthony	Anthony / Eliza	Parish Clerk.
1832	Jan 19	**Hodges**, Mary	William	Scripture Reader.
	Feb 12	**Quilty**, Mary	John / Ellen,	Plasterer and slater
	Mar 4	**Hodgins**, James	Edmond / Jane	A constable.
	Jul 1	**Odell**, Caroline E.	Major T./ Jane Caroline	Ballingarry.
	Jul 15	**Cox**, Elizabeth	William	Ballineale.
	Jul 27	**Peppard**, Grace Eliz. Dowdal	John / Thomasina	Kilbeg
	Aug 12	**Switzer**, John Christopher	John, jnr./ Mary, nee Hodgins.	
	Aug xx	**Daxon**, Elizabeth	R. Dickson / Aphra	Ballingarry.
	Aug 21	**Gubbings**, Sarah Olivia	Revd. Thomas	Ballingarry.
	Sep 10	-------, William	A foundling	Ballingarry.
	Nov 23	**Standish**, Valentine	Richard	Frankfort.
1833	Jan 14	**Cox**, John	John	Ballynoe.
	Mar 10	**Healy**, Mary Anne	John / Mary	Ballingarry.
	Mar 14	**Hanrahan**, John	Laurence	Caherhennessy
	Mar 17	**O'Donnell**, Catherine	Elizabeth	
		(alias Hick, widow of Patt, late 50th Regiment of Foot.)		
	May 5	**Odell**, Isabella Catherine	Robert	Ballingarry.
	Sep 17	**Lebert**, Frances	Anthony / Eliza	Ballingarry.
	Oct 13	-----, Thomas	A foundling	Ballingarry.
1834	Jun 22	**Robinson**, Eliza	William / Mary Anne	A constable.
	May 23	**Quilty**, Anne	John / Ellen	Ballingarry.
	Oct 5	**Cox**, Frances	William	Ballyneale.
	Oct 12	**Switzer**, Jane	John	Ballingarry.
	Oct 15	**Standish**, Montgomery Agnew	Richard	Frankfort.
1834	- - - - -	**Hayes**, Bridget	Daniel / Mary	A weaver.
	- - - - -	**Cullinan**, Mary	Michael / Mary	Ballingarry.
1835	Jan 14	**Cox**, Elizabeth	John / Barbara	Ballyneale.
	Jun 23	**Scanlan**, Michael	William / Aphra	Ballyknockane
	Oct xx	**Dennehy**, Jeremiah	Daniel / Catherine	Grammer Teacher
1836	Jan 26	**Odell**, Helena Mary	John / Eliza H.	Odelville.
	Mar 6	**Odell**, Mary Charlotte	John	Ballingarry.
	Jun 24	**Hanrahan**, William	Laurence	Caherhennessy

Year	Date	Name	Parent(s)	Townland
1836	Jul 27	**Scanlan,** Constance Fennell	Matthew / Emily	Ballinaha
	Aug 20	**Scanlan,** Fanny	William	Ballyknockane
	Sep 4	**Sullivan,** John	William	Cappanihane.
	Oct 9	**Switzer,** Edward	John / Eliza	Ballingarry.
	Nov 15	**Echlin,** William	Henry	Ballingarry.
1837	Feb 17	**Dennehy,** Edmund	Daniel	Ballingarry.
	Mar 1	**Quilty,** Ellen	John/ Ellen	Ballingarry.
	Mar 21	**Cox,** William	William	Ballynoe.
	Mar 31	**Moore,** Eliza Louisa	James / Louisa	Glebe House
	Aug 7	**Brown,** Mildred	Wm./ Mildred	Springmount
	Nov 12	**Cox,** William Sidney	John / Barbara	Ballyneale.
	Dec 3	**Odell,** Annette	Robert / Eliza	Med. Doctor.
	Dec 27	-----, Ruth	A foundling	Ballingarry
	xxx xx	**Hayes,** John	Daniel / Mary	Ballingarry.
1838	Feb 11	**Odell,** Alexander	Alexander / Catherine	Ballyagran.
	Feb 21	**Scanlan,** John Brown	William / Aphra	Ballyknockane
	Mar 28	**Scanlan,** Frances	Matthew / Emily	Ballinaha.
1838	Apr 11	**Cox,** Ormsby (2nd son)	William / Elizabeth	Ballynoe.
	Apr 13	**Langford,** William	John Peter / Mary	Ballynoe.
	Jul 29	**Standish,** Jane	Richard	Frankfort.
1839	10 Feb	**Switzer,** Margaret	John	Ballingarry.
	25 Apr	**Culhane,** Maria	Michael / Sarah	Castletown.
	28 Apr	**Odell,** Emma	Robert	Ballingarry.
	Jun 23	**Slater,** John	John	Ballingarry.
	Aug 2	**Scanlan,** William	William / Aphra	Ballyknockane
	Aug 2	**Brown,** John	Wm./ Mildred	Fortwilliam
	Aug 19	-----, Mary	A foundling	Ballingarry.
1840	Jan 13	**Stuart,** Letitia Anne Matilda	Alex /	Vicar
	Feb 23	**Brown,** John	Henry / Sarah Elizabeth	Solicitor
	Feb 20	**Scanlan,** Aphra Phoebe	Matthew	Ballinaha.
	Feb x	**Patterson,** Elizabeth	James	Ballingarry.
	Mar 3	**Cox,** Vowel Sampson	John / Barbara	Ballyneale
	Aug 12	**Scanlan,** Michael	Hugh / Sarah	Kilbeg.
	Dec 4	**Dowling,** John	John / Grace	The Grove.
	-------	**Hayes,** Margaret	Daniel / Mary	Ballingarry.

Year	Date	Name	Parent(s)	Townland
1841	Apr 28	**Gubbins**, Alice	Rev. Geo./ Dorothea J.	The Glebe.
	May 10	**Dennehy**, Margaret	Daniel	Ballingarry.
	xxx xx	**Keily**, Simon	Michael / Jane	Ballingarry.
	Jul xx	**Odell**, Robert William	Robert, Med. Dr.	B'gy. Castle.
	Aug 29	**Chapman**, Selina (Shoemaker)	William / Mary	Monkstown.
1841	Sep 29	**Patterson**, Anne Jane	James	Ballingarry.
	Oct 21	**Scanlan**, Hugh Wheeler	William / Aphra	Ballyknockane
	Oct 28	**Scanlan**, Michael	Matthew	Ballinaha.
	Nov 26	**Standish**, Mary Frederika	Richard	Frankfort.
	--- --	**Reidy**, William	James / Mary	Ballingarry.
	--- --	**Alfred**, John	Robert / Jane	Head Const.
1842	Jan 5	**Brown**, Jane	Henry, a solicitor.	O'Brien's Br.
	May 9	**Ryan**, Richard Alexr.	Alexander	Ballingarry.
	Aug X	**Cox**, Barbara	John	Ballyneal.
	Sep 14	**Odell**, Edmund Cripps	Robert	The Castle.
	--- --	**Alfred**, Michael	Robert / Jane	Head Const.
1843	Jan 7	**Scanlan**, Aphra	Matthew / Meliora	Ballinaha.
	Jan 17	**Gubbins**, Edward Nugent	George	The Glebe.
	Feb 10	**Stark**, Elizabeth (Shoemaker)	Henry / Ellen	Coolruss.
	Feb 11	**Scanlan**, Matthew	William / Aphra	Ballyknockane
	Feb 14	**Cox**, Alice	William / Eliza	Ballynoe
	Jun xx	**Hosford**, Barbara Frances	James / Barbara Police Sergeant,	Castletown.
	Aug 6	**Patterson**, Maria	James	Ballingarry.
	Sep	**O'Kelly**, Vowel (Gatekeeper)	Patrick / Bridget	Ballinoe.
	Sep 14	**Quilty**, Millicent	John / Ellen	
	Dec 4	**Odell**, Richard	Robert / Eliza	The Castle.
	--- --	**Keily**, Jane	Michael / Jane	Ballingarry.
	--- --	**Chapman**, Edward	William / Mary	Shoemaker
1844	Feb 10	**Ryan**, Southwell John	Alexander / Catherine	Shoemaker
	May 4	**Scanlan**, Frances Constance	Hugh Wheeler / Sarah	Kilbeg.

Year	Date	Name	Parent(s)	Townland
1844	Jun 16	**Gubbins**, Georgina	George Gough	Ballingarry.
	Jun 30	**Keily**, Simon	Michael / Jane	Ballingarry.
	Jul 10	**Scanlan**, James Fisher	William / Aphra	Ballyknockane
	Jul 22	**Brown**, Thomas	Henry	O'Brien's Br.
	Oct 6	**Cox,** Catherine Georgina	John	Ballyneale.
	--- --	**Mahony**, Ellen	John	Limerick.
1845	Jan 3	**Keily**, Michael	Michael / Jane	Ballingarry.
	Apr 15	**de Massy**, George Thomas	W.H./ Mary Frances	Glenwilliam.
	Jun 8	**Odell**, Elizabeth Phoebe	Robert	The Castle.
	Jul 20	**Patterson**, William	James / Anne Jane	Scrip.Reader
	Sep 6	**Hunt,** Meliora Catherine	Damon / Sarah	Kilvestrone, Galway
	Sep 9	**Reidy**, Ellen	James	Knockfierna
	Dec xx	-----, Matilda	A foundling	Ballyhahil
	Dec 3	**Odell**, Meliora Dorothea	Thomas / Ann	The Cottage
	Dec 15	**Gubbins**, Henrietta	George	The Glebe.
	--- --	**Hayes**, Richard	Daniel / Mary	Ballingarry.
1846	Apr 6	**Ryan**, Francis Henry	Alexander	- - - - - - -
	May 20	**Griffin**, Bessie Maria Inez (Woodstock Cottage, A Gentleman.)	George / Aphra	Woodstock.
	Aug 24	**Massy**, William Hamo	William Hamo de	Glenwilliam.
	Sep 7	**O'Brien**, Margaret Anne	Michael / Mary	Shoemaker.
	Sep 24	**Bryan**, Margaret	Thomas / Eliza	Parish Clerk.
	Oct 22	**Quilty**, William	John / Ellen	Ballingarry.
	Oct --	**Cox**, Robert George	John / Barbara	Ballinaha.
	Oct 26	**Cleary**, Anne	John / Ellen	Schoolmaster.
1847	Mar 20	**Bennett**, Rosa	Thomas / Johanna	Listowel.
	--	**Scanlan**, Thomas Richard	William	Ballyknockane
	Jun --	**Odell**, Thomas Alexander;	Thomas / Anne	The Cottage.
	Aug 8	**Gubbins**, Eliz.Dorothea	Geo./ Dorothea	The Glebe.
	Aug 15	**Griffin**, Bridget Geraldine	Geo./ Aphra	The Abbey, Rathkeale
	Sep 20	**Odell,** William	Robert	Ballingarry.
	Nov 25	**Hunt**, Vere Dawson	Dawson / Sarah Pierce	Odellville.
	Dec 11	**Brown**, Samuel	Hugh / Mary.	64th Reg.Foot
	Dec 15	**McMinamy** ?, Agnes (Police Sergeant)	James / Barbara	Knockfierna.

Year	Date	Name	Parent(s)	Townland
1848	Jan 6	**Hay,** William	James / Margaret	64th Reg. Foot.
	Feb 26	**Bredim,** Alexander	Robert / Mary	64th Reg. Foot
	Apr 27	**Reidy,** Margaret	James / Mary	Ballingarry.
	May 9	**Patterson,** Maria }		
		Patterson, Olvinia } Twins	James	Ballingarry.
	Jun 11	**Cox,** George Hugh	John / Barbara	Ballinaha
	Aug 29	**Curtin,** Thomas	William / Mary	Ballingarry.
	Sep 7	**Odell,** Emily Bloomfield	Thos. Henry / Anne	The Cottage.
	Dec --	**Griffin,** Frances Aphra	George / Aphra	Rathkeale.
1849	Jan 7	**Vander-Kiste,** Margaret Elizia Constantia	John / Margaret	Dublin
	Feb 15	**Tighe,** Eliza	James / Prudence	Policeman, Bruree
	May 11	**Power,** Bessie Maria	Richard / Bessie	Ballinakill
	May 27	**Brett,** Ellen	Charles / Mary	Soldier.
	Jul 26	**Gubbins,** Wm.Launcelotte	Geo./ Dorothea	The Glebe .
	Aug 31	**Quinlan,** George	William / Margaret	Groom.
	Oct 2	**Sweeney,** Michael	Michael / Ansty	
	Oct 08	**Cleary,** Mary	John / Ellen	Schoolmaster.
	--- --	**Jones,** William	William / Eliza	Scrip. Reader.
1850	Feb 27	**Bryan,** Robert	Thomas / Eliza	Knockfierna.
	Mar 3	**O'Kelly,** Mary Anne	Pat / Bridget,	Inspector, Irish Police.
	Jun 12	**Dowling,** Edmond	Thos./ Johanna	Ballingarry.
	Jun 27	**Browne,** Sara Elizabeth	John / Eliza	Schoolmaster.
	Aug 03	**Power,** Anne Helena	Richard Pierce / Elizabeth Maria a.k.a. Bessie	Ballinakill.
	Oct 19	**Curtin,** John	William / Mary	Ballingarry.
1851	Feb 01	**Mahony,** James	Patrick / Catherine	
	Mar 3	**Odell,** William	William / Mary	Ballingarry.
	Mar 3	**Gubbins,** Arthur Gough	Geo./ Doro. Jane	The Glebe.
	Apr 13	**Odell,** Phoebe	Dr. Robert / Eliza	Ballingarry.
	May 24	**Gardiner,** Julia May (policeman)	William / Julia	Ballinoe
	Nov 9	**Donahy,** Jeremiah	Daniel / Catherine	Scrip. Reader
	Nov 15	**Downes,** James	James / Margaret	Ballingarry.
	Dec 26	**Power,** Meliora	Daniel / Kate	Ashborough.
1852	Feb 12	**Power,** Samuel Dickson	Richard / Bessie	Ballinakill

Year	Date	Name	Parent(s)	Townland
1852	Apr 4	**Noonan,** Ellen	Wm./ Margaret	Carpenter.
	Apr 4	**Berry,** Robert Edward. (Schoolmaster)	Thos. / Cath. Louisa	Knockfierna.
	Apr 07	**Browne,** Maria Catherine	John / Eliza	Parish Clerk
	Oct 15	**Gubbins,** Joseph Maynard	George / D. Jane	The Vicar
	Dec 13	**Stackpoole,** Frederick George. (Schoolmaster)	Thomas / Maria	Adare.
1853	Mar 01	**Power,** Edward Dickson	Dan. D./ Kate	Ashborough
	Apr --	**Power,** George Massy	Robt.P./ Bessie	Ballinakill.
	Jul 29	**Airey,** Mary	Robert / Mary	Whitesmith
	Nov 13	**Wilkinson,** William Percival. Baptised by C. Wilkinson, Curate. Meala Brae, Salop, at	Thomas William / Helena Rosalie St. Oswald's	
	Dec 16	**Clarke,** William	Laurence / Anne	Scrip. Reader
	--- --	**Mick,** Richard	Richard / Mary	Lisamota
1854	Feb 11	**Berry,** Maria Alice	Thomas	Knockfierna
	Mar 6	**Barrett,** May Ann Louisa	Mark / Mary Ann	Schoolmaster
	May 02	**Browne,** John Thomas	John / Eliza	Schoolmaster.
	Jul 21	**Halpin,** Henry Ross (Henry, a curate and his wife, Elizabeth Gaston)	William Henry	Ballingarry
	Aug 10	**Power,** Annabell Honoria	Dan.D./ Kate	Ashborough.
	Aug 11	**Lynch,** William	William / Mary	Knockfierna.
	Aug 12	**Cleary,** John Christopher	John / Ellen	Schoolmaster.
	Aug 20	**Graydon,** Samuel. (Henry a policeman)	Henry / Margaret	Knockfierna.
	Sep 27	**Downes,** Michael Wm. Pat	James / Mary	
1855	Jan 06	**Power,** Richard	Richard / Bessie	Ballinakill.
	Apr 07	**Brennan,** Jane	Denis / Jane	Glenwilliam.
	May 04	**Patterson,** Maria (James is a Scripture Reader.)	James / Anne Jane	Knockfierna.
	May 23	**Gubbins,** Charles Decianas O'Grady. and his wife, Dorothea Jane.	George Gough,	the Vicar The Glebe.
	Jul 19	**Halpin,** Hugh Gaston	Wm Henry / Eliz	Curate.
	Aug --	**Browne,** George Henry	John / Eliza	Schoolmaster.
	Dec 03	**Alfred,** Thomas	Robert / Jane	Head Constable
1856	Aug 07	**Shaughnessy,** John	John / Margaret	Glenwilliam.
	--- --	**Power,** Hamo Massy	Robt.P./ Bessie	Ballinakill.

Year	Date	Name	Parent(s)	Townland
1857	Feb 17	**Laffan**, Julia	Thomas / Jane	Slater
	Jun 11	**Graydon**, William	Henry / Margaret	Knockfierna.
	Aug 02	**Power,** John Thos. Smith	Danl.D / Kate	Ashborough.
	Nov 01	**Cronin**, Patrick	Michael / Catherine	
1858	Jun 10	**Brown,** William James	John / Eliza	Schoolmaster.
	Jun 17	**Sharpe**, Rebecca	Thomas / Fanny	Scrip.Reader.
	Aug 14	**Mick**, Clarinda }		
		Mick, Charlotte { Twins	Richard / Mary	Lisamota
	Dec 17	**O'Neil**, Margaret	Daniel / Anne	Schoolmaster.
1859	Feb 03	**Kiggell,** Anne Eliza Lucy	Samuel / Emily	G'wm Castle.
	Jul 19	**Sharpe**, Sarah	Thomas / Fanny	
	Aug 29	**Mick,** John	Richard / Mary	Lisamota.
1860	Feb 09	**Conyers,** Edw. Fitzgerald (F. = Fitzgerald.)	Grady F./Helena	Liskennett.
	Apr 23	**Madagan,** Edward	William/Julia	Schoolmaster.
	Jul 06	**Power,** John Thomas	Edward Jas./Bridget	Soldier.
	Sep 04	**Kiggell,** Lucy Emily.	Lancelot John/ Meliora	Wilton, R'keale
1861	Jan 26	**Sharpe,** William	Thomas / Fanny	Scrip. Reader.
	Mar 02	**Atkinson**, Emma Anne	Edward/Emma	Glenwilliam.
	Mar 31	**Greenham,** Frederick G.	Richard/Rebecca a steward,	Kilmacow
	May 06	**Shaughnessy**, Margaret	John/Margaret	Glenwilliam.
	Nov 06	**Conyers,** Francis Spring Grady.	Grady F. /Helena	Liskennett.
1862	Jun 01	**Hodgson**, Emily Mary	Laurence John	G'wm Castle.
	Jul 19	**Delmage**, James	William Julia a steward,	Ashboro'
	Sep 05	**Coe,** Mary Harriette	Samuel/Anne	Constable.
	Sep 11	**Mick,** Leonard	Richard/Mary	Lisamota.
	Oct 02	**Kiggell**, Lancelot Edward	Lan.J./Meliora,	Wilton, R'keale.
1863	Jan 01	**Fitzgerald**, Rosanna	James/Mary Anne	
	Jan 23	**Atkinson**, Thomas Richard Durbin.	Edward/Emma	Glenwilliam
	Aug 07	**Morony**, Eliza Helena	Edmund/Helena.M.	Odellville.
	Aug 31	**Lagier,** Elizabeth	Henry/Eliza	Ashborough
1864	Feb 08	**Conyers,** Charles Augustine	Grady/Helena	Liskennett.
	Apr 13	**Airey,** Richard	John/Eliza	Whitesmith.
	Sep 05	**Coe**, Thomas	Samuel/Anne	Head Constable
	Oct 02	**Cronin**, Honora	Michael/Cath.	Knockfierna.

Year	Date	Name	Parent(s)	Townland
1865	Apr 24	**Johnson**, -------	Charles/Marcella	Pensioner.
	Sep 26	**Morony**, Geraldine	Edm./H. Mary	Odellville.
1866	Aug 1	**Bale**, Eliza Anne Matilda William a Musician in the Vicarage.	William/Matilda	
1867	Mar 22	**Hewett**, William Nicholas William a Naval Officer.	William Nicholas/ Geraldine Glenwilliam.	
1868	Jan 16	**Swindle**, Edward	Richard/Mary	Constable
1869	Apr 13	**Swindle**, Richard Morgan	Richard/Mary	Constable.

Marriages in Ballingarry 1800 - 1858.

1800	Jul 22.	Martha Ann **Scanlan** to Mister **Wadefoot**. No name given.
1801	Feb 5	Robert **Fetherston**, M.D. to Widow **Austin** of Liskennett.
	Feb 10	Thomas **Mahony** to Margaret **Purcell** of Ballinaruga.
	Apr 17	John **Brown** of Danesfort to Margaret **Odell**, Governess at Grove House.
1805	Jan 7	T. A. **Odell**, Odelville to Miss Meliosa **Browne**, Danesfort, at Kilmacow Church.
	Jan 20	John Hunt **Navingham**, Co. Tipperary to Constance **Monkton**, Ashborough
1807	Jul 30	James **Raymond** to Miss Aphra **Odell**.
1808	31	Miss Grace **Odell**, The Turrett, Ballingarry to Charles **Smyth**.
1810	Apr 24	Miss Mabella **Graves** to John **Croker**, Croom Castle.
1813	Sep 8	Michael Conyers **Darcy** to Mary **Upston**.
1814	Jul 10	James **McYivia ?**, Sergt. East India Co., to Catherine **Sentry?**. Both of Ballingarry. Names could be ***McDevitt & Scully*** ?
1818	Feb 18	Robert **Gardiner**, Adare to Susanna **Hill**, Ballingarry.
1819	Apr 29	Eliza Maria **Odell**, 4th dau. Wm., The Grove to George **Massy**, Glenwilliam
1822	Feb 3	Hugh **Switzer** to Julia **Donegan**.
	Aug 11	John **Powel**, Corporal,1st Rifle Brigade & Mary **Doody**.
1823	Feb 11	Margaret **Harte** to David **Fuller**, a police constable.
1824	Jun 24	Mary **Benson** to Thomas **Dyer**, Private;1st Btn. Rifle Brig.
1825	Oct 27	Richard **Daxon** to Aphra Dent **Scanlan**, dau. Michael, Ballyknockane.
1826	Jan 8	John **Davis**, police constable to Mary **Ancot**, Governess, the Grove House.
	Nov 23	Thomas **Sullivan** to Julia **Cagney**, alias ***Jameson***.
1828	Aug 27	Edmond **Odell**, Ashborough to Miss Maria **Bernard**.

	Sep 24	William **Odell** to Miss Catherine **Condon**.
	Nov 25	Henry **Harte**, Gortroe to Sarah **Odell**.
1829	Jul 20	John **White,** Kilmurry to Miss Aphrasia Augusta **Cox**.
	Sep 20	John **Switzer** to Mary **Hodgins**.
1831	Jun 22	James **Condon** to Catherine **Molloy**.
	Jul 12	Edmond **Lloyd** to Miss Anne **Locke** in Kilmeedy Church.
	Dec 29	Hugh **Baker** to Sybella Mockler **Graves**.
1832	Jan 3	Thomas Harrison **Baker** to Catherine Anne **Graves**.
1834	Apr 15	Rev. Richard **Maunsell** to Miss Frances **Brown**.
1835	Jun 16	Philip Francis **Drought**, Co. Tipperary to Margaret Elizabeth **Graves**.
	Jul 20	Henry **O'Dell,** Ballyhahill to Thomasina **O'Dell,** Ballingarry.
	Sep 11	Thomas **Locke**, Castleview to Mary Ann **Evans,** Knockaderry House. Married in Kilmeedy.
1836	Feb 5	Rev. Thomas **Gubbings**, to Anne Maria S. **Evans**. Married in Kilmallock.
1838	Oct 29	John **Dowling**, a Tutor, to Grace **Odell**, daughter of Major Thomas.
1839	May 14	Hugh Wheeler **Scanlan** to Sarah **Brown** in Drehidtrasna Church.
1840	Jul 16	Edward **Eyres,** Journeyman Baker, Askeaton, to Eliza **McCormick** of Askeaton. Married in Ballingarry
1841	Mar 10	Richard **Maunsell,** 2nd Fusiliers to Mary **Odell**, daughter of Major Odell, The Grove. Married in Croagh.
	Nov 1	William **Odell,** Askeaton to Constance **Scanlan,** formerly Ballyknockane, now Kilbeg.
1845	Apr 23	George **Griffin** to Aphra **Massy**.
	Nov 25	Mary **Christie** to Michael **O'Brien**.
1846	Jan 28	Belinda S. **Gubbins** to Arthur **Vincent**.
1849	Jun 24	Terence **Connor** to Johanna **Purtell**.
1850	Sep 30	Mary **Heeime** to John **Mason**.
1851	Feb 3	John **Cronin** to Mary **Ready**, widow, nee **Hickey**.
	Dec 11	John **Mason** to Johanna **Quin**.
1852	Dec 28	William **Madagan** to Julia Anne **Laffan**.
1853	Mar 7	Jeremiah **Meehan** to Margaret **O'Connell**.
1855	May 22	Terence **Gore** to Catherine **Hanrahan**.
1856	Sep 15	Catherine **McEniry** to Michael **Cronin**.
1857	Mar 4	Michael **Leady** to Jane **Mullard**.
1858	Jun 15	Henry **Graydon** to Margaret **Quill**.
	Aug 19	Louisa Mary **Gubbins** to James Henry **Cullom**.

Burials in Ballingarry 1800-1872.

Year	Date	Name	Place
1800	Jul 18	**Monkton**, Miles.	
1802		**Jackson,** Walker,	Castle Jackson.
	Aug 2	**Jackson,** Clifford,	Castle Jackson.
		Scanlan, Michael, snr.,	Ballinaha.
		Cox, Ellen, wife of Hugh,	Ballinoe.
		dau. of Michael., snr.	Ballinaha.
1803	Feb 19	**Fitzgibbon,** Mrs., wife of Mick.	Ballingarry.
	Jul 15	**Fitzgibbon,** Michael., a weaver.	Ballingarry.
1804	Sep 8	**Clanchy,** Mrs Ann.	Glenwilliam.
	Dec 3	**Hurley,** Widow.	
1808	Apr 5	**Powel,** Mrs., age 71.	
1809	Dec 2	**Shelton,** Robert.	
1810	Jul 4	**Jackson**, Miles.	Limerick.
	Oct 22	**Cox,** William.	Ballinoe.
	Nov 8	**Mason,** Widow.	Limerick.
1811	Mar 15	**Taylor,** John. 5th Rgt. Drag.	
		Royal Irish Inniskilliners Brought from Ennis	
	Nov 9	**Fitzgerald**, Mrs., wife of David	Ballingarry.
1812	Jan 18	**Scanlan,** Mrs., widow of late Michael.	Ballinaha.
1817	Sep 13	**Phinn,** W. A.	Newcastle.
		Buried in Ballingarry Church grounds.	
1818	Jan 4	**Odell**, Mrs.	The Turrett.
		Ballingarry	
	Apr 8	**Darcy,** Mrs.	Newcastle.
	Apr 9	**Odell,** William, son of Col.William,	The Grove.
1820	Apr 28	**Graves,** Rev. John, age 69.	Ballingarry.
	Apr --	**Cox,** William, age 80.	
	Nov 20	**Cox,** Mrs., age 40. approx.	
1821	Apr --	**Cox,** Hugh , age 48.	
	Nov 4	**Grimes,** Revd. Edward, D.D., Vicar.	
1822	Jan 6	**Monkton,** Nicholas, age 70.	
	Mar 12	**Cox,** Mary, age 50, widow of William.	Ballinoe.
	Aug 20	**Scanlan,** Thomas, age 46.	Brook Lodge.
1823	Jan 24	**O'Grady,** Mrs. Catherine, age 61.	Newcastle.
	May 11	**Odell,** Henry, son of Major Odell.	
	Sep 20	**Scanlan,** Captain Michael L., age 58.	Ballyknockane.
	Sep 28	**Monkton,** Mrs. Anne, wife of George.	Ballingarry.
	Oct 10	**Odell,** Mary, wife of Reginald William Butler O.	Rathkeale.
1824	Jan 27	**Harte,** Sir Richard, age 84. Knight of Coolruss.	Buried in C'town.

	May 23	**Monkton,** Clifford, age 30.	
	Oct 22	**Shelton,** John, age 66.	Rossmore.
	Dec 4	**Odell,** Henry, son of Robert.	
1825	Feb 20	**Odell,** John, age 13, son of Thomas.	Newcastle.
	Sep 13	**O'Dwyer,** Mrs. Martha, age 80 approx.	
1826	Apr 28	**Odell,** Jane, age 53, widow of William.	Clonee.
	Dec 29	**Crips,** Maria Louise, age 18.	Buried in Castletown.
		(2nd daughter of Edmond, deceased, and Mary)	
1827	Feb 25	**Moore,** Martha, dau. Wm. and Martha.	The Grove.
	Oct 9	**Dwyer,** Mrs., age 43, wife of James.	Liskennet.
1828	Aug 3	**Monkton,** Mary Anne, age 18, dau. of George.	
1829	Aug 28	**Odell,** William Fitzwilliam, son Robert and Catherine	
	Sep 11	**Ryan,** Southwell, age 50.	Formerly Clerk of the Parish.
1830	Feb 6	**Monckton,** Sophia, age 18 mts., daughter of Miles.	
	Mar 25	**Lynch,** William, Surgeon, The Dispensary,	Ballingarry.
	May 20	**Harkness,** ------, age 11 mts., son of a Police Constable.	
	Dec 17	**O'Dell,** Colonel Thomas, age 77.	
1831	May 16	**Odell,** Reverend William Butler, age 84.	
	Nov 2	**Monkton,** Marianne, alias **Powys,** age 23, wife of Miles.	
	Dec 1	**Cussen,** Margaret, age 23, dau. of Laurence.	Rockhill.
1832	Apr 14	**Yielding,** Jane, a widow.	
	Apr 14	**Marker,** Anne, age 70, widow of Connell.	Rathkeale.
	May 13	**Sullivan,** Caroline Sarah, age 20, Tullilease.	Buried in Cloncagh.
	Oct 28	**Odell,** John, age 20, son of William and Sally.	
1833	Mar 7	**Wilkinson,** Mrs., age 45, alias **Upton.**	
1834	--- ---	--------, Thomas, age 8 months	A foundling.
	Apr 2	**Dwyer,** John, age 60. Counsellor	Ballingarry.
1835	Feb 7	**Cox,** Miss. Buried in Limerick.	Ballinoe.
	Mar 9	**Massy,** George, age 75. Buried in Rathkeale.	Glenwilliam.
	Apr 6	**Cox,** Catherine, wife of John	
	-	**Moore,** Mrs., wife of M.	
	Dec 27	**Healy,** John, Parish Clerk.	Buried in Askeaton
1837	Aug 17	**Brown,** Mildred, dau. of Wm./Mildred	Fortwilliam.
	Nov 21	**Odell,** Catherine, age 30, wife William Fitzwilliam O.	
	Dec 10	**Moore,** William, age 35. Scotch Steward.	Ballingarry.

1838	Feb 14	**Newasham,** Constance, alias ***Monckton,*** a widow of cholera.	
	Feb 16	**Odell,** Miss Charlotte, age 43, of cholera, dau. of William.	
	May 23	**Monckton,** Margaret, age 84, a widow.	Ballingarry.
	Oct 17	**Odell,** William, age 28.	Ballingarry.
1839	Apr 3	**Lloyd,** Edward, age 72, formerly Castlemahon.	Kanturk.
	Jun 16	**Graves,** Thomas, age 40.	Woodstock Cottage
	Oct 29	**Odell,** John, age 86.	Ballyhahill.
1840	Jul 15	**Browne,** Ellen, age 86.	
	Sep 11	**Gubbins,** George Gough, age 1½, son of Vicar	Ballingarry.
	Oct 14	**Moore,** John, age 60.	Land Steward.
1841	Apr 30	**Monckton,** George, age 50, formerly Ashboro'	Limerick
	Dec 26	**Odell,** John, age 24	Shannon View.
1842	Apr 30	**Odell,** Thomas Alexander, age 70	Odle Ville.
	Sep 15	**Scanlan,** Aphra Phoebe, age 2yrs. 7mts.	Ballinahaha.
	Nov 05	**O'Dell,** Catherine, age 79.	Ballyhahill.
	Dec 15	**Casey,** James, age 39.	Limerick.
1843	Mar 19	**Graves,** Catherine Anne, age 68, wife of Rev. John, The Glebe.	
	Mar 27	**O'Dell,** Kate, age 28.	Ballingarry.
	Jun 24	**Hasford,** Eliza Jane, age 3.	Castletown.
	Sep 17	**Massy,** Hugh, age 15.	Odleville.
	Nov 03	**Hickie,** Mary Anne, age 11.	Ballingarry.
	Nov 08	**Casey,** -----, age 40.	Limerick.
	Nov 24	**Casey,** Dobbin, age 67, formerly Athlacca	Limerick.
1844	Apr 03	**Ryan,** Mrs. Lucinda, age 72.	Ballyhahill.
	May 31	**Keily,** Michael, age 32.	Ballingarry.
1845	May 03	**Odell,** Thomas, age 25.	Shannon View.
	--- --	**Ryan,** Southwell John, age 1 year.	Ballingarry.
1846	Feb 25	**Odell,** Thomas, age 68, Barrister at Law	Shannon View.
	Nov 10	**Alexander,** James, age 73.	Ballingarry.
1847	May --	**Sullivan,** Dr. William, M.D., age 35.	Buried in Clouncagh.
	Jul 01	**O'Brien,** Michael, age 21.	Ballingarry.
	Jul 04	**Keily,** Michael. Infant.	Ballingarry.
	Aug 14	**Ryan,** Mary, age 56.	Ballingarry.
	Nov 05	**Odell,** Alexander, Esq., age 39.	Ballyhagran Cottage.
	Nov 25	**Quilty,** William, age 1½ years.	Ballingarry.

1848	Feb 03	**Lloyd**, John, age 23.	Heathfield.
	Mar 28	**Hayes**, Daniel, age 50.	Ballingarry.
	Apr 15	**Scanlan**, Francis, age 74.	Kilbeg.
	Apr 15	**Donald**, Miss Elizabeth, age 1$^1/_2$ years.	Ballingarry.
	May 26	**de Massy**, William Hamo, age 28. Glenwilliam Castle.	
	May 27	**Scanlan**, Hugh Wheeler, age 41.	Kilbeg.
	Jun 05	**Sullivan**, Henry W., age 33.	Buried in Clouncagh.
	Jul 14	**Pattison**, Florinda, age 4mts. Twin sister.	Ballingarry.
	Jul 28	**Shelton**, John Willington, age 57.	Monkstown.
	Dec 09	**Cox**, George Hugh, age 6 months.	Ballyneale.
1849	Jan --	**Ryan**, Alexander, age 40.	Ballingarry.
	Jan 19	**Cronin**, James, age 11.	Lisamota.
	Jan 24	**Odell**, Meliora, age 62.	Odleville.
	Mar 26	**Curtin**, Thomas, age 6 months.	Ballingarry.
	Apr --	**Ryan**, Edward Southwell, age 30.	Ballingarry.
	Jul 02	**Odell**, Mrs. Sarah, age 65.	Ballingarry.
	Jul 17	**Sullivan**, Mrs. Mary A., age 61, Chesterfield.	Brd. in C'cagh.
1850	Jan 01	**Moloney**, Eliza, age 10.	Ballingarry.
	Feb 12	**Sullivan**, Major James, age 71, (83rd Regt. Officiator, the Rev. ***Aske.***)	Chesterfield Brd. in C'cagh.
	Mar 11	**Airey**, Margaret, age 13.	Ballingarry.
	Apr 07	**Lloyd**, Edward, age 28.	Heathfield.
	Jun 18	**Cronin**, Mary, age 17.	Ballingarry.
	Sep 29	**Chapman**, Margaret, age 11.	Ballingarry.
1851	Jan 25	**Hanrahan**, Mary, age 3$^1/_2$ years.	Ballingarry.
	Jun 25	**Odell**, John, age 45.	Odellville.
	Dec 09	**Odell**, Eliza, age 40.	Odellville.
1852	Jan 15	**Power**, Meliora, baby.	Ashborough.
	Mar 07	**Jones**, George, age 14.	Ballingarry.
	Apr 09	**Cronin**, Margaret, age 10.	Ballingarry.
	Jun 09	**Kennedy**, Martin, age 8. (Officiator, the Revd. William ***Barland.***)	Ballingarry.
	Jun 21	**Hennessy**, Maria, age 43.	Knockfierna.
	Jul 21	**Hogan**, David, age 14.	Ballingarry.
1852	Jul 29	**Cox**, Alice, age 8 years.	Ballynoe.
1853	Feb 23	**Odell**, Crone, age 62.	Ballykevan.
	May 18	**Noonan**, Ellen, age 1 year. (Officiating, the Rev. W. Henry ***Halpin,*** Curate.)	Ballingarry.

	Oct 26	**O'Sullivan,** Margaret, age 22.	Glin
1854	Aug 08	**Irwin,** Jack, age 11.	Ballingarry.
	Aug 12	**Alexander,** Elizabeth, age 65.	Ballingarry.
	Sep 30	**Browne,** John Thomas, age 3$^1/_2$ years.	Ballingarry.
	Nov 07	**Cronin,** Patrick, age 11.	Ballingarry.
1855	Feb 26	**Lynch,** William, age 70.	Knockfierna.
	May 10	**Mason,** Mary Anne, age 22.	Knockfierna.
	Jun 04	**Shaughnessy,** Anne, age 23.	Knockfierna.
	Aug 08	**Browne,** Thomas, age 74.	Ballingarry.
	Oct 06	**Cox,** John, age 86, County Limerick Coroner	Ballinamona.
1856	Jan 03	**Lloyd,** James, age 30.	Heathfield.
	Mar 02	**Scanlan,** Michael, age 64.	Kilbeg.
	Jun 21	**Quill,** Johanna, age 14.	Knockfierna.
	Oct 19	**Odell,** Richard Maunsell, age 72.	Ballingarry.
	--- --	**Evans,** Jane, age 79.	Rathkeale.
1857	Feb 27	**Cronin,** Bridget, age 60.	Ballingarry.
	May 05	**Mahony,** Ellen, age 15.	Ballingarry.
	Aug 02	**Lloyd,** Mrs. Frances, age 54.	Tarbert.
1858	Mar 05	**Cripps,** Mrs. Mary, age 82.	Ballingarry
	Jul 13	**Power,** Mrs. Bessie Maria, age 35.	Ballinakill.
1859	Mar 05	**Scanlan,** Thomas, age 55.	Craig Cottage.
	Apr 08	**Laffan,** Julia, a baby. Officiator, Rev Mr. **Baker.**	
	Oct 07	**Murphy,** Michael, age 70.	
	Oct 15	**Madigan,** William, age 2$^1/_2$ yrs.	
	Nov 22	**Neville,** Mrs. Constance, age 20.	Dundalk.
	Dec 26	**Tighe,** James, age 52, a Police constable.	Glenwilliam.
1861	Mar 08	**Odell,** Selina, age 24.	Officiator,
		Michael H. **Cotter,** Curate.	
	Apr 17	**Mahony,** Catherine, age 60. Officiator, Rev Patrick **Moinch?**	
	Oct --	**Leary,** Michael. aged 75.	
1862	Apr --	**Powell,** Harriette, aged 2.	Officiator, Revd.
		Elliott ***O'Donnell.***	
1863	Oct 23	**Scanlan,** John, aged 17.	Kilbeg.
1864	Jan 04	**Brown,** Anne, aged 80.	
	Mar 14	**Gubbins,** Georgina, age 19yrs, 8mts, 3days.	The Glebe.
1865	Feb 16	**Odell,** Robert, age 56.	
	Apr 07	**Power,** Daniel Dickson, age 56.	Mallow St., Limerick.
	Nov 24	**Odell,** William, pensioner, age 67.	Killaheen, parish of Kilconnell
		(Officiator, the Revd. Clement **Richardson**.)	

1866	Mar 26	**Montford,** Mrs. Bridget, age 60. Officiator, Rev. ***Stenson***, Croom
	Mar 29	**Hamilton,** Mrs. Wilhelmina Frances, age 34. Tarbert
	May 24	**Brown,** Edward, age 74. Wilton, Rathkeale
	May 29	**Wilkinson,** Clennell Spearman, age 7. St. Oswald's.
	Jul 03	**Airey,** John, age 10 months. Ballingarry.
	Nov 24	**Lloyd,** Mrs. Anne, age 70. Heathfield.
	Dec 16	**Thompson,** Anne, age 63. Relict of the Rector, Croagh
1867	Feb 21	**Odell,** Mrs. Elizabeth Anne, age 63. Ballingarry.
	May 01	**Bouchier,** Grace Alice, age 3 months. Ballykevin.
	Aug 15	**Lloyd,** Edward, age 74. Heathfield Officiator, Rev. Tyrell ***Evans***
	Sep 10	**Lloyd,** Miss Margaret, age 48. Heathfield.
	Nov 02	**Morony,** Edmond, age 74. Odelville
1868	Nov 15	**Scanlan,** Frances M., age 90. Ballyknockane.
1869	Mar 19	**Cox,** John, age 35. Limerick.
	Jun 01	**Cox**, John, age 63. Ballyneale. Officiator, Rev John ***Westropp***
	Jul 17	**Cox,** Barbara. Ballyneale.
	Dec 24	**Odell,** Mrs. Anne (Crone), age 86. Rathkeale.
1870	Nov 08	**Patterson,** Mrs. Anne Jane, age 59. Knockfierna.
1871	Apr 18	**O'Dell,** Mrs. Mary, age 80. Morgans, Askeaton.
1872	Feb 09	**Cox**, Mrs. Elizabeth, age 70. Ballynoe.

The following families have been identified as living in Ballingarry from the Church of Ireland Parish records held on microfilm in the National Archives.

1848	**Airy**, Robert, Ballingarry. A Whitesmith. Wife Mary and children. John, born 1841 and William, born 1848.
1849	**Bank,** Elias. Wife Catherine and James, 16.
1870	**Bouchier,** Joseph Henry, Ballykevin. Wife Julia Anne and children. Anne, Feb. 09, 1864. James Henry, Oct 09, 1865. Grace Alice, Jan 27, 1867. Henry, Mar 21, 1868 and John Thomas, Feb 11, 1870.
1870	**Cox,** Robert, Ballinamona. Wife Catherine and children. John Hugh, Oct 18, 1860. Anne, Jan 25, 1862. Grace and Kate, twins, Feb 07, 1865. Robert Maunsell, Oct 25, 1866 and Mary Elizabeth, Apr 24, 1870.
1849	**Cronin,** Patrick. Labourer. Wife Bridget and children. John, 17. Mary, 15, Margaret, 09 and Patrick, 07.

1839	**Cronin,** Thomas, Ballingarry. Wife Mary and children. Margaret, born 1837 and Catherine, born 1839.
1850	**Curtin,** William. Wife Mary and children. Johanna, born May 27, 1849. John, born Nov. 18, 1850
1851	**Curtin,** Patrick, Kilmacow. Carpenter. Wife Catherine and children. Catherine, born 1841. Hanora born 1843. Alice born 1846 and Patrick born 1851.
1844	**Downes,** James, Ballingarry. Wife Mary and children. Michael, born 1842 and John, born 1844.
1843	**Guiry,** William, Knockfierna. Wife Margaret and children. John, born 1838. Michael born 1841 and Margaret born 1843.
1849	**Hanrahan,** John, labourer. Wife Norry and children. Bridget, 19. Laurence, 16. Catherine, 13. James, 11. Bessie, 9 and Mary, 1.
1852	**Hanrahan,** Patrick, Ballingarry. Wife Bridget and children. Patrick, born 1831. Ellen, born 1834 and Michael, born 1843.
1849	**Hayes,** Daniel. A Weaver. Wife Mary and children. Bridget, 14. Ellen, 13. John, 11. Margaret, 8 and Richard, 5.
1850	**Hogan,** Michael, Ballingarry. A Weaver. Wife Fanny and children. John, born 1834. Mary, born 1840. Peter, born 1845 and Ellen, born 1850.
1849	**Kenedy,** Martin, Ballingarry. A Shoemaker. Wife Mary and children. Eliza, born 1840 and Ellen, born 1842.
1843	**Leo,** John, Ballingarry. Wife Bridget and children. Mary, born 1840. Bridget, born 1842 and John, born 1843.
1842	**Mahony,** Patrick, Ballingarry. Wife Catherine and children. Patrick, born 1840 and Michael born 1842.
1849	**Mahony,** Patrick. Kilmacow. Carpenter. Wife Catherine and children. Catherine, born 1841. Hanora, born 1843. Alice, born 1846 and Patrick, born 1851.
1852	**Mason,** John, Lisduane. Wife Johanna and children. Mary Anne, born 1832. Matilda, born 1834. John, born 1836. Hanna, born 1839. Eliza, born 1841. Edmund, born 1842. Bridget ?, born 1844 (difficult to read the name). Denis, born 1846 and Ellen, born 1849.
1835	**McEniry,** David, Knockfierna. Wife Hanora and children. Catherine, born 1835. Thomas, born 1837. David, born 1839. Denis, born 1841 and Patrick, born 1843.
1849	**Montfort,** George, a soldier. Mary, his wife and daughter Bridget, aged 9.

1838   **Noonan,** William, Ballingarry. A carpenter. His wife, Ellen and children Margaret, born 1838. Catherine, born 1842. Mary, born 1846. Edward, born 1847. Ellen, born Apr 4, 1852 and John, born Jun 30, 1855.

1870   **Shine,** William, Lisamota Castle. A farmer. Wife Catherine and children. Richard William, Sep 7, 1856. Helena Mary, Sep 5, 1861. Susan Caroline, Oct 11, 1863. John, Apr 24, 1865. Eliza Sarah, Aug 11, 1867. William, Nov 8, 1868. Amelia, Jan 22, 1870.

It would appear William married twice. Richard's mother is shown as Catherine. Emily is William's wife in 1870.

1835   **Tracy,** John. Knockfierna. Wife Margaret and children. Margaret born 1835 and John, born 1837.

1849   **Vincent,** George, father and his son George, aged 9.

List of residents in Ballingarry 1845 - 1850 - 1855.

(Extracted from the Church of Ireland parish records in the National Archives.)

1845

John, Margaret and William **Alexander,** Ballingarry. James **Brown,** Ballingarry. James and Thomas **Bryan,** Ballingarry. William **Buckley,** Ballingarry. Mary **Cluntie,** The Glebe. Bessie, Hosa and Mary **Cox,** Ballynoe. John **Dallon,** Ballingarry. Mary **Fisher,** Ballyknockane. Margaret **Hanrahan,** Ballingarry Bessy and Sarah **Harding,** Lisduane. James **Keily** and Thomas **Kingsley,** Ballingarry. Edward **Langford,** Ballynoe. Aphra, Bessy, Fanny and Godfrey **Massy,** Odellville. Maria **McKenna,** The Glebe. Fanny, Lucy and William **Nash,** Fort Edmund. Anne, Caroline and Edmund **O'Dell,** The Grove. Isabella and Selina **O'Dell,** Ballingarry. Joseph and Michael **O'Brien,** Ballingarry. James **Patterson,** Ballingarry. Mary **Power,** Fortwilliam. William Michael **Roberts,** Ballingarry. Alexander, Catherine, George and Henry **Ryan,** Ballingarry. Henry **Sampie,** Ballingarry. Bessy and Hugh **Scanlan,** Kilbeg. Elizabeth **Smith,** The Glebe. Anne and James **Sparling,** Mount Brown. John, Richard, Thomas and William **Standish,** Frankfort. John **Quilty,** Ballingarry and Mary **Reidy,** Knockfierna.

1850

Mary and Robert **Airy.** Lizette **Beaupeare.** Minny **Brown.** Mary **Chapman.** Miss **Conely.** Bessie, Snr., Eliza, Fanny, John,snr., John,jnr. and Robert **Cox.** Bridget, John, Michael and Michael, snr. **Cronin.** Mary and William **Curtin.** Aphra and Bessie

Daxone. Edmund **Denehy**. Catherine **Donahy**. James and Mary **Downes**. William **Gardiner**. Elizabeth O. G. **Gubbins**. Margaret and William **Guiry**. Bridget, Honora, John, Kate and Susanna **Hanrahan**. David and Mary **Hayes**. Andrew **Kearney**. Catherine and Mary **Mahony**. Frederick **Massy**. William **Mullins**. Margaret and William **Noonan**. Ann, Elizabeth Helena, Helena, Margaret Lucy, Mary Charlotte, Robert, Med. Dr. and Thomas Henry **O'Dell**. Nancy and Fanny **Peppard**. Kate and Maurice **Power**. Fanny, Michael and William **Scanlan**. Joseph **Taylor** and Thomas **Wilson**.

1855

Airy, John
Barrett, Charles
Cansbie? Kate
Cox, William, William Sydney and Ormsby.
Cronin, Catherine and Thomas
Gore, Terence
Guiry, John and Michael
Hayes, John and Mary
Johnson, Louisa
Langford, Margaret E. and Mary.
Leader, Ellen
Leary, Ellen and Michael
Lynch, Mary
Mahony, Michael
Mick, Peter
Noonan, Margaret
Patterson, Anne J. and Elizabeth
Scanlan, Michael H.
Tracy, John and Margaret

Alford, John
Blake, Johanna
Clarke, Mary

Dowling, Grace, Julia and Kate.
Gubbins, Alice
Hanrahan, Bessie, Ellen and James
Hogan, Fanny, John and Mary
Kelly, Catherine and Johanna.
Lawrenson, Sarah
Leahy, Ellen
Lee, Bridget
Mason, Johanna, John,Snr and John,jnr.
McEniry, David, Honora and Thomas
Mullard, Jane
Odell, Annette, Emma and Robert
Rochford, Thomas
Shaughnessy, John and Margaret